THE
LORD'S
PRAYER

THE
LORD'S
PRAYER
BRIDGE TO A
BETTER WORLD

C. G. WEERAMANTRY

LIGUORI/TRIUMPH
LIGUORI, MISSOURI

Published by Liguori/Triumph
An Imprint of Liguori Publications
Liguori, Missouri

Library of Congress Cataloging-in-Publication Data

Weeramantry, C. G..
    The Lord's prayer : bridge to a better world / C. G. Weeramantry — 1st ed.
      p. cm.
    Includes bibliographical references and index.
    ISBN 0-7648-0181-3
    1. Lord's prayer. 2. Christianity and justice. I. Title.
BV230.W34   1998
226.9'6'06—dc21   97-52262

Unless otherwise indicated, scripture quotations are from the *Today's English Version*, Second Edition, copyright © 1992 by American Bible Society. Used by permission.

Copyright © 1998 by C. G. Weeramantry
Printed in the United States of America
02 01 00 99 98 5 4 3 2 1
First Edition

OUR FATHER
WHO ART IN HEAVEN,
HALLOWED BE THY NAME.
THY KINGDOM COME
THY WILL BE DONE,
ON EARTH AS IT IS IN HEAVEN.
GIVE US THIS DAY OUR DAILY BREAD;
AND FORGIVE US OUR TRESPASSES,
AS WE FORGIVE THOSE WHO TRESPASS
   AGAINST US,
AND LEAD US NOT INTO TEMPTATION,
BUT DELIVER US FROM EVIL.
AMEN.

To my grandchildren and their generation
that they may know a world which is as close
to the kingdom of heaven
as universal effort can make it.

"What is faith worth if it is not translated into action?"
—Mahatma Gandhi

"No longer can we afford the luxury of passing by on the other side. Such folly was once called moral failure; today it will lead to universal suicide."
—Martin Luther King, Jr., in a sermon referring to the parable of the Good Samaritan

"Probably every generation sees itself as charged with remaking the world. Mine, however, knows that its task will not be merely to remake the world. Its task is even greater: to keep the world from destroying itself."
—Albert Camus

"I will write peace on your wings and you will fly all over the world."
—Sadako Sasaki, aged 12. Died 1955 of leukemia after exposure to radiation in Hiroshima

CONTENTS

PREFACE

T his book is about justice—justice for all peoples, justice at all levels of society, justice that avoids tensions and wars, justice that is the path to peace. It finds its inspiration in a concentration of practical wisdom, unrivaled in its width of coverage and brevity of expression : the Lord's Prayer.

In the hope of reaching people of goodwill of all faiths and walks of life, this book has been written free of doctrinal assumptions. It does not claim to be a theological or juristic work, and it requires no theological or juristic knowledge of its readers. It is addressed to humanity at large, and not to Christians alone, for the Prayer is the common inheritance of all sections of the human family—not the exclusive possession of some.

In the search for the practical wisdom underlying the Prayer, this study draws upon the literature of all religions. As Pope John Paul II has observed in his recent book, *Crossing the Threshold of Hope*, "We should be amazed at the number of common elements [in these religions]," and he notes that the Church is on the lookout for "seeds of the Word" present in other religions. And so the reader will find some of those common elements, corresponding in their entirety with the spirit and ideals of the Prayer, throughout these pages.

Though this book concentrates on a minute section of the scriptures of but one religion, it deals with the fundamental human dignities that underlie them all. Though it touches the spiritual, it is anchored to the practical. Though focused on the city of God, it is concerned with the city of man. It thus becomes, in practical terms, a book for those who desire to eliminate war, to strive for peace, to banish want, and to enthrone justice. It seeks to ensure that humanity does not plunge to its destruction in the twenty-first century by continuing to tread the path it has chosen in the twentieth.

By distilling from the Prayer the legal principles deeply ingrained within it, this work seeks a new vision for a new century—and, indeed, a new millennium—a vision of governance "on earth as it is in heaven."

There is today a global flood tide of millennial speculation and enthusiasm, and a concentration upon ways of bettering the human condition as this new era dawns. This book aims at offering to this outpouring of thought and goodwill a globally oriented perspective on the reservoirs of power and wisdom lying within the Lord's Prayer. These wait to be channeled toward achieving world order in the new millennium, if only a route can be excavated between the lofty principles of the Prayer and the seemingly intractable problems of our age. It is my hope that through this fresh analysis, the Prayer, which has in the past attracted a torrent of theological writing, will be seen to reveal fresh nuances of meaning with deep practical relevance to the quandaries that face humanity as it enters this age of unprecedented danger and unprecedented opportunity.

ACKNOWLEDGMENTS

I have benefited greatly from the comments of friends and colleagues too numerous to mention, who have at various stages encouraged me to go ahead with this work, at times when its very novelty seemed daunting. Chief Justice Brennan of the High Court of Australia gave me considerable encouragement in the early stages of this work.

I also owe a debt of gratitude to Dr. Kumar Amarasekara of the Faculty of Law of Monash University, whose constant exhortations to me to write a work on law and Christianity acted as a catalyst to set me off on this endeavor.

I thank my literary agent David Levy for his wise guidance and advice at all stages since the manuscript first took shape, and my publishers, Liguori/ Triumph and, in particular, Patricia Kossmann, for their interest, enthusiasm, and discerning suggestions at various stages of this work.

My heartfelt thanks are also due to my secretary, Miss Maureen Sullivan, for her dedicated attention to this work through more drafts than she or I can remember.

Finally, and by no means the least of my debts, is the gratitude I owe to my family for their selfless, cheerful, and unwavering support over the years in an endeavor which would not otherwise have seen the light of day.

PART ONE

HARNESSING
THE POWER
OF THE PRAYER

CHAPTER 1

A PRAYER FOR
THE THIRD MILLENNIUM

W e live in the midst of terrorism, genocide, racism, torture, narcotics, militarism, arms races, hijacking, environmental devastation, and human rights violations of every kind. The events in Afghanistan, Bosnia, Cambodia, Chechnya, Rwanda, and Somalia highlight our inadequacies. Even as this book goes to press, some forty-eight armed conflicts rage around the world. From the Olympic Park at Atlanta to the subways of Tokyo, the sparkle of vibrant life gives way in a frightening instant to the specter of unexpected death. From the killing fields of Yugoslavia to the rubble of Oklahoma, good people everywhere feel helpless in projecting their values into the violent world around them. More than 130 wars of the postwar "peace" have shed more blood than both World Wars put together. We hear of organized rape and orchestrated carnage. Our perils seem endless, our problems insoluble. The world is in turmoil, international order defenseless, the values of civilization in retreat.

We end the second millennium on a note of failed expectations of peace and grim forebodings of doom. As one war-torn century draws to a close, another century of cruelty and violence seems poised to succeed it. Unless we change track. But how?

There is another picture of the human condition painted for us by the greatest lawgiver of Christian civilization. It is a picture of the equality and dignity of every human being. A picture of love and brotherhood and sisterhood. A picture of social concern and responsibility. A picture of peace. Its setting is universalism. Its object is the reign of justice, good faith, and fair dealing. Its basis is forgiveness, resistance to temptation, and the trampling down of evil. Without negating our material needs, it points to higher values than profit and power, nobler means than the bullet and the banknote, broader principles than individualism and racism, deeper loyalties than sect or nation. The picture painted is of a city of man that resembles the city of God, of a new Jerusalem brought down to earth. That picture is painted in brilliant miniature in the Lord's Prayer.

Is there a bridge between these two contrasting scenarios, along which the saving graces of the second can move into the first? How can these two kingdoms—the Kingdom of God and the kingdom of humanity—be brought closer together?

The last four hundred years have seen a steady widening of the gap between them. Far from coming closer together, they are drifting further into isolation from each other. They have become kingdoms apart. The values and restraints taken for granted in the one are rejected in the other. Hence the misery, the conflict, the degradation of the human condition to depths unknown before. Hence the virtual snuffing out of humanity's age-old dream, expressed by Isaiah, and engraved at the United Nations Headquarters in New York, that nations "shall beat their swords into plowshares and their spears into pruning hooks. Nation shall not lift up sword against nation, neither shall they learn war any more." Are there no means of rekindling the fading embers of that eternal dream?

The Great Divide Between Law and Religion

The religious wars of the seventeenth century ended the immemorial relationship between religion and law. When in the seventeenth and eighteenth centuries the pioneers of modern international law made a conscious break from religion, they did so for a very good reason: The religious wars of their times demanded an increasingly secular approach. That era sought a principle of international order founded on human reason and experience, rather than on the quicksands of disputed religious dogma. That divide has widened with each succeeding generation. Historical and intellectual influences continue to condemn the entry of religious values into the public arena as unfashionable, unacademic, and visionary.

Today, all religions have learned that they must accept one another and coexist for the foreseeable future. Modern scholarship reveals more clearly than ever before the essential unity of the principles of human conduct enjoined by the great religions—principles that have imprinted themselves on the hearts and minds of entire nations.

International law is still in that formative phase wherein it must continually draw upon equity, ethics, and the moral sense of mankind to nourish its developing principles. Far from demanding a distancing from religion, our times demand that we urgently strengthen the moral base that underpins international law and order. Though it is evident that the rationale for distancing international order from religion no longer exists, we are still captives of a school of thought that arose in vastly different circumstances—and was undoubtedly the appropriate approach for that day and age.

Derided by academic pedantry, distanced by legal formalism, obscured by theological complexity, crippled by sectarian narrowness, religion tends to be treated as inert dogma, rather than an active ameliorator of the human condition.

Tomorrow's world order will be based on active cooperation, seeking to fuse out of the world's different historical and cultural backgrounds a set of common principles. All must cooperate, or all will perish. This era of cooperation demands that the legal essence distilled from each culture be brought to the common service of the international order. Law need no longer distance itself from the *values* of religion (as opposed to *dogma* and *ritual*).

Relevance of Religion to Practical Law and Order

Modern scholarship is demonstrating religion's relevance to social ordering. Even in a field so remote from morality as statecraft, recent studies[1] describe major foreign policy blunders resulting from ignorance of religion's role in society. A former president of the United States, in his Foreword to one of these works, stresses the constructive role of religious values in global trouble spots.[2] Contemporary analyses of the causes of world disorder[3] are showing that global unrest is due largely to lack of understanding of other cultures. A principal source of such misunderstanding is the lack of appreciation of the shared religious values of these different civilizations. The role of cultural factors in international diplomacy, especially in the field of human rights, is attracting increasing scholarly attention.[4]

The same applies also in the world of law—human rights, international law, conflict resolution. All of these are heavily dependent on morality, and morality draws deeply from religion. They lose powerful nourishment if we cut them away from their inspirational roots. We blunder profoundly if we disregard the impact on practical social conduct of the wealth of moral guidance offered by religion.

A bridge must be found to carry the strength of religious values into these practical realms. That bridge could be the Lord's Prayer. Its simplicity conceals its profoundness; its brevity conceals its range. It is a prayer that commands universal respect.

For Christianity, there can be no better practical beginning than to study what relevant principles of human rights and law are encapsulated in the Lord's Prayer, acknowledged from the earliest times to be a succinct summary of the whole gospel. The wealth of scholarly commentary the Prayer has attracted is eloquent testimony to the multiple strands of meaning woven into its every word. The powerful and hitherto unsuspected links between the Prayer and modern human rights doctrine will intensify the strong groundswell of world opinion that is deeply committed to basic morality and goodwill. That growing volume of opinion is becoming increasingly impatient at its helplessness in stemming the tide of inhumanity that engulfs the world. Not only scholars, theologians, lawyers, and statesmen, but also a vast body of concerned citizens of all faiths, are casting around desperately to find some anchors to steady the vessel of civilization that is adrift and rocking dangerously.

The Legal Content of the Prayer

For twenty centuries studies of the Prayer have concentrated on theology. Yet it is an unexplored treasure house of *legal* and *human rights* concepts: good faith, fair dealing, free will, trusteeship, intergenerational fairness, social use of property, communal responsibility, economic and social rights and duties, fair trial, equity, just punishment, affirmative action, nondiscrimination, nonviolence, universalism, conciliation, peace. Every word resonates with law and justice.

Take the first word "Our." All humanity is cast in one group, addressing its common superior. Differences of race, sex, color, language, learning, or rank melt away. All supplicants are equal. Second, everyone, however destitute or despised, has dignity sufficient to speak directly to God. Third, this dignity is irremovable. No potentate, whether emperor or pope, can come between the individual and that dignity.

Equality, dignity, and inalienability of rights—the three pillars of today's vast human rights edifice—are thus implicit in the first word. Analyzed similarly, the Prayer's fifty-six words become an armory of human rights and international law concepts. A volume could be written on such implications of each word of the Prayer (and, indeed, this work is a condensation of a larger work by the author). The present volume concentrates on *forgiveness* and *temptation*, but here is a sampling of what can be extracted from the other words.

"Father" implies: love. Brotherhood and sisterhood. Peace. Dispute resolution. Collective responsibility. Impartial justice. A higher law. Affirmative action. Cooperation. Nonviolence. Social rights and duties. Intergenerational fairness.

"Kingdom" is rich with meaning. A kingdom of justice, the characteristics of which are love, truth, justice, fellowship, equality, dignity, compassion, kindness, peace, good faith, fair dealing. No forced labor, no discrimination, no exploitation, no torture, no slavery. John Wesley saw heaven as a state to be enjoyed on earth, Martin Luther as a state to be attained through deeds. The Prayer is a reminder that heavenly duty must be performed on earthly soil.

"Come" is a resounding call to action, to end our moral paralysis in the face of injustice. We must work to achieve the justice of God's kingdom on earth. Complacency is a sin against the Prayer. In a world teeming with injustice, we do little to end it till it knocks on our door. The new Jerusalem does not descend from heaven to earth when we bid it to come and sit back with folded arms.

"Thy will be done" involves another commitment—not only to accept God's will, but also to *do* God's will; not merely to abstain from evil, but to *do* good. Resistance to temptation. Resistance to complacency. The Prayer calls for *active* Christianity, not passive resignation. By whom is this will to be *done* except by us? Where should this process of change begin—among the Eskimos of Lapland, the islanders of the Pacific, the peoples of the Congo, or among the peoples of the world's most powerful nations, many of them Christians for centuries, many of them frequent reciters of the Prayer? God's will will not *happen* on earth, it must be *done* on earth, and each recitation of the Prayer is a commitment to action. It is a principle of law that one must not say one thing and do another. In traditional legal language, one cannot blow hot and cold. The Prayer, if it is to be meaningful, calls for *action*, and was never meant to end with pious *recitation*.

"Daily bread" embraces economic rights—food, clothing, shelter—and shows the Prayer's intense practicality. It implies economic rights, fair wages, employment, the right to development. The word "daily" is also a warning: No cornering of markets. No antisocial accumulations of vast surplus. No hoarding or profiteering, for we cannot ask for bread for ourselves while taking bread out of the mouths of others. We must also conserve our environment, because we cannot stretch out one hand for food and with the other destroy the environment that creates it.

"Trespasses" comprises the whole domain of moral conduct, not merely abstention from sin and crime. Many trespasses today are invisible: the trespasses of corporate wrongdoing, white-collar crime, underdevelopment, economic domination. The Prayer delves deep into each individual's conscience, reaching areas that no legal regulations can police.

"Forgive" cleanses social poisons through forgiveness, not retaliation. No vendettas, no paying off old grudges, no lingering hatreds, no blood feuds. The Prayer embodies a perfect measure of justice, for we are forgiven only as we forgive.

"Temptation" tells us that we enjoy free will—to do good, to abstain from evil, or to commit evil actively. The choice is ours. Temptations lie all around us and many new species are being created all the time. "Be vigilant," says the Prayer, reminding us that the responsibility for decision lies in our hands alone.

The Prayer, then, is a road map showing us how to avoid the one-way track to disaster that awaits us in the twenty-first century if we continue being guided by the same principles of self-centeredness, hatred, and greed that characterized the twentieth. Radiant in his moral splendor, the founder of Christianity has charted a course for us through other avenues — universal love, forgiveness, and resistance to temptation. The range of these temptations has expanded enormously since the time Jesus addressed a simple peasant audience in a pastoral society.

"Deliver us from evil" highlights the need for spiritual values to guide us away from the proliferating sources of evil that beset modern society. The power of these values must not be underestimated, for religion molds the moral stances of four billion out of the world's population of nearly six billion people. This portion of the scriptures of one religion, when thus analyzed for its practical legal content, can perhaps stimulate similar studies in other religions, helping the world translate precept into practice before time runs out.

Justice and the Prayer

Jesus himself faced social problems as intense as any the world faces today, and his conduct in facing them gives us guidance, example, and inspiration. He did not avoid them or turn away from them as worldly problems of no concern to a man of spirituality. Jesus' approach was to humanize law and legal structures, making them serve man, rather than the institutions they entrenched. He faced imperialism at its height (the Roman), tyranny at its worst (the Herodian), and exploitation at its most acute (of the poor by the rulers, both imperial and Jewish, as well as by the rich). Gross discrimination (between Roman and non-Roman, Jew and Gentile), religious intolerance, mass infanticide, genocide, the most barbaric forms of torture—all of these were accommodated within a legal structure that honored the letter of the law, but lacked humanistic vision. Jesus did not run away from them or become a recluse in the face of their barbarity. He faced these problems squarely—spiritually, intellectually, and physically. That is the example he left behind, an example he fortified by a sublime body of spiritual teaching; a wealth of spiritual teaching and human rights principles lies encapsulated in the Lord's Prayer—if we but notice, and heed, its prescriptions for conduct.

Our Century of Last Opportunity

This century opened in a blaze of hope. A fanfare of voices from across the world demanded peace on earth and the banishment of war. A glittering Peace Conference assembled for this purpose at The Hague in 1899. The new century, so bright in promise when it began, withered into a century of *lost* opportunity. The century about to begin, in a fresh glow of expectation, will be our century of *last* opportunity, for if humanity should blunder once more, it will receive no further chance. We are caught in a web of self-centeredness, hatred, and greed. These forces have cast their long shadows over the century that is about to begin. ("The next century will be religious or it will not be at all," said André Malraux.) The world desperately needs to tap the wisdom of the Prayer in order to guide us into a century of renewed hope.

But have we relaid the tracks that have thus far led us to war and devastation, torture and genocide, gas chambers and ethnic cleansing, terrorism and despair? Or are we careering along, oblivious that we are on a one-way track to disaster?

In its capacity for the infliction of human suffering, the nineteenth century had surpassed all previous centuries. It had achieved new levels of efficiency in the regimentation of resources for the slaughter of enemy populations. Conscience-stricken, the peoples of the world were raising their voices in protest. Peace societies proliferated across the world. They numbered over four hundred by the turn of the century. They pressed for a conference to end all wars. The century of Napoleon, the military genius, Bismarck, the Iron Chancellor, and Clausewitz, the philosopher of war, began to hear arguments that sounded strange to the ears of statesmen accustomed to conducting wars from the gilded comfort of their palaces.

The brash new voices were asserting, in the face of the accepted political tradition of the time, that the slaughter of tens of thousands of vigorous young men in the prime of their youth might not be the most rational means of proving the justice of one's cause. The conference table might possibly be resorted to, *before* the business of slaughter commenced, for purposes of conciliation and arbitration. "Peace on earth: goodwill to men," a cry heard twenty centuries ago, began to echo through the corridors of power. It was greeted as revolutionary new doctrine.

However, the clamor for peace reached a crescendo pitch. It was heard by the crowned heads of the day. It pierced even the fortifications of the Kremlin that housed one of the most absolute monarchies on earth. The Czar of Russia took the initiative. The United States threw its weight behind his efforts. Thus it was that in the last year of that war-torn century, nations great and small sent emissaries to The Hague. They made plans to lead humanity to a golden future free of the scourge of war. The conference went further along the path to establishing a machinery for global justice than any other conference in recorded history. The angels' nativity song of peace and goodwill, repeated by Christian Europe every Christmas Day for nearly twenty centuries, drew closer than ever to fulfillment. Serious action seemed about to replace mechanical repetition of these hallowed sentiments.

The logic of the new position appeared compelling, however much it might fly in the face of tradition and accepted wisdom. It was strengthened by the cries of mangled and dying soldiers reechoing from smoking battlefields, and the wails of bereaved wives and mothers rising plaintively from shattered homes. A new era of hope had dawned.

That hope was blighted. "Progress" and "civilization" had not stood still in the intervening years, with the advent of machine guns and poison gas.

World War I mowed down the flower of the world's youth with far greater efficiency, thanks to these new weapons. World War II notched up the efficiency of slaughter even further with aerial bombardment and suffocation in the gas chambers. We prepare for World War III by spending trillions of dollars on marvels of scientific ingenuity that could annihilate our species and all life with it. As we mass manufacture everything in this age of technology, so also we mass manufacture death and suffering.

The result of all these "advances" has been that the century meant to be a child of hope has turned into a monument to despair. It ends in an epidemic of violence, destruction, and dejection. We urgently need a means of preventing this century's bonfires from burning into the next. In that century, peace will not be a desirable option but a compelling imperative.

While the world looks on, mesmerized in fascinated fear, dreadful new chapters are added to the "long and lamentable catalogue of human crime." A new tribalism raises its head. One by one, the settled bastions of law and order surrender. The principles and structures of civilized coexistence seem to be in terminal decay. Justice is in retreat, its authority under challenge, its content under ridicule.

Sensitivity to the sufferings of others is dulled, as the grossest brutalities are flashed every hour on television screens to an audience whose scale is unprecedented in human history. Impressions of the success of might over right, thus dramatically demonstrated, flood out from the centers of oppression to reach a world public whose disillusionment increases by the day. The contention of the ancient Sophists that a fistful of might is worth a bagful of right seems to receive new confirmation every day. The vision of humanity's ability some day to reach a sunlit plateau of international cooperation recedes inexorably before the vision of a headlong descent into primitive lawlessness. The world seems soaked in injustice.

Such is the scene that greets us as this century closes and such will be the note on which the new century will begin—the last in which humankind still has the ability to choose between progress and destruction.

Percipient observers of the human scene, writing even in the first half of this century, have noted these options and how fast they are closing. Either

a renascent *Homo sapiens* struggles on to a new, a harder, and a happier world dominion, or he blunders down the slopes of failure…in the wake of all the monster reptiles and beasts that have flourished and lorded it on the earth before him, to his ultimate extinction....This is no guess that is put before you, no fantasy; it is a plain and reasoned assembling of known facts in their natural order and relationship. It faces you. Meet it or shirk it, this is the present outlook for mankind.[5]

This century of *last* opportunity to correct the errors of the century of *lost* opportunity may well be the century of *least* opportunity for peace, if we ignore the call to universalism, the warning against trespasses, and the call for forgiveness that reverberates magisterially throughout the Lord's Prayer.

CHAPTER 2

THE POWER
OF THE PRAYER

The Lord's Prayer is a prayer for all time. Ringing out across the ages, it has in every generation enjoyed a central place in Christian thought and worship. It is also a prayer for all times: joy and celebration, pain and sorrow, birth and death, sickness and health, reunions and farewells. There is no aspect of the human condition to which it is not intensely relevant. It is recited by hundreds of millions of people in hundreds of millions of situations.

The Prayer sounds a clarion call for justice in our dealings with every human being, every community, every nation. Even a modicum of compliance with the principles of justice it encapsulates would have saved us from ending the second millennium with the Prayer's underlying philosophy unimplemented, its social message unrecognized, its practical principles violated.

Mechanical and ceremonial repetition of the Prayer—and there is no dearth of this—is no substitute for compliance with its inner core of meaning. Its width needs to be comprehended, its depths explored, its wealth of practical guidance recognized. Though the Prayer is laden with what the Proverbs of Solomon describe as "instruction in wise dealing, righteousness, justice and equity" (Proverbs of Solomon, 1:3), the practical instruction it contains tends to be passed over by most reciters who focus only on its spiritual content.

Though successive generations of Christians have treated it with the utmost reverence, they have tended to see it as a purely religious pronouncement. Though they have solemnly repeated it, even at the commencement of their parliaments and congresses, they have failed to translate it into principles of practical law and government. Though its social message is self-evident, they have encrusted it with theology and ritual. Often reduced to rote recitation, its sweeping practical prescriptions for human conduct remain largely unperceived.

What are the strengths of the Prayer that make it such a powerful instrument for justice?

Centrality to Christian Doctrine

At one end of the spectrum of knowledge and experience, the Lord's Prayer is among the earliest prayers a child learns to lisp. At the other, outstanding philosophers see it as embodying the quintessence of Christian teaching.

This special reverence for the Prayer is discernible from the earliest days of Christianity. In the second century, for instance, Clement of Alexandria stressed the need to reverence the Prayer as a vessel of infinite knowledge. Tertullian, one of the preeminent writers of the early Church, described it as a summary of the whole gospel and a prayer book of the entire Church (Tertullian, *De Oratione*, 1.PL 1, 1155). Saint Augustine observed that there is nothing in all the words of the holy prayers in scripture that is not contained within it (St. Augustine, Ep. 130, 12.22; PL 33, 503), and Saint Thomas Aquinas praised it as "the most perfect of prayers" (St. Thomas Aquinas, *S. Th.*, II-II, 83,9). In our own age, it has been described as "the quintessential prayer of the Church."[1]

Intellectual Content

The Prayer, apart from its doctrinal content, has been an intellectual inspiration to scholars throughout the ages. Works upon it range from such early tracts as that of Saint Augustine in the fifth century, through those of such giants as Thomas Aquinas, Desiderius Erasmus, and Martin Luther, down to the most recent profusion of books upon the subject. Among others who have written upon it are such diverse personalities as Sir Matthew Hale, the seventeenth-century Chief Justice of England; William Blake, the poet; Saint Teresa of Avila; Aldous Huxley, the philosopher; and Cardinal Wyszynski.

Library searches, by no means comprehensive, show over a thousand books specifically devoted to the Prayer. Apart from scores of works that describe themselves as sermons or commentaries on the Lord's Prayer, many of them draw attention to the variety of possible approaches to the Prayer. Some of the more intriguing titles are: *Could You Not Tarry One Hour?*; *Help! I Don't Know How to Pray; The Lord's Prayer in the Light of Yoga; Bold to Say; The Prayer of Integral Liberation; Laws of Progress in the*

Lord's Prayer; The Politics of the Kingdom: A Study of the Lord's Prayer; A Journalist Looks at the Lord's Prayer; and *An Octave of Song, A Rainbow of Hope.*

And these titles are only the English-language works! French, Spanish, and German studies also abound, adding to the deluge of writing stimulated by its remarkable inspirational and intellectual content. It is also interesting to note that Hugo Grotius, the father of international law, wrote a short comment on the Lord's Prayer in seven pages of verse, which could be sung to the tune of the twelfth Psalm.[2]

Timelessness

The Prayer is timeless—as much a prayer for the third millennium as it was for the first and second. It is a prayer for the global society of the future, as it was for the parochial society of days gone by.

Since the Prayer exists not merely in the spiritual realm but is also firmly anchored to practicalities, it calls for a continuing effort, in the changing contexts of each age, to apply and interpret its maxims to meet the problems of the day. The village, the tribe, and the province, which bounded the vision of the generation that received the Prayer, have rolled back their frontiers even beyond those of nation-states, revealing vistas of the vast global community to which we all belong. That society is universally oriented, technologically penetrated, and industrially dominated. Its problems are of a new order that could scarcely be visualized by prior generations and, least of all, by the simple rural communities that were its immediate recipients.

Analyses worked out for the parochial societies of the past, valuable though they are, need reconsideration in the light of problems unprecedented in the annals of human experience. The Christian message needs to be interpreted to meet the new problems resulting from the dominance of technology[3] and of corporate organization. Economic crimes may cause damage just as extensively as crimes of violence. Yet, in the former, the moral imperative tends to be submerged from view, since such crimes do not involve physical force. Hence, the relevance of the Prayer is overlooked.

Social patterns and global problems, unforeseen and unforeseeable by the audience who received the Prayer—and indeed by generations of later commentators—need, therefore, to be urgently addressed. Many of these problems concern legal and human rights, which are profoundly relevant to the needs of the twenty-first century when all mankind must learn to live as a family, or perish. As humanity glances anxiously toward the onset of the next century, it needs the guidance not merely of law, but of the laws that stand behind the law.

A Code of Social Conduct

A mine of spiritual instruction and earthly wisdom, the Lord's Prayer is also a code of social conduct. Nearly a hundred human rights principles, vital to human survival in the next millennium, lie embedded within it, waiting to be quarried (see Appendix). They are not activated, as their presence is not recognized in this code of conduct, which carries the supreme authority of the author of the Prayer.

Free of theological intricacies, liturgical niceties, and dogmatic assertions, this Prayer, which is more than a prayer, sets out a code of conduct that is more than a code. It deals simultaneously with the framework of the individual's relationship with God and with all other human beings. In one short prayer, a marvel of comprehensiveness and brevity, the supreme exponent of the Christian way of life—Christ, the lawgiver—formulates for all time a set of principles covering every facet of human conduct.

Christological research has tended to concentrate on Christ as priest and prophet, and not on Christ as the supreme lawgiver of the Christian world. These writings have scarcely explored Christ's teachings as laying the foundations for the fundamental rights of humankind.

One would expect the legal systems of the Christian world—and they are among the world's most influential—to take their spirit and philosophy from Christ's explicit teachings about law. Surprisingly, they have gone principally in the opposite direction, while professing loyalty to Christian principles. Neglecting the spirit of the law for the letter, they have elevated property and power and diminished the worth of the human person. They often see the law with a fine eye to all its embroidered intricacies, but not the social purpose behind it.

This vast treasure house of legal and human rights principles is relevant equally to the lawyer and to the layman, to the Christian and to the non-Christian, to those who pray and to those who do not.

Practicality

Many a prayer, rich in doctrinal content, loses sight of the practicalities of living. A prime characteristic of the Prayer is that, while being a sublime piece of spiritual teaching, it does not lose sight of humanity's material needs. This notion is captured in the petition relating to daily bread, thus giving recognition at the more basic level to the fact that there are economic and physical needs that religion cannot afford to neglect. It is a down-to-earth prayer, anchored to the ground where humanity must pass its existence—however much it may long for the heavenly state that is its goal.

In the parlance of modern human rights discourse, the Prayer does not lose sight of the areas of social and economic rights. Long before international legal discourse recognized the need for economic rights, the Prayer accorded them a place of high importance. While nourishing the soul with spiritual food, it recognized the body's need for nourishment with daily bread. Bread is symbolic of that which is necessary for the sustenance of life with dignity: food, clothing, shelter, education, employment. These need to be in adequate supply. At the same time, the word "daily" is an eloquent sermon on the need for moderation in our requests and expectations. With the maximum economy of language, the need is recognized and its limitations defined.

The Prayer's concern with practicality does not end here. Practicality suffuses the Prayer throughout, from its first word to the last, for each word is replete with practical implications of a legal, social, ethical, economic, parochial, national, and international nature. The Prayer translates itself forcefully into authoritative principles relating to every aspect of our daily life in society.

The more one ponders it, the more one wonders at its inexhaustible content.

The Prayer's conciseness and directness render it an extremely handy prayer for frequent use. It cuts through the encrustations of accumulated theology and ritual and drills to the core of Christ's message. The pressures of life often leave the average person with little time for elaborate or complicated prayers. Though brief, the Lord's Prayer is not so compressed as to omit essentials and curtail the sweep and vision befitting a dialogue with the Infinite. Rather, as both down-to-earth people and philosophers have attested with admiration, the Prayer crystallizes the quintessential wisdom of Christian doctrine. Its intent is to be an exercise in simple and genuine piety. It rejects the trappings that often clutter up the very process of prayer. It contains no flourishes, no traditional recitals, no invocations of prior prophets, no learned formulas. "In praying do not heap up empty phrases as the Gentiles do; for they think they will be heard for their many words. Do not be like them….Pray then like this" (Matthew 6:7–9). These words that precede Christ's teaching of the Prayer capture its spirit—a spirit that infuses it with simplicity and sincerity, power and practicality.

In the words of the *New Jerome Biblical Commentary,* "Jesus' bequest of the 'Our Father' to his disciples will not only teach them how to pray but especially how to live and act as his followers."[4]

The battle-hardened Duke of Wellington, when questioned about religious instruction for his soldiers, said that all they needed to know about Christianity was contained in the Lord's Prayer.

The French essayist Montaigne observed of the Prayer, "I would have all good Christians to say the *Pater Noster*, and if no other prayer, at least not to omit that….It is the only prayer I use in every place, at all times and upon every accident."[5] In many monastic orders, it was considered so important that lay brothers were permitted to recite the Prayer a certain number of times every day instead of the Divine Office.[6] Saint Francis of Assisi, for example, recommended to his brothers that the Prayer be recited twenty-four times in the morning and as often as possible throughout the day.[7]

Authority and Eminence

The Prayer carries the fundamental authority of its Author, who taught it as the recommended form of prayer in response to the disciples' specific request that they be taught how to pray. Other prayers, such as the Rosary, which are built around the *Ave Maria*, also accord a place of honor to the Lord's Prayer. One need note little more than that there is no other expressly formulated prayer in the Christian prayer book that goes back in its formulation to Jesus himself. Jesus did indeed pray other prayers as, for example, when he prayed for all his followers that they may all be one and that Jesus may be in them and them in him (John 17:20–26), but those were not prayers for general use.

This is not to say anything in diminution of the many other prayers beloved of Christians. Indeed, what has been described as a great treasury of prayers is available to Christians: Mary's song of praise, the *Magnificat*; the *Gloria in Excelsis Deo* of the angelic chorus on the first Christmas night; the *Kyrie*; the *Agnus Dei*; and the Jesus Prayer, to mention a few.[8] For the devout Christian they will always have a place of honor and devotion. Yet they are songs of praise or invocation, rather than summaries of belief or doctrine.

The Nicene Creed is, of course, a summary of doctrine but was formulated after much debate by a council of the early Church. It is not recited regularly by the lay Christian, and it is too long for frequent practical use. Nor can the Creed be understood by a little child when it enters areas of dogma and doctrine well beyond childhood's level of understanding.

Treating the Lord's Prayer as a universal prayer is no reflection on other religions, for the Prayer contains no presuppositions beyond allegiance to a universal and supreme source of life. It embodies a code of righteous conduct that is universally applicable. Thus people of all religions can identify with its central theme, and there is inherent within it a tolerance of all religious faiths. Its only assumption is the centrality of that magisterial power that guides and governs all things animate and inanimate.

Relevance to Modern Youth

The demand of youth for social relevance

The Prayer's remarkable combination of the practically relevant with the morally sublime carries a special message for the youth of today. Impatient of dogma and technicalities, they grope around, in the midst of manifest social injustices, for some religious guidance to provide them with the pillars on which to build their world order of the future. They look around their immediate world and find organized religion expending vast resources and energies on the outward forms of worship, while all around them there proliferate the problems of the hungry, the naked, the deprived, and the persecuted to whose needs Jesus pointedly drew attention. Touched by these problems, and seeking inspiration and leadership from the churches, they tend to be disappointed.

An epidemic of disillusionment is sweeping through the younger generation. The boundless wealth of inspiration available in religion thus fails

to combine with the boundless enthusiasm available in youth. That enthusiasm trickles into the sands, as far as a large number of youth are concerned.
Churches are not seen by many of today's youth as expending sufficient
effort in transforming moral teaching into practical conduct, religious precept into "daily bread."

The confusion of youth by the separation of faith from reason

Youth has further been confused by the separation of faith from reason, as
the two are portrayed as mutually exclusive. Throughout the nineteenth
century, the Church taught blind faith, and the universities taught intellectual rationalism. The mind of youth was confused, and that confusion still
continues.

Today science is showing us that the two approaches are not mutually
exclusive. At its highest levels, science hovers on the borders of the metaphysical, and the old distinctions between mind and matter are breaking
down. Neither religious nor educational institutions can today afford such
rigid separations in their teachings. As the psychologist C. G. Jung observed
in the early part of this century, the world was then reaping the fruit of
nineteenth-century education.[9] We should not repeat this dichotomy today.

Religion as supporter of the established order

It is important, if youth is not to continue to be alienated, that an institution
that they rightly view as a prime inspirational source of social reform should
not be seen by them as a supporter of the *status quo*, even when all the
equities that religion stands for cry out for change.

Martin Luther King, Jr. had strong words of criticism on these lines—
perhaps not entirely unjustified. The great American Nobel laureate, with
his penetrating insight into the social malaise of his time, observed:

> If today's church does not recapture the sacrificial spirit of the early
> church, it will lose its authenticity, forfeit the loyalty of millions, and
> be dismissed as an irrelevant social club with no meaning for the twen-
> tieth century. Every day I meet young people whose disappointment
> with the church has turned into outright disgust.[10]

These are telling comments, uttered as they were by a charismatic figure as deeply Christian in spirit and in practice as any this century has seen. Stripped clear of generations of church organization and centuries of theological writings, the Lord's Prayer comes to us direct from the lips of the Founder, setting out with limpid clarity, and in language understood by any teenager, a message vibrant with the call for reform of our iniquitous social order. With its unique combination of practicality and spirituality, the Prayer can powerfully focus youth's attention on the truth that heavenly duty needs to be performed on earthly soil. It does not stand aloof from the contemporary problems of humanity, but homes in on them with saving values and a moving call to action. It can be an answer to the quest of youth for a practical relationship between religion and social reform.

The divisiveness of religion

Another alienating factor is what youth perceives as the divisiveness of religion.

All religions in one way or another provide such divisive factors in their more narrow and doctrinaire interpretations. That divisiveness is further accentuated by formalistic rituals, abstruse dogma, and a constant repetition of abstract moralities unrelated to their practical application on the ground. Even within the fold of Christianity, there is a vast conflict between different denominations, which sometimes surfaces—as in Ireland—in violence and bloodshed. Relations between Christianity and other religions are not as understanding as they should be, having regard to the vast areas of moral principle on which they tread common ground. If the churches would provide inspirational leadership in this latter regard, one would not perhaps hear so often the comment of the younger generation that they accept Christianity but reject "Churchianity"—a set of narrow Church-made rules with which they cannot identify.

The right of youth to a share in the management of the future

The twenty-first century belongs to the youth of today, and it is they who will make or break the human future.

Youth suffers most in the conflicts of every age, yet bears the least share of the blame for causing those conflicts. It is thrust into the front line of the battle but is not even in the back rooms of the power play that produces them. It is the idealistic element of the human race, but is thrown by its elders into the role of destroyers of each other's dreams. It has cause for dissatisfaction with the way in which its rich moral inheritance has been mangled by its elders.[11]

Every principle in the Lord's Prayer is one with which the youth of today can readily identify, if it is presented to them on the practical basis that constitutes the core of its structure. As already noted, it is universal: Non-Christians can relate to it as well as Christians. Out of its sweeping concepts today's youth can extract sufficient principles to galvanize them in their dream of building that world order—more practical, more just, more universal, more conducive to peace—for which they yearn.

A better future for all can only be built on imagination and hope, on visions and dreams. Youth is rich in this regard, but there is no place for daydreams in the corridors of power or in the gilded mansions of the establishment. The Prayer opens a door to such a vista, for its goal is no less than the establishment on earth of the kingdom of heaven. This is a goal that goes even beyond the fondest dreams of youth. Presented this way, youth will respond to its call.

A society that fully practices the principles of the Prayer would of course reach

> Amazing heights of boundless Power
> Unfathomable depths of Love.[12]

but this is too much to hope for.

Yet a greater compliance with the principles of the Prayer will considerably hasten our progression toward a just society in which we can truly say, "Thy kingdom come, thy will be done on earth as it is in heaven."

CHAPTER 3

THE FRAMEWORK
OF THE PRAYER

The opening words "Our Father" provide the framework within which the Prayer is set. They cover *all* human relationships from a universal perspective, for they place *all* human beings together, as members of a common family. These first two words, therefore, are a fitting name for the Prayer.

A. "OUR"

The word carries the connotation of membership in a community. With community membership comes the concept of affirmative action to help those in the community who are in dire need. With equal membership of a common community comes the concept also of a unity in the basic rules by which all members are governed.

The Concept of Equality

The seamless web of humanity

The reader will see immediately the significance of a word that addresses a common Father and proclaims the existence of a common group who so address Him. Within the circle thus placed together in a single group, and addressing a common Creator or source of their being, there are no divisions. God is a common Father, alike to them all.

All human beings are placed in a single group bonded in a common relationship to their Creator and united by commonality of origin and dependence. Divisions of sex, color, age, race, wealth, learning, and birth disappear. Aristocracies and superiorities of all descriptions are flattened out. It "breaks boundaries separating rich and poor, hale and halt, men and women, clean and unclean, saint and sinner."[1]

> God purposely chose what the world considers nonsense in order to shame the wise, and he chose what the world considers weak in order to shame the powerful. He chose what the world looks down on and despises, and thinks is nothing, in order to destroy what the world thinks is important (1 Corinthians 1:27–28).

Neither wisdom nor physical strength nor social status can smother the principle of equality that is thus enthroned.

Absence of a religious elect

Whereas the prayers of the time of Jesus recalled many special gifts and tasks awaiting a chosen people, not one of those is mentioned in the Lord's Prayer.[2] Nor is there any reference to Christians being intermediaries between God and the nations in such terms as their being "a guide to the blind, a light to those who are in darkness, a corrector of the foolish, a teacher of children."[3] Nor is there any reference to a special order of learned or priestly people entrusted with special religious powers who served as a channel through which the Father should be addressed.

Helen Wodehouse, in her insightful work *Inner Light*,[4] gave expression to the idea of a direct approach to God in a very plain-spoken manner when she wrote:

> We think we must climb to a certain height of goodness before we can reach God. But…if we are in a hole the Way begins in the hole. The moment we set our face in the same direction as His, we are walking with God.

However low, therefore, a person may be in his or her level of education or spirituality, that person is not an underprivileged member of the flock. If he or she should turn toward God, uttering a prayer that requires no elitism or learning for it to be repeated with feeling, that person is at once upon the upward road that leads direct to the source of all life and power. The track may be long and arduous, but the vital first step is taken, for, in the words of the Chinese proverb, a journey of a thousand miles begins with the first step. The Lord's Prayer makes this first step available to all without distinction, irrespective of learning, position, or status.

In other words, there is no exclusivity in the Lord's Prayer. No distinctions, no secret incantations, no barriers. It is a prayer for all; and just as its utterance elevates the sinner, so also it elevates the saint.

> Finally, the Lord's Prayer is not a prayer for a community or a church; any particular quality of faith or revelation, historical election or eschatological promise, cult or law, disappears in the equality with which the children of God stand before their Father.[5]

The individual, freed of the shackles of the past, faces and communicates with his or her Maker with a new confidence born of the conferment of this supreme dignity. The peasant in his field of mud spoke from the same pedestal of dignity as the Czar in his palace of marble.

The Concept of Dignity

Dignity resulting from direct communication with the Father

To give the individual the right thus to address God directly was to invest him or her with the greatest dignity. No priest or bishop or pope, no nobleman or king or emperor, could do any better. The Prayer was a great leveler, but it leveled up rather than leveled down. Every individual was elevated to the level of dignity previously enjoyed only by the privileged few.

Rev. Robert Schuller, in his little booklet on *Five Negative Emotions,*[6] puts this aspect in down-to-earth language when he says:

> The Lord's Prayer heals us of our inferiority. Call it lack of self-esteem, lack of self-respect or lack of self-worth….The Lord's Prayer gives me pride and humility, both in perfect measure, at the same time. How? Why, 'Our Father' wow! If God is my Father, then I have a good bloodline. *I am somebody.*

The daughter of Louis XV of France is said to have told one of her ladies in waiting, whom she thought to have been disrespectful to her, "Do you not know that I am the king's daughter?" to which the lady is said to have replied, "And I am a child of God."[7]

Paul, in his Epistle to the Galatians, gives expression to this same concept when he writes:

> To show that you are his sons, God sent the Spirit of his Son into our hearts, the Spirit who cries out, "Father, my Father." So then, you are no longer a slave but a son. And since you are his son, God will give you all that he has for his sons. (Galatians 4:6–7. See also Romans 8:10–17.)

Origen, one of the early commentators on the Prayer, refers in his *De Oratione* to the "boldness of speech" on the part of Jesus in addressing God as Father, which goes beyond Jewish practice.[8] Origen made the point that "In the Old Testament there is no prayer invoking God in the name of the Father." The Christian community has for centuries treated the right to pray directly to the Father as a special privilege, for prior to Vatican II the time-honored formula introducing the Prayer in the Roman Missal read: "Admonished by your teachings and instructed by divine institution, we *dare to say*: 'Our Father…'"

Dignity resulting from the oneness of Jesus with his flock

Jesus joins his followers in this Prayer. He does not set himself in a class apart from them but is one of them—part and parcel of the community that together addresses the common father in adoration and supplication. He prayed in the desert and on the hilltops, in the fields and by the sea, and indeed on the cross itself, addressing himself to the same Father he asked his followers to invoke.

The fact that Jesus, the supreme embodiment of human dignity among Christians, is a member of the group that addresses the Father gives every member of that group a new dignity—a dignity that no act of man can take away. The word "our" as used in the Prayer would bring Jesus himself into the community that addresses the Father. The implications from the standpoint of human dignity are profound.

Dignity of every human being reinforced by Jesus' own conduct

Jesus consorted with the poor and humble, with sinners and children, and paid no particular attention to worldly rank and privilege. "Whoever would be great among you must be your servant, and whoever would be first among you must be slave of all." The variety of people to whom he turned his attention is striking: the blind, the lame, the crippled, the poor, the hungry, the miserable, the lepers, the prostitutes, the tax collectors, the children, the persecuted, the downtrodden, those who were overburdened, the rabble, the sinners, those who labored, and those who were possessed by unclean spirits. He reached out to the whole gamut of humanity, however lowly. They were all his brothers and sisters, with no ranking among them.[9]

Indeed, to seek out the future leaders of his religion he did not search the ranks of the spiritually or academically elite, even though this might earn their lifelong antagonism. He sought out the humble, addressed their needs, and preached to them at their level of understanding, thus propelling some of the most ordinary people to the highest levels of spiritual attainment. Just as he distanced himself from the elitism of wealth and position by the manner of his life, he distanced himself from the elitism of mysticism and learning through the substance of his teaching.

Through express statements of oneness with all, irrespective of rank or background, he drove home this lesson of equality: "Whoever does what my Father in heaven wants him to do is my brother, my sister, and my mother" (Matthew 12:50). We also have the teaching (Matthew 22:34–40) that next to love of God the greatest of all commandments is "Love your neighbor as you love yourself." There are no ranks or distinctions among the category of neighbors. They must all be equally loved and equally served. On love of God and of one's neighbors depend "The whole Law of Moses and the teachings of the prophets" (Matthew 22:40).

Dignity resulting from God's empathy with the supplicant

The God addressed in the Lord's Prayer is a caring God. By contrast, the Greek and Roman gods were conceived as ruling humanity from high Olympus, without any sense of nearness to them in their joys or sorrows. They were so far above humans as to be incapable of being affected by human actions. In the words of Sallustius, who wrote an authoritative treatise on the ancient gods in a last reaction against Christianity:

> God does not rejoice—for that which rejoices also grieves; nor is he angered—for to be angered is a passion; nor is he appeased by gifts—if he were he would be conquered by pleasure.[10]

The Epicureans saw the gods as totally detached from the world, the Stoics as unable to experience any feelings at all. Such was the impersonal deity of classical philosophy.

Against this background, the Prayer made a breakthrough in bringing about a greater closeness to God and thereby immensely raising the level of dignity of every individual human being. The concept of dignity, as thus taught in the Prayer, can be summarized in the words of a modern writer on the Lord's Prayer:

> If God is *our* Father, then our fellow man is our brother…Nationalism, racialism, snobbery, class distinction, the color bar, apartheid, stand uncompromisingly condemned in the two words which open our Lord's Prayer. If we pray those words and hate or despise our brother man, then the prayer is a mockery and we make ourselves liars.[11]

The Concept of Irremovability of Rights

Modern human rights theory sees human rights as inhering in the human person by reason of his or her humanity, and not as flowing from the grant or generosity of any state or ruler. The very fact of humanness invests every person with those rights, which none can take away. Not even the individual who possesses these rights can trade them away.

In the field of human rights, it was not without a strenuous intellectual battle that this concept was won. Thomas Hobbes (1588-1679), and other famous exponents of absolute sovereignty theories, sought to argue that all rights lay at the disposal of the sovereign and that the individual's rights could be taken away at the sovereign's pleasure. John Locke (1632–1704) was a pioneer among Western philosophers in arguing that there were certain rights that were irremovable and that inhered in every human being by virtue of being a human being. The thinking of Locke on this matter passed into the American *Declaration of Independence,* 1776, and the French declaration of *The Rights of Man and of the Citizen*, 1789. It contains the core principles of modern human rights doctrine. Locke, in formulating his theory, was much influenced by the Christian notion of the dignity of every human being.

The direct relationship between every individual and his or her creator, as enshrined in the Lord's Prayer, means that no empires of power can interpose themselves between the individual and the Source. The Prayer swept away with one stroke the whole apparatus of secular, religious, or learned privilege, revealing the individual in all his dignity and majesty—a dignity and majesty that, because it was recognized by God, could not be taken away by man. That notion, through its influence on human rights doctrine, has contributed much to human liberty on a global scale today.

The concept of inalienability is now enshrined in the Preamble to the *Universal Declaration of Human Rights*, which stresses, at the very outset of this memorable document, the recognition of the *inalienable* rights of all members of the human family as one of the pillars of freedom, justice, and peace in the world.

Pope John XXIII's *Pacem in terris* harmonizes religious teaching and human rights doctrine:

> It is our earnest wish that the United Nations Organization may become ever more equal to the magnitude and nobility of its tasks, and that the day may come when every human being will find therein an effective safeguard for the rights which derive directly from his dignity as a person, and which are therefore universal, inviolable and inalienable rights.

The Concept of Community

The words "our" and "we" and "us," eight times repeated in the Prayer, emphasize that one is not praying for oneself alone. One prays as a member of a group or community, and one cannot pray for oneself without at the same time praying for others. In the words of John Donne,[12] "No man is an island, entire of itself; every man is a piece of the continent, a part of the main."

The first message in the Prayer is a message against selfishness or self-centeredness. Every time they pray, those who use the Prayer "are reminded that they are a brotherhood, a society, a Holy Church, or family, of which the members are mutually responsible for one another's welfare."[13]

With community come mutual duties. One cannot shut oneself up in an individualistic shell and disclaim interest in the needs or the welfare of one's neighbor. "One cannot say, as Cain, 'Am I my brother's keeper?'"[14] As a member of a group, the individual identifies with the group in its activities, its prayers, and its needs. There is a strong rejection of such aspects of individualism as encourage a person to build up assets and possessions in such a manner as to damage the interests of the community, or fiercely compete with his neighbor for the appropriation of scarce resources. Charity toward all, love for one's neighbor, solicitude for the poor, and the brotherhood of man are incompatible with these attitudes.

The notion of collective duties assumes special relevance for our time, for the problems the human family faces today are so immense that it is only by collective action and collective discharge of responsibility that they can be meaningfully addressed. Vast problems such as those associated with world poverty and environmental degradation need such a collective effort. If we are called upon to pray collectively and to invoke blessings upon ourselves collectively, there must be collective obligations attaching to the benefits we hope to receive. Society cannot function on the basis only of the fulfillment of individual obligations, for there is a limit to what individuals can do. There have to be collective obligations as well—and the more so when the most urgent of our problems, on which our very survival depends, can only be solved by collective action. To pray collectively and insist on acting individually is a contradiction in terms.

The first word of the Lord's Prayer thus extends outward and horizontally toward all fellow human beings, bonding them together in a single community, as contrasted with the second word, "Father," which extends upward and vertically, linking each of them to their common source by ties of parental affection and authority.

The Concept of Universality

For the concept of the indivisibility of the human family so clearly underlying the Prayer itself, we have a powerful confirmation from the gospels. In answer to the lawyer who asked "What must I do to receive eternal life?" Jesus said: "Love the Lord thy God with all thy heart, with all thy soul, with all thy strength, and with all thy mind"; and "Love your neighbor as you love yourself" (Luke 10:25,27). The lawyer perhaps felt rebuffed by this unexpectedly simple answer, and sought to regain his standing with his audience by pursuing the matter legalistically. He asked a further definitional question in the manner beloved of lawyers, for lawyers pride themselves on their precision of thought and language. "And who is my neighbor?" he taunted, hoping perhaps to expose a looseness of thinking on Jesus' part, which would restore his own scholarly authority.

Back came the answer in a parable that has reverberated through the ages: the story of the Good Samaritan. The question could not have been more dramatically or completely answered, for, contrary to the attitudes of the time, the parable powerfully brings out the extension of the concept of community to foreigners as well, the people from Samaria being so regarded.

The analogy bursts through any concept of a special group of chosen elite. The circle of neighbors who constitute a common community is thus vastly extended beyond the borders that circumscribed it in contemporary thought. In the context of today's more closely interlinked world and vastly extended visibility of all nations, the Good Samaritan concept of neighborliness will correspondingly expand.

The life of Jesus also bears out this view of humanity as a single group that he was anxious to serve in its entirety. The people he helped included Samaritans, Romans, and Greeks. For example, in the group of ten lepers healed on the outskirts of a town on the borders of Samaria and Galilee, one was a Samaritan (Luke 17:11–19)—and this indeed was the only one who returned to give him thanks.

It follows from the notion of equal membership of a common community that there is a unity in the rules by which all members are governed. A set of obligations common to all and not varying from one group to another becomes the basis on which society is ordered. This notion has great value as providing a base for a universal code of human obligations and rights. Irrespective of such local and national differences as may exist from state to state, there is also a common and universal code that must apply to all humans by virtue of their humanity.

A major criticism of the *Universal Declaration of Human Rights* has been that it tends to concentrate on rights rather than duties. In the Prayer, on the other hand, it is the concept of universal duty, rather than rights, that receives emphasis. When each individual conforms in his or her conduct to that set of obligations, the obligations toward his or her fellow human beings fall into place. The vertical relationship properly tended leads to a proper ordering of the horizontal relationships between person and person.

The Concept of a Higher Law

There has been a search throughout history for a higher principle or law that stands above all man-made law. The Lord's Prayer offers one means of doing so, by basing human rights and duties upon a higher principle than the purely mundane. Those whose belief systems are God-based would see this higher principle as based on God's will, while those who do not would see other bases for it, which have been variously figured out throughout the long history of thinking about a higher (or natural) law. What is important is the acceptance of a higher set of values than merely mundane considerations as illuminating the path of law and of human rights and duties.

Theoretically, the painful historical process by which modern human rights were achieved would not have been necessary if the central relationship emphasized in the opening words of the Lord's Prayer had been paid due attention.

The Concept of Social Rights and Duties

The Western political tradition tended to obscure the importance of social, economic, and cultural rights, for the historical process by which they evolved tended to concentrate on the civil and political rights that each individual could win from those exercising authority over him. Other rights could supposedly follow, once these rights were established, but they were scarcely the subject of detailed discussion.

The major political revolutions, and the writings associated with them, had concentrated on wresting from despotic authority the civil and political rights that that authority withheld from its subjects. Magna Carta, the Cromwellian Revolution in England, the "Glorious Revolution" of 1688, the French Revolution—all of these aimed at achieving civil and political rights for the people by forcing the authority withholding them to accord due recognition to such rights. The concept of social, economic, and cultural rights was long delayed in achieving equal acceptance in Western legal theory.

So much was this the case that even after the era of modern human rights began, with the enactment of the *Universal Declaration of Human Rights* in 1948, it took eighteen years before economic, social, and cultural rights were placed on a footing of equality with civil and political rights by the simultaneous adoption in 1966 of the twin Covenants: the International

Covenant on Civil and Political Rights and the International Covenant on Economic, Social and Cultural Rights.

To interpose a legalistic dividing line between these two sets of rights creates an unnecessary cleavage in the totality of human rights doctrine that would not be possible according to the central principles underlying the Lord's Prayer. As will be evident also from the discussions of other words in the Prayer, the Prayer takes within its compass the economic and social position of the individual in a manner that is consonant with the most modern approach toward human rights. For example, it does not refrain from referring to the mundane need for "daily bread," which would today be described as an economic right.

The Concept of Ecumenism

The word "our," as observed earlier, joins together in a common bond the whole family of humanity. Among those who profess the Christian faith, there is no room for any divisions, for all Christians alike can with equal sincerity utter every word of the Lord's Prayer. Fine doctrinal distinctions and the tomes of philosophers and theologians sometimes blur the essentials under clouds of verbiage. The resulting differences of interpretation and belief divided the common fold of Christians into antagonistic and sometimes warring groups. Yet the Lord's Prayer, which is central to all of them without exception, offers a bond of unity that none can destroy. Perhaps modern-day ecumenism can lean more heavily on the Lord's Prayer for its basic arguments. By so doing, it can avoid attitudes of antagonism and intolerance that have led so often in history to basic denials of freedom of thought and conscience.

The faithful are taught to pray not merely individually but also together. It is not "my" father who is addressed but "our" father. The presupposition is that, apart from its use by individuals, this is a collective prayer. There is here a clear indication of joint worship that transcends all barriers among the churches.

For all these reasons, it can be said that the opening word of the Prayer gives us a vision that sweeps to the frontiers of legal thought.

B. "FATHER"

Connotations of God's Fatherhood

The transcending of gender

The word "father" in the Prayer transcends considerations of gender. It is a word with all the loving and protective connotations of parenthood. We may recall in this context the words of Isaiah, "I will comfort you…as a mother comforts her child" (Isaiah 66:13; see, also, 49:15). Attributes of the divinity have thus not been exclusively paternal in scripture. The discussions in this volume regard the feminine and the maternal as no different in symbolism from the masculine and the paternal, with all the associated attributes of loving and protective parenthood.

Closeness

As Father Leonardo Boff points out in his work on the Lord's Prayer,[15] the word "father" is used by Jesus as many as 170 times in the gospels (4 in Mark; 15 in Luke; 42 in Matthew; and 109 in John). It is said to convey the sort of love and immediacy of the affectionate word "dad" or "daddy."

The closeness of the word "father" is emphasized also when we recall that in Jesus' time two Semitic languages were used in Palestine. Hebrew was the language of the Bible, Aramaic the language of everyday life. The word "Abba" is Aramaic, a comparatively ordinary and colloquial word contrasting strongly with the elevated and august language in which the Bible referred to God, the Holy One. The deliberate use of the simple and informal expression, in contrast to the dignified and formal terms traditionally used, drove home to Jesus' listeners in a special way the lessons of immediacy, intimacy, and love that he was seeking to convey. We may lose this flavor of closeness if we merely recite the word "father," which is rather more formal, without this awareness of the word actually used by Jesus.

As the Father's love flows to every human being, love flows from every human being to every other. It would be a negation of the concept of love if it were manifested by the individual only toward God, for that would be a truncated and incomplete form of love. The flood of love flowing earthward from heaven does not stop abruptly at each individual, but flows outward through and from each individual to every other.

Mahatma Gandhi said that love is the strongest force the world possesses and yet it is the humblest imaginable.[16] And Ralph Waldo Emerson, the preeminent American philosopher, put it even more strongly when he wrote in his *Essay on Love* that "Love is our highest word and the synonym of God."[17] Little wonder that Jesus, in depicting the Almighty to his followers, should have chosen the analogy of a parent, with all its love-impregnated connotations. Various practical duties follow when one switches from the wavelength of theology to that of social relationship and law.

Justice and Peace

As depicted in the Lord's Prayer, love is a concept that interlocks with justice, for love irresistibly spells out a variety of duties toward others. This aspect was well analyzed by Konrad Braun, a judge of the Berlin Court of Appeal until he was dismissed by the Nazi Government. In his powerful monograph on the interlocking nature of the relationship between love and justice, he argued that justice in all human relationships is the path that love takes in society.[18] Love, therefore, is "the highest standard by which justice on all stages is tested and corrected."[19]

It is implicit also in the father analogy that all disputes among children will be judged according to standards of justice. Not only would the equality prevailing among them be disturbed if one could gain unjust advantages at the expense of another, but the metaphor of fatherhood itself breaks down if injustice can prevail among the members of the father's family and be tolerated without interference by the father.

The Old Testament likewise depicted God as embodying justice and insisting on justice in conduct, rather than the outward forms of religion.

> Do you think I want all these sacrifices you keep offering to me?...Stop all this evil that I see you doing. Yes, stop doing evil and learn to do right. See that justice is done—help those who are oppressed, give orphans their rights, and defend widows (Isaiah 1:11, 16–17).

Such reflections are valuable in reinforcing the notion that, if God is love, God is justice as well.

From the consideration of common parenthood follows a duty among all children to keep the peace. Nothing can be more irreconcilable with the concept of common fatherhood than for the children to rebel against their common father by killing each other. "[W]hosoever shall smite thee on thy right cheek, turn to him the other also" (Matthew 5:39, KJV), and "love your enemies and pray for those who persecute you, so that you may become the sons of your Father in heaven" (Matthew 5:44–45) were surely not words to be received with cynicism and treated with disdain when it suited the purpose in hand. Indeed, these are the teachings that closely precede the formulation of the Lord's Prayer and offer the key to the spirit of love and brotherhood permeating it. These are all brought together in the Beatitudes of the Sermon on the Mount: "Blessed are the peacemakers: for they shall be called the children of God" (Matthew 5:9, KJV).

All that has been said of the inferences that follow from the fatherhood image does not of course exhaust the attributes of God as understood by the Christian. The rich analogy of fatherhood takes one only to the threshold of the spiritual mansion in which one contemplates the concept of divinity. The depiction of God as a father does not in any way militate against the principle Saint Thomas Aquinas formulated so well when he wrote: "The highest knowledge we can have of God in this life is to know that He is above all we can think concerning him."[20] The use of the father analogy does not confine the notion of divinity within the limits of our concepts of fatherhood, but only makes use of the attributes of fatherhood as a starting point for an understanding of the concept of divinity.

Before closing this discussion of the key word "father" in our day, it is perhaps appropriate to consider some psychological theories that emphasize the human craving for an authority figure, which in Freudian language may be described as "the father complex." Out of our feelings of inferiority, insecurity, and fear we are said to conjure up an image that embodies the opposite of these feelings. We cling to it doggedly, though we know it is an illusion. It lulls us into feelings of security, resignation, and avoidance of reality. Accepting the illusion as a reality, we confine ourselves within it and escape from reality.

In the first place, while there is an attitude of resignation to the will of God, the Prayer does not teach passive resignation to our lot. There is, rather, a call to action in straining every nerve to better our environment—socially, politically, economically, legally, internationally, and in every way. (This aspect is elaborated upon in the chapter "Thy Will Be Done.") If we commit ourselves to the ideal that we should have a regime "on earth as it is in heaven," nothing short of our maximum effort is called for. The image represents not an attitude of resignation, but a philosophy of hope.

Second, we are not deluding ourselves in accepting the existence of a superior power. All human experience, and every branch of science—chemistry, physics, botany, zoology, medicine, astronomy—is daily teaching us how much more immense and intricate is the order of the universe than we could possibly have perceived earlier.

Third, there is no incompatibility between the thoughts of an all-powerful Creator ruling the universe and the thought that that Creator has a real interest in oneself. For the believing Christian, this is made easier by the express words of scripture to that effect. Other religions likewise make this clear.

A fourth consideration is that free will is a central principle recognized by the Prayer. The call for protection against temptation recognizes that there is a freedom to act otherwise. The call for forgiveness of sins recognizes that we set our own standards in our forgiveness of others. The entire Prayer is framed for a free-willing individual and not for an automaton mechanically implementing the Father's will.

Fifth, far from a father remote from us in spirit, the image we have is one of a loving and caring father.

Sixth, we do not diminish ourselves by the father image as is implicit in Freudian thought. We do not abandon our judgment or authority. We do not cower helplessly under the protection of an all-powerful father. Rather, our own dignity is enhanced, and our will is liberated.

Finally, as I observed at the beginning of this chapter, the connotations of the fatherhood image are not gender-based.

The fatherhood image, far from encouraging childish dependence, stimulates social responsibility. Far from inducing quiescence, it is an urgent call to action. Far from being an evasion of reality, it focuses attention on the real problems of starvation, disease, violence, and waste that we see all around us. In terms of Jesus' teachings, these are the Father's intimate concerns, for what is done for suffering humanity is done for the Father himself. In short, the fatherhood image provides us with an ideal that rises gigantic above all the petty squabbles and ambitions that have bedeviled humanity's eternal quest for justice.

CHAPTER 4

READING THE PRAYER

Jesus' Attitude to Prayer

Our starting point is Jesus' own attitude toward prayer, for it is not the mere recital of a prayer that matters, but the reciter's attitude toward it.

We know from Luke's Gospel in particular that Jesus was continually in prayer. In fact, Luke gives over twenty references to Christ's teaching on prayer and to his own practice of prayer. Prayer for Jesus was a continuing dialogue with the Father, and indeed it is in this sense that the Lord's Prayer needs to be regarded. It was a dialogue resorted to on a daily basis, in good times and in bad, and was a conversation rather than an emergency appeal. As a continuing conversation, it set the tone for one's daily life.

Indeed, this fact probably lay behind the disciples' request to Jesus to teach them how to pray. It is not that there was any dearth of well-known prayers in the Jewish tradition, which was particularly rich in this respect. Rather, what the disciples were seeking was probably an insight into such matters as one's relationship with God, and the priorities and fundamentals that should be uppermost in one's attitude and requests. One notes that Jesus is recorded as saying "This, then, is how you should pray…" (Matthew 6:9), thus showing that what was provided was a pattern or model, rather than a set formula.

A powerful aid to the interpretation of the Prayer is Jesus' abhorrence of insincerity in all its forms. Among these are:

- Ritualistic repetition of a prayer. This makes prayer a meaningless mechanical exercise. "And in praying do not heap up empty phrases as the Gentiles do; for they think they will be heard for their many words" (Matthew 6:7). In Matthew's Gospel these are the words that immediately precede the Lord's Prayer, thus offering a particularly important approach to its interpretation. The conciseness of the Prayer underlines this message, for empty verbiage has no place in it.

• Ostentatious prayer aimed at creating an impression of piety, rather than at sincere communication with God. "When you pray, you must not be like the hypocrites; for they love to stand and pray at the street corners, that they may be seen by men." Prayer, as taught by Jesus, is a dialogue with God rather than an exhibition of religiosity, and the directness of the dialogue imparts greater earnestness to the words used.

• The utterance of a prayer without one's full intention of abiding by the tenets of conduct implicit within it. In the Prayer, as in Christianity in general, profession and practice are "grappled" to each other "with hoops of steel." Thus, if various values are embodied in the Prayer, and one repeats the Prayer, there is a commitment to abiding by those values. Jesus' teaching on this is embodied in his criticism of the Pharisees and scribes in terms of Isaiah:

> This people honors me with their lips
> but their heart is far from me.

• Prayer unaccompanied by requisite reflection. The Prayer is meant, not for reflexive recitation, but for reflective meditation. The long hours spent by Jesus in quiet meditation, as in the Garden of Gethsemane or the forty days in the desert, are a pointer to the deep reflection that he expected to be devoted to prayer. Reflection is perhaps the middle process in the triad of affirmation, internalization, and application. Any proper interpretation must take the Prayer through all these three stages and not stop at the affirmation, which is only the preliminary—and perhaps least important—stage.

• Prayer unaccompanied by appropriate action. The need for appropriate action is taught in the parable of the Good Samaritan, often seen as the practical corollary to the Lord's Prayer. Celestial aspirations are coupled with terrestrial duties. Prayer unaccompanied by the requisite external actions, such as the prayer presumably uttered by the Pharisee and Levite who passed by the injured man without giving him assistance, is valueless. In the words of James (2:14–17):

My brothers, what good is it for someone to say that he has faith if his actions do not prove it? Can that faith save him? Suppose there are brothers or sisters who need clothes and don't have enough to eat. What good is there in your saying to them, "God bless you! Keep warm and eat well!"—if you don't give them the necessities of life? So it is with faith: if it is alone and includes no actions, then it is dead.

- Prayer unaccompanied by love or charity. Jesus' characterization of love of one's neighbors as the greatest of the commandments, and, along with love of God, as containing a summary of all the commandments, gives an indication of the internalization of prayer that he stressed so greatly.
- Emphasis on procedure over substance. Jesus did not attach any particular significance to the times of prayer, the accouterments of prayer, the places of prayer, the mediaries of prayer, or the formulas of prayer. These aspects were not sacred. What was sacred was the substance of the prayer, the thought and concentration with which it was uttered, and the resolution to act in accordance with it.

Method and Spirit of Interpretation

With due acknowledgement to other schools of thought, my purpose in this book is to relate the principles embedded in the Prayer to the practical problems of today's world. Practical problems call for a practical, rather than a theological or doctrinal, approach to interpretation.

In Ignazio Silone's *The Story of a Humble Christian*, Cardinal Caetoni says, "You can't govern with the *Pater Noster*." This scarcely does justice to the wealth of practical law-and-order material that can be quarried out of the Prayer.

One is conscious of the impossibility of considering the Lord's Prayer totally apart from all theological and doctrinal considerations. However, the practical orientation adopted in the study could, for what it is worth, take its place alongside other interpretations to add something to the rich stock of universal thought that has been channeled into the understanding of this universal prayer. It is true that modern interpretations, especially in the last third of the twentieth century, have spread out into the realm of sociological studies,[1] but there has not, as far as I am able to discern, been a detailed inquiry into the practical field of human rights *and* the legal regulation of social conduct.

Such a perspective assumes considerable importance, since the legal regulation of society lags so far behind the moral sentiments of the community as to be disturbingly inadequate. The softening influence of religious and moral values on purely legal regulation makes urgent the task of achieving a law-oriented analysis of scripture.

There is a great wealth of learning within the Church on the interpretation of the scriptures, and an entire discipline (hermeneutics) has grown up around this activity. Hermeneutics covers the threefold task of communicating the scriptures to others, translation from one language to another, and the work of commentary and explanation.[2]

Hermeneutics brings out clearly the conflict between literal interpretation and interpretations that go beyond the literal sense. Indeed the history of biblical interpretation in the Catholic Church seems to represent a series of swings from the primacy of literal interpretation to the primacy of the spiritual aspects of scripture.[3] For example, the literal exegesis of Jerome, or the school of Saint Victor in the Middle Ages, were "quickly swallowed up in a more attractive movement that stressed the theological or spiritual aspects of scripture almost to the exclusion of literal exegesis."[4] Constant interpretation also performs the valuable task of stripping off dead dogma and concentrating attention on the heart of the scriptural message.

There is great richness in this tradition, and it needs to be drawn upon. In regard to the Lord's Prayer itself, a leading commentary has noted: "At every turning point of Christian history the Lord's Prayer itself has seemed to need new interpretation."[5] From the time of the early Church Fathers there have been attempts to probe the meaning of the Prayer in accordance with the needs of changing times, and some of these interpretations have been of far-ranging importance. Origen in the fourth century expounded it in a study that Greek theology followed for centuries; and Tertullian (c. 155–222) and Cyprian (c. 200–258) interpreted it for the African Church. Augustine's fifth-century interpretation for the West held sway in the Middle Ages,[6] while the needs of those seeking a break away from that settled state were reflected in commentaries such as those of Nicholas of Cusa (1401–

1464) and Meister Eckhart (1260–1327). Martin Luther made many expositions of the Prayer for the Reformation and, down to the liberation theology of today,[7] the Prayer has been the subject of continuing comment.

The need for constant interpretation of the sacred texts has been well expressed for the Jewish tradition, in terms that "Each generation in turn...could receive through its experience and intelligence the eternally expanding word of the Divine Lawgiver."[8] As human experience expands, our understanding of the language of the Lord's Prayer should expand correspondingly; instead, it often tends to be kept confined within its ancient receptacles of meaning. Interpretations that may have been adequate to the needs of the past do not in many areas reach through to the unprecedented problem areas of our time. Indeed, throughout intellectual history—whether in law, literature, philosophy, or religion—the work of the interpreter has been vital in keeping ancient teaching in line with modern reality.

The need for constant adaptation in the face of social and factual change was elegantly expressed by Pope Pius XII, in addressing the Tenth International Congress of Historians on September 7, 1955, when he said that it was in this way that the Church "penetrates into the moral foundations of the living community."[9]

An important message of Jesus was that the letter of the law should yield to its spirit. Harsh and literal interpretations were to yield to softer interpretations more consonant with the object and purposes that impregnate the text. This was the basis for the severe castigation of lawyers by Jesus in at least three places in the New Testament.

In the words of a recent writer:

Lawyers generally get a bad press in the New Testament. However, a close reading will reveal that our Lord's anger was directed not at the class but at particular beliefs and actions of the scribes and the pharisees. Hypocrisy, formalism, pride, the abuse of power, the bondage of wealth—these were among the specific sins so explicitly attacked by Jesus, sins that are not the exclusive domain of the legal profession but ones to which we lawyers are very prone.[10]

It would be irony indeed if the formal interpretations Jesus protested against were applied to the words of Jesus himself. It would compound the irony if we were to note that the rigid letter against which Jesus revolted was the letter of the original text of the scriptures in question, while the words of Jesus that we now construe were not his actual words, but words that have come to us through a series of translations from Greek texts that themselves were translations of Jesus' words.

The Prologue addressed to Leo X by Cardinal Ximenes in the sixteenth century encapsulated the traditions of the biblical humanists when it noted that:

> Certainly, since there can be no word, no combination of letters, from which there does not arise and as it were spring forth, the most concealed senses of the heavenly wisdom; and…the most learned interpreter cannot explain more than one of these….[11]

The search for the spirit of Jesus' words throws upon the present generation a heavy responsibility to seek to understand its ancient wisdom in the light of today's needs and tomorrow's problems.

Eight Aids to Understanding the Lord's Prayer

There are at least eight aids that may be used for understanding the Lord's Prayer, which may be likened to concentric and ever-widening circles drawn around the core word.

1. Interpretation of the word according to its natural and ordinary meaning, bearing in mind that the English version we read is only a translation, and probably a translation upon a translation.
2. Interpretation of the word according to the context of the entire Prayer of which it forms a part.
3. In case of doubt, light may be thrown upon the passage by the Sermon on the Mount, in the midst of which it is set.
4. Where there is still doubt, the other express teachings of Jesus can be used to shed light upon the matter. In particular, Jesus' teachings and attitude to prayer will shed light on how the Prayer should be interpreted.
5. If further inquiry be necessary, the conduct and example of the life of Jesus can be called in aid. His entire life was a protest against hypocrisy, mercenary attitudes, injustice, formalism and

legalism, and against those in authority who had lost sight of their fundamental obligation of service to the community.

6. It must be remembered that Jesus taught against the background of the Old Testament to which he himself alluded, as in his specific references to Isaiah. Except where Jesus specifically repudiated Old Testament teachings, these scriptures could be an important source for the illumination of Jesus' teaching. For example, the expositions on justice of Amos (5:21–24) and Micah (6:6–8), showing it to be so central that other external responses to God are meaningless without it, could be used for this purpose. It is not without significance that such words as "justification," "just," and "justly" occur in the Bible about seven hundred and fifty times.[12] In the words of Micah:

> What he requires of us is this: to do what is just,
> to show constant love; and to live in humble
> fellowship with our God (6:8).

7. If what may be described as the primary sources, as outlined above, are exhausted, one may look for guidance in the secondary sources of the teachings and writings of the disciples.
8. As a weaker, but still legitimate source of illumination in case of doubt, the writings of learned theologians and commentators— though here we are on more debatable ground.

Many commentaries on the Prayer often tend to skip from stage 1 to stage 8 without an adequate exploration of the concentric circles of interpretation that lie between.

Cross-Cultural Perspectives

A great number of studies of Christianity and Christian doctrine tend to be inward-looking, researching Christianity from within the confines of Christian belief and teaching and not reaching outward to the vast sources of wisdom available in other cultures and religions, which could considerably illuminate an understanding of Christianity itself.

"And what should they know of England who only England know?" is an adage applicable not merely in the sphere of history or literature, but also of religion. If we overcome the narrowness of approach that often characterizes research on Christian doctrine, we will find that the boundaries of our study and understanding expand visibly.

We cannot fail to take note of the richness of thought contained in such religions as Hinduism, Buddhism, Judaism, and Islam and the richness of the literature and indeed the language in which notions regarding God and his majesty are expressed.

The Hindu scriptures contain exquisite and detailed descriptions of the majesty and attributes of God, set out in the cadences of the Sanskrit language, which Sir William Jones, the English Sanskritic scholar, has extolled as "more perfect than the Greek, more copious than the Latin and more exquisitely refined than either."[13] Similar descriptions appear in the Koran in language so beautiful that Marmaduke Pickthall has described it as "that inimitable symphony, the very sounds of which move men to tears and ecstasy."[14] Such literature provides perspectives in plenty that are not to be rejected. As an eminent multicultural scholar has observed, in referring to the world's great religious scriptures:

> Great poems in different languages have different values but they all are poetry, and the spiritual visions of man come all from One Light. In them, we have Lamps of Fire that burn to the glory of God.[15]

Thought about God and his majesty, couched in such lofty language, must afford flashes of insight on the nature and attributes of the supreme divinity. Over the centuries such literature has accumulated wisdom concerning the great cosmic principles that underlie humanity's concept of the divinity and people's relationship with it. To the same extent that the majesty, the omnipotence, the compassion, and the other attributes of the divinity are common ground among the theistic religions, we are closing upon ourselves windows that will light up our understanding of these shared themes.

Likewise, if one is attempting to understand fully, conceptual implications in such notions as compassion, justice, equity, and mercy, the Buddhist scriptures are among the world's richest repositories of finely analyzed discussions of these concepts. Notions that are simply mentioned by generic name in scripture have been dissected and taken apart into their component elements by the fine scalpels of Buddhist analytical thought.

I hope that the glimpses of other religions' scriptures interspersed throughout this work will render our interpretations of the Lord's Prayer richer and more meaningful by drawing upon the splendors of universal thought. The rich and varied nuances that impregnate the Christian scriptures can sometimes receive a new radiance through rays of inspiration coming from other scriptures, just as those others can be lighted up by inspiration from the Christian.

PART TWO

HIGHROADS TO
WORLD ORDER

INTRODUCTION

The themes of forgiveness and temptation are central messages of the Prayer. They are integrally linked, and it is perhaps not by accident that the Prayer places them alongside each other. The two petitions are beautifully matched and balanced. We look backward to the past and ask for forgiveness of the wrongs we have done, then look forward to the future and ask that we be protected from doing wrong. The Prayer relating to forgiveness is also beautifully balanced within itself, for we can only ask forgiveness to the extent we forgive others.

This section of the book concentrates on the core themes of forgiveness and temptation, for there can be no hope for humanity in the next century unless we practice forgiveness and resist the multitude of temptations peculiar to our age, which assail us at every level.

The world is torn with disputes arising from wrongs done in the past, and grievances carried into the future. As long as the wrongs linger unforgiven, they keep resentment alive, and resentment feeds upon itself. It leads to reprisals, and the reprisals to new resentments. Unless that vicious spiral is broken, the lack of forgiveness has soon turned itself into hatred. The international tensions that swirl around us are largely the result of attitudes of hatred that have simmered long in silent resentment, before being translated into action. Genocide does not suddenly unleash itself without a long gestation period of hatred breeding quietly and steadily in the recesses of the mind.

We are entering the next century beset by racial hatreds, tribal hatreds, class hatreds, political hatreds, religious hatreds, economic hatreds, social hatreds, attitudinal hatreds, and linguistic hatreds. These hatreds are fed on painful memories of unforgiven wrongs. If the Christian notion of forgiveness had been practiced at the earliest stages of misunderstanding, the first ripples of anger would long ago have been dissipated.

The Prayer thus shows us a direct route to a more peaceful world: the route of forgiveness.

The world is also caught in a web of continuing temptations to trespass upon the rights and sensitivities of others. And the available means of doing so are getting easier, the results ever more attractive. Never before has humanity been exposed to such a powerful combination of temptations. The Prayer's warnings against temptation need to be considered in the light of these new developments.

In this Part, we shall first examine the path of forgiveness (Chapter 5), then the concept of resistance to temptation (Chapters 6 through 8), and finally the roadblocks obstructing our way (Chapters 9 through 15).

CHAPTER 5

"FORGIVE US...
AS WE FORGIVE THEM"

Centrality of the Concept of Forgiveness

...ssage, and forgiveness is one of the ...tations of love. The concept of for- ...s "a high-point of Christian prayer."[1] ...Lord's Prayer as well.

...n more than one score. In the first ...s to require forgiveness of enemies ...ace, it is the one plea in the Lord's ...h he develops explicitly in the Sermon ...inion with the qualities of the Divine, ...forgive one another as God in Christ ...it becomes for Christians the standard ...he yardstick of Divine justice to man. ...the notion of the mercifulness of God. ...ss of sin. Forgiveness thus becomes a ...ory of Mary Magdalene; the sinner on ...m; the adulterous woman against whom none dared to cast the first stone; the specific authority to forgive sin given by Jesus to the apostles. All of these highlight the concept of forgiveness as a fundamental theme of Christian theology.

The standard of forgiveness Christianity prescribes is dramatically de-scribed in Matthew (18:21–22):

Then Peter came to Jesus and asked, "Lord, if my brother keeps on sinning against me, how many times do I have to forgive him? Seven times?" "No, not seven times," answered Jesus, but seventy times seven."

This is immediately followed by the parable of the servant who, forgiven his debt by his king, proceeds to deny forgiveness to his fellow servant who owes him a debt.

Indeed, the concept of forgiveness reaches its zenith in the gospels in the awesome moment when Jesus, at the height of excruciating suffering on the cross, cries out "Father, forgive them for they know not what they do."

The Basic Yardstick of Christian Justice

The words under consideration provide the basic yardstick of Christian justice.

The Christian undertakes that he will do unto others as he would be done by and announces his expectation that he will be judged by the standards he adopts toward others. This concept is so important that immediately after formulating the Lord's Prayer, Jesus repeats it in specific terms: "For if you forgive men their trespasses, your heavenly Father also will forgive you; but if you do not forgive men their trespasses, neither will your Father forgive your trespasses" (Matthew 6:14–15).

The theme that the measure you give will be the measure you get is echoed throughout the gospels. For example we read in Matthew: "Do not judge others, so that God will not judge you, for God will judge you in the same way as you judge others, and he will apply to you the same rules you apply to others" (Matthew 7:1–2). Later in the same gospel we have the likening of the kingdom of heaven to a king settling accounts with his servants. The servant on whom the king had mercy did not treat his own debtor with mercy, whereupon he received from the king the same treatment that he had meted out to his debtors (Matthew 18:23–35).

It is clear from the express words of the Prayer and from their amplification in such illustrations that the standard of forgiveness which the supplicant can expect is in a sense fixed by the supplicant himself. As Gregory of Nyssa has written, "Be yourself your own judge; give yourself the sentence of acquittal."[3]

However, as is made clear from the scriptures, and is also stressed in the scriptures of other religions (for example, in Buddhism), the motive or reason for doing good must not be the expectation of reward for the good deed in question, but the inherent desire to do good. That good consequences will follow is immaterial and should not be an element in the reckoning, except that initially it may help one to get on the right track.

This basic yardstick of Christian justice is twinned by the basic yardstick of Christian conduct and perhaps springs from it, for "...all things whatsoever ye would that men should do to you, do ye even so to them: for this is the law and the prophets" (Matthew 7:12, KJV).

The Link Between Forgiveness and Love

It cannot be stressed enough that the Lord's Prayer is a universalistic message, based upon love for all humanity. That love cannot be divided into segments. It is one and entire. An individual cannot love part of the human family and not love another part. One cannot love those who do good to us and not love those who do us harm. To do so would be to compartmentalize love in a manner that destroys its very quality. If there is no forgiveness of one who has done wrong, there is no love for that person. And if there is no love for that person, the entire concept of love is impaired through the denial of its universality.

Forgiving a Wrong vs. Ignoring a Wrong

Implicit in the Prayer is the requirement of forgiveness of wrongs done by others. We must forgive those who trespass against us, for it is by the standard of our forgiveness that we ourselves will be forgiven.

But a distinction should be made between forgiving a wrong and ignoring a wrong. Elsewhere we discuss the evils to society of complacency and paralysis in the face of wrongdoing to others. Forgiveness does not mean turning a blind eye, for that may amount to condoning, which brings one close to guilt in the continuation of wrongdoing. Interest must be shown in protesting against the wrongdoing, devising means to prevent its repetition or continuance, helping society in its efforts at compensating the loss and suffering caused to the victim, and encouraging international efforts to bring such wrongdoing under control if it is of a widespread nature.

For lack of appreciation of this distinction, wrongdoing to others is often treated as though it has happened in another universe of activity—a universe so remote that one is not drawn into it, either by way of protest and preventive activity, or by way of forgiveness. The Prayer involves the utterer in such distant wrongdoing, not only in thought (through forgiveness), but also in action (through protest and prevention).

Passive Forgiveness vs. Active Forgiveness

All that has been said thus far relates to what may be described as "passive" forgiveness, that is, the state of mentally forgiving the wrongs done to oneself. One wipes the slate clean of hostile or revengeful thoughts. It is important to stress, however, that the Christian standard of forgiveness goes far beyond this. One is required not merely to forgive those who have caused harm to us but, indeed, to turn this into the "active" sentiment of loving them. One is called upon to love one's enemies and persecutors. Christ speaks of this as a distinctive mark of Christian love (Matthew 5:43). It is thus open to the individual to carry forward the standard by which he is to be judged beyond mere forgiveness for his sins, to the stage of being actively loved despite his sins. If he is to earn this standard of judgment, he should attempt to practice it toward others, difficult though it may be.

This concept was well expressed by Henry Ward Beecher, the American Congregationalist preacher:

> "I can forgive but I cannot forget" is only another way of saying, "I will not forgive." A forgiveness ought to be like a cancelled note, torn in two and burned up, so that it can never be shown against the man.[4]

The Nature of True Forgiveness

Forgiveness is thus not a matter of merely external conduct, but is primarily an internal process that occurs in the forum of one's own conscience. The manifestation through external conduct is a necessary consequence of that internal process. True forgiveness does not occur through a merely external act indicating that one is not pursuing a wrongdoer by external action. One does not forgive a debt by merely taking no action upon it. Something more is required: The forgiveness must be internalized in the heart of the wrongdoer.

Scriptural authority for this cannot be stronger. After the powerful parable of the wicked servant who did not forgive his fellow servant, although he himself had been forgiven by his Lord, Jesus goes on to sum up the lesson of the parable in these terms: That is how my Father in heaven will treat every one of you unless you forgive your brother *from your heart*

(Matthew 18:35). External acts of forgiveness are rendered complete only by such an internal frame of mind.

True forgiveness, then, must be total and complete. Christians are required to elevate the level of their forgiveness to match the level of Divine forgiveness. In Paul's words, they are required to be "kind and tender-hearted to one another, and *forgive one another, as God has forgiven you through Christ*" (Ephesians 4:32).

Legal and Moral Justice

This consideration highlights the nobility of Christianity's moral standard of justice, and the shortcomings of merely legal justice, which is administered by man. Of the many differences that stand out, these are the most obvious:

- Moral justice reaches into the sphere not only of action but also of thought. Legal justice punishes only the act, leaving thought unpunished, however sinful it may be, so long as it is unaccompanied by action. Moral justice condemns the guilty intention and the wicked thought that the law is quite unable to reach.
- Even in the realm of actual action, there is a vast area of wrongdoing that the law does not punish because the law cannot reach it. This may be because the law does not provide for such actions owing to a lacuna or loophole in the law, or because the law has simply not geared itself to that area of activity.
- Legal justice moves into operation only upon legal proof. Many a wrongful action goes unpunished for lack of witnesses or because even the genuine witness does not stand up well to cross-examination in court and is disbelieved or considered unreliable. In many an act of legal wrongdoing, there may be no witness at all. Moral justice is independent of the requirement of proof.
- The apparatus of detection available for legal justice is naturally not perfect. Vast segments of wrongful conduct pass undetected for this reason. No thought or action escapes the scrutiny of moral justice.
- Legal justice is formal and depends upon a number of procedural steps and rules of evidence. A failure to comply with any significant requisite of form means that the entire edifice of the case collapses. Moral justice is independent of formality.
- The law does not punish, except in that very limited area of wrong-

doing that it classes as criminal. The criminal law covers only a very small segment of human activity. Much of the larger segment falls within the area described as civil law; and the most that civil law can do is to order compensation, not punishment.

- The scale of compensation offered by the law varies in its impact upon the individual, for it depends upon the state of his fortune. A fine of five hundred dollars may mean next to nothing to a millionaire, but may mean weeks of privation to the family of a poor wage earner. One is reminded of the ancient Roman story of an affluent freeman who desired to show his contempt for a law imposing a fine of a certain monetary sum for every offense of assaulting a slave. With a slave in attendance behind him carrying a basket of coins, he set out on a public road assaulting every slave he encountered, while the slave tossed the appropriate coins to the victim. He was demonstrating that the punishment did not affect him at all.

- It is only in a very small proportion of cases that the legal punishment or award exactly matches the offense—even if the law can reach the conduct in question, and even if the requirements of legal proof are satisfied.

Moral justice quite clearly overcomes all these defects. It is to one's sense of moral justice in the forum of one's own conscience that the Lord's Prayer is addressed. Indeed, the Lord's Prayer goes a step further than moral justice in its ordinary connotations, for while moral justice would merely balance the scales between wrongdoing and punishment, Christian justice introduces the further notion of forgiveness. Properly analyzed, it goes even beyond forgiveness and requires the person who has been wronged to love the wrongdoer.

The Prayer offers a clear precondition to forgiveness: The offender must himself forgive. The matter does not end there, but a more precise scale than anything any law can devise is also provided—namely, that one can ask for forgiveness of one's own wrongdoings only to the exact extent that one is prepared to forgive the wrongdoing of others to oneself.

One could therefore arrange justice in three basic categories, in ascending order of excellence:

legal justice → moral justice → Christian justice as required by the
                                    Lord's Prayer

CHAPTER 6

"OUR TRESPASSES..."

The word "trespass," for present purposes, is construed as a shortcoming in righteousness of conduct. This chapter does not restrict itself to conduct that amounts to a crime in the eyes of the state, or a sin in the eyes of the Church.[1] "Crimes" and "sins" tend to be encapsulated within legal and theological definitions, and much ingenuity is often expended on arguing whether a given piece of conduct falls within the definition.

It would indeed be a pity if the sweeping range of the word "trespass" is whittled down and circumscribed by the concept of sin. Words such as "sin" miss the many nuances and shades of unrighteousness in conduct that fall within the ambit of the word "trespass." The issue is further complicated by fine theological definitions of "mortal" and "venial" sin.

The substitution of the word "sins" for "trespasses" robs this part of the Prayer of its rich flavor of a call to righteousness as a standard of conduct. We are left with the negative perception that we must not commit a sin, but we are not called to the active observance of a standard of righteousness that is the Prayer's guiding principle of conduct. While it would be righteous conduct to assist a friend when he or she is in distress, failure to do so may not be a sin. To exclude an exhortation to such righteousness from the Prayer seems to run contrary to its spirit.

The Lord's Prayer is impregnated with the notion that God will treat us as we treat others. The standards we adopt in our dealings with others are the only standards by which we can claim to be judged. Hence, the prayer that we be forgiven our trespasses cannot be limited to the case of the commission of sin.

In other words, we should, in interpreting these words, engage in a search for standards of righteous conduct, rather than standards of delinquency; positive standards of action, rather than merely negative standards of abstention from wrong. Standards of delinquency are no doubt included within the meaning of the word, but that is not all the word contains.

We should therefore view the word "trespass" as not dependent on the concept of sin, but as meaning simply any act that falls short of righteous or moral conduct. We shall concentrate on conduct that, whether it be a sin or not in the formal sense, is a trespass upon righteousness. However slight the deviation, it would fall within the contemplation of the Prayer. It may not be a sin, for example, to fail to visit one's sick neighbor when he or she is in the hospital, but it could be a trespass against neighborly duty.

Viewed in this light, this word "trespass" has an enormous sweep of meaning that is easily missed if we think of it only in terms of sin.

The Ten Commandments and the Lord's Prayer

The word "trespasses" incorporates the Ten Commandments into the Lord's Prayer, for anyone surely commits a trespass who violates the commandments. Yet the word is wider in its connotations, for it comprises a whole range of obligations stretching far beyond the specific commandments brought down from Mount Sinai. Prohibitions such as those against murder, adultery, theft, and bearing false witness are laws in the strict sense, but "trespasses" reach far out into areas of morality not covered by strict law.

The Ten Commandments, or Decalogue, was not even in Jesus' time a complete charter of morality, for it laid down only basic rules, not the whole framework of moral conduct. As expressed in a modern classic on Catholicism, "It is important to note that *the Decalogue was not intended as the ultimate norm of all morality*. On the contrary, it barely touches upon individual moral obligations."[2] We must therefore range further afield in our quest for the meaning of "trespasses" as used in the Prayer. It is in the light of the moral message of Jesus that the word "trespass" needs to be construed. That moral message is found in the vast expanses of moral territory covered in such teachings as the Beatitudes of the Sermon on the Mount and the nature of the kingdom of God, as well as in such parables as that of the Good Samaritan. The Lord's Prayer covers the whole of that moral territory and, although keeping the Ten Commandments is part of the duty of every Christian, the word "trespasses" in the Prayer extends beyond mere obedience to the commandments.

A parallel can be drawn with obedience to the penal laws of a state, which do not constitute the totality of the fabric of legal obligations. The latter reach far wider than the specific prohibitions and commands of the law.

Even if one confines oneself to the particular laws contained in the Ten Commandments, their specific words assume a much wider meaning in our age than could have been appreciated when they were first revealed.

Merely by way of illustrating this proposition, let us consider just one commandment: "Thou shalt not steal."

Of course, it would be a trespass within the meaning of the Lord's Prayer to indulge in theft. But what constitutes theft when viewed against the background of the twenty-first or, for that matter, the twentieth, century? The ambit of the offense has surely broadened from the simple physical appropriation of another's property, which occupied center stage in the concept of theft many centuries ago.

Today the wrongful deprivation of another's property can take myriad forms not even envisaged in earlier ages. Taking that which rightfully belongs to future generations—intergenerational theft it could be called—is a prime example. Using economic pressure to extract financial or other benefits from a poor country is another, for as a result, that which belongs to the people of that poor country is drained away in a manner that can be worse than theft and, in fact, resembles extortion. Also, as mentioned earlier in the book, theft of information by computer crime is another new form of theft peculiar to our age. And theft of ideas or "intellectual property" is yet another.

In other words, our approach to the wording of the commandments, implicitly contained in the Lord's Prayer, must be expansive, taking into account the changed global milieu that is essential to a proper understanding of these words for our age.

Commandments such as "Thou shalt not kill" and "Thou shalt not bear false witness against thy neighbor" take on similarly extended meanings in the light of modern conditions.

The Expanding Scope of Obligations

Viewed thus, the concept of trespass in the twenty-first century will need fresh study more than most other sections of the Prayer, for the obligations imposed upon ordinary people will far transcend, in complexity and scope, all that the Church and the most learned theologians have expounded over the preceding centuries.

The time has come when, in interpreting the phrase "our trespasses," we should not confine ourselves to the narrow visibility of sin as discernible in the context of a simple and parochial society. In the complex, technologically oriented and economically dominated global society of the twenty-first century, such a vision is not only totally inadequate but fraught with infinite danger to the very survival of the human species.

Where do we stand, for example, on matters such as environmental degradation, affluent lifestyles that absorb disproportionate earth resources, racial discrimination, white-collar crime, nuclear and chemical weapons, and the abuse of modern technology in myriad ways? None of these were known to the audience who heard the Lord's Prayer when it was formulated, and none of them are likely to have been seriously contemplated in any ages prior to our own. Each one of these areas, if neglected, can cause misery on a colossal scale, affecting the lives of millions. Their suffering could range from agonizing deaths through starvation and malnutrition to grotesque mutilation, through toxic waste, of children yet unborn. Yet, the law does not adequately handle these problems, leaving them in the twilight area of difficult problems for which no clear guidance is available. Church guidance on the moral aspects involved is scanty, for these new issues are not the subject of systematic doctrinal writing and hence receive only sporadic attention in the ordinary teachings of those in religious authority. True, some encyclicals and pastoral letters address these questions, yet these problems have not been comprehensively examined.

The Widening Gulf Between Moral and Legal Precepts

There has always been a gulf between conduct that is legally prohibited and conduct that is morally blameworthy. That gulf is growing exponentially.

In this vast unpoliced area of obligations not prohibited, censured, or punished by law lie some obligations whose breach is enormously more damaging and blameworthy than some of the most heinous crimes upon the statute book.

A clear message emerging from the increasing power now becoming available to affect the lives of others is that legal protections are becoming woefully inadequate—much more inadequate than they have ever been before to protect humans from the cruelty or thoughtlessness of other humans. The power to influence others has grown exponentially through the increase and concentration of economic power, political power, media power, and technological power. All of these are racing ahead while the law remains comparatively stationary. They are, in short, racing out of legal control while the law stands by, watching helplessly from the sidelines. The gap between morality and legal regulation was perhaps never so wide as it is now, and the need for a sense of moral obligation to bridge this gap was never so great. In fact, it becomes more urgent by the day. It is consequently the imperative obligation of every moral system—and religious systems occupy the predominant place among moral systems—to spend its most concentrated efforts on addressing these problems. They cannot much longer be consigned to the "too hard" basket wherein they have lain unaddressed for too long. Perhaps it is in this area that the great religious systems of the world face their most momentous contemporary challenge: in squaring religious teaching with the practical problems facing humanity.

Yesterday's Horizons and Today's Expectations

The word "trespasses" offers a valuable key to the urgent task of increasing the relevance of religious teaching to the practical problems of today.

Such matters as honesty in one's transactions, abstention from physical violence, and moral propriety in matters of sexual conduct, largely adequate in yesterday's social milieu, cannot limit the contours of "trespasses" in this age. Moreover, what is meant by the victim of one's trespasses—one's "neighbor"—has expanded enormously in scope under the impact of modern conditions. The citizens of China, Nigeria, or Peru are in many respects immediate neighbors to one another, as they are to the citizens of the United States, owing to modern technology that brings them into instant communication (as through satellite and Internet) and makes their acts impact directly on one another (as through environmental degradation).

The accredited spokespersons of organized religion often formulate their answers to today's problems in terms of yesterday's understanding of the reach of such words as "trespasses" and "neighbor." As a result, advances in adapting religious teaching to new circumstances often proceed not from acknowledged leaders but from adventurous spirits on the peripheries of religious power. Many basic problems of modern society thus remain largely unaddressed. The route to greater relevance perhaps lies in analyzing in a practical context the unprecedented temptations offered today for conduct adversely affecting one's neighbors. In the interknit nature of today's global society, one must view the term not merely parochially but nationally, not merely nationally but internationally.

To speak of traveling around the globe in a week was to speak nonsense until the twentieth century. To speak of instantaneous communication between distant countries, of instant transmission of pictures across the globe, to speak of pollution of the earth's entire atmosphere or of the seas, of global climatic change, of splicing the genetic building blocks of living things, of man-made satellites in space, or of transmitting letters by electronic means, was to smack of the ludicrous. Concepts tailored to an age when such things were impossibilities are still our working tools in the fields of law and religion. They are no longer comprehensive enough and must be reconsidered in the light of the unprecedented power given by technology, and the unprecedented interactions and chain reactions it has set up among all inhabitants of the planet.

The "trespass" that could be committed in an earlier age was only the trespass that the technology and social organization of that age saw as a possibility. Today, trespasses far beyond the imagination of that age are possible. Must we not widen our appreciation of the word accordingly? The powers that any one of us has today of committing a trespass upon the rights of a distant person in an Arctic igloo or a tropical rain forest are much greater than any that prior centuries could have visualized. Must not the practical meaning of the word expand as the power to trespass expands?

The obligations of human beings expand and alter as their power expands and alters, for power unbridled by obligation becomes power abused. It is a cardinal law based on the observation of human conduct that any power available to man will be used for self-centered purposes even though such use may hurt another—unless restraints either internally imposed by morality or externally imposed by law hold that increased power in check. Bioethical advances, nuclear power, and computerized invasions of privacy are among these new areas of power that have bred new obligations unknown in an earlier age.

Some abstract moral propositions are difficult to prove, but not the proposition that expanding power begets expanding obligations. Of this, our age provides us with dramatic proof, for unless our greatly heightened powers are reined in by corresponding obligations, the destruction of the human species—indeed the destruction of all life forms on the planet—can be assured.

The boundless nature of the notion of duty that we have been considering here makes it patently clear that the notion of right and wrong cannot be "cabin'd, cribb'd, and confin'd" within the letter of any definition, however comprehensive.

In the absence of any possibility of definition, each individual's conscience must be his or her guide. A striking passage from Ecclesiasticus brings home this point:

> [L]et the counsel of thine own heart stand...For a man's mind is sometimes wont to tell him more than seven watchmen that sit in a high tower... (37:13–14).

It will not do to shut one's eyes to the wider ramifications of one's action or inaction and thus to blur one's perceptions of their likely impact on others, who are now our "neighbors" upon a tightly knit planet. Indeed, this expansion of responsibility takes place not merely in the dimension of space, but also in the dimension of time. Our enhanced physical powers mean also that they can reach further into the future, thereby affecting the rights of future generations. This has given rise to the new concept of intergenerational duty, thus imposing on us an entirely fresh set of obligations. Generations of the future whom we do not know are affected by our actions in a very real way when we, as their trustees of the earth and its resources, use our vastly increased technological power to abuse our trust. Not only do we appropriate to our generation the nonrenewable resources of the earth, but we also damage the ecosystem of our common home for thousands of years to come. An individual conscience that becomes sensitized to these new dimensions of trespass will have a surer guide to avoiding "trespass" than it does now.

Quite often, in discussions on the apportionment of responsibility for wrongs committed on a global scale, there is a tendency, when the matter is raised, to argue that the real perpetrators of the wrong who should be taken to task are way out there—so why trouble me? It's "their" responsibility, and "they" should take remedial action. Turning this around, however, the individual so protesting is not unwilling to take the benefits that he might reap from the iniquitous practice under consideration.

One is reminded of the days of slavery when God-fearing people, churchgoing in the best tradition, would enjoy the benefits of the slave trade in their homes, seemingly guiltless because the whip of oppression was wielded by the stern slave master out there in the plantations and not by them. In apportioning guilt or assessing obligations, one could not possibly omit consideration of such people's role, especially if they accepted without protest the proceeds of that iniquity. Was this not a "trespass" of the kind that is reproduced a millionfold in the world of today?

Apartheid in the twentieth century shows how the problem expands and, with its expansion, so also the circle of responsibility expands. It was not only people in South Africa who were taking the benefits of apartheid, but people worldwide. The purchase of South African goods without protest helped to entrench the system and, but for international protest against the system of apartheid, it would have continued much longer before being dismantled.

Protest across the globe sensitized the conscience of many a global citizen who might otherwise have taken the benefits of apartheid not knowing to what extent the impairment of human dignity would have been furthered by unthinking acceptance and encouragement. Global movements against South African goods and global protest in such areas as sports participation mounted the necessary pressure to help in dismantling this elaborately constructed apparatus of discrimination.

The principles emerging from these two examples have much applicability in working out notions of duty and responsibility for the ever greater global problems of the environment, Third World starvation, and nuclear and chemical weaponry that wreak havoc in the lives of those who are yet children. To remain unresponsive to these problems that undermine the basis of the human future is surely to commit a trespass in the fullest sense of that word. It is a trespass upon one's duty in this age—a duty, moreover, that imposes so much obligation upon its citizens. As the U.S. Catholic bishops pointed out in their 1983 pastoral letter, "mutual security and survival require a new vision of the world as one interdependent planet."[3]

The Dilemma of Ignorance

A recognized ground on which one can avoid culpability in matters of morality and even of law is lack of knowledge that one is committing a breach. However, if the knowledge is available and one willfully desists from obtaining it, the ignorance resulting from the willful denial to oneself of the facts cannot be pleaded as an excuse.

It may be argued that such an approach involves a standard so rigorous as to assign it to the category of the impossible. Moreover, today's problems, diverse as they are, render it beyond the competence of any one individual to assimilate the facts pertinent to all the great global issues of our time. To add to the problem, the version of news and views presented to the world's citizens on important global issues contains a large amount of distortion and misinformation. It is thus beyond anyone's competence to pierce this smoke screen to reach the facts as they really are.

Indeed, the one-way flow of information from the developed to the developing worlds has created such acute problems as to prompt the demand for a new world information order, with a two-way flow of information. However, for lack of support and resources this proposal has unfortunately fallen by the wayside.[4]

All these are factors of the utmost importance, and they need to be addressed. In many an instance it will be found that a well-meaning person is perpetuating misery on a massive scale when he or she acts in relation to a matter concerning Third World poverty without a full picture of the facts and, indeed, on the basis of a great deal of misinformation. The hope that we should be forgiven our trespasses perhaps requires a more diligent effort to avoid the commission of a trespass through unawareness—when information is available to us. This is a more compelling consideration in an age when information travels instantly and in great abundance across national boundaries than when the movement of knowledge was sluggish. To shut oneself off from available information, if relevant to a course of action that can minimize human misery, may well be a failure of Christian duty, a trespass directly within the ambit of the Lord's Prayer.

Varying Standards of Morality

Lon L. Fuller, the noted American jurist, has illuminated the area of relative moral standards in his book, *The Morality of Law*.[5] He draws attention to the fact that standards of morality and duty can vary from those of the sinner to the saint, with a whole universe of different standards lying between them. Thus the standards of duty that the Gandhis and the Mother Teresas of this world would deem imperative may not impose any sort of duty on others who impose a lesser standard on themselves. The *counsel* of perfection is at one end of the scale, and the *command* of duty at the other.

There is a distinction between the morality of duty (moral standards with which we must all comply if life in society is to be possible) and the morality of aspiration (the morality of excellence). Some will deem their own conduct to be blameworthy if it fails to comply with the morality of aspiration. Others, more self-centered, would not give such failure a thought. The law cannot impose standards above those of the morality of duty, but the Lord's Prayer does.

There is, in other words, a vast range of standards of duty along the scale, rising up from the level of the morality of duty to the level of the morality of aspiration. At what point does failure to comply amount to a trespass in terms of the Prayer? It is for each individual to decide, conscious that the standard chosen will be that by which the individual would in turn be judged. The higher one ranges up the scale in setting a standard for oneself, the more compassionate would be the judgment that person would in turn receive.

The point in the scale of morality at which failure to act in a desirable manner becomes a trespass can vary, depending upon the numerous surrounding circumstances that make up a different background for every individual. It is idle for outside observers to stipulate that point or formulate the governing standard. The duty to support a child is a duty imposed by morality as well as law. So, also, in many systems, is the duty to support an aged parent. But the law cannot possibly take in that vast range of situations where a duty unquestionably exists in morality or equity, though not in law. In such cases, every person must consider whether he or she is in breach of such a duty and whether the course of conduct he or she chooses to pursue is such as to constitute a trespass in terms of the Prayer. What is important is that each individual be sensitized to this issue, which tends to be swept under the carpet if one thinks only in terms of sin.

Am I My Brother's Keeper?

Moving beyond the preceding considerations, we come to a reflection of the way in which the insights of religion can help in improving not merely the standards of individual conduct, but the law itself.

A classic case in modern English law—the case of the snail in the ginger beer bottle—offers a good example. In *Donoghue* v. *Stevenson*,[6] decided in 1932, Christian concepts of duty to one's neighbor were used to expand the circle of persons to whom a manufacturer owed a legal duty. Though manufactured products were now distributed through a chain of contracts, extending from the manufacturer to the ultimate consumer, the law still afforded a remedy for defective goods only where there was a direct relationship between consumer and manufacturer. A lady, drinking ginger beer from a bottle purchased by her friend from a retailer, suffered a nervous shock when she saw a dead snail in the bottle she had purchased. The manufacturer was many steps removed from her in the chain of supply. Lord Atkin, one of England's outstanding judges, broke through the inadequacies of the law by reliance on the Christian principle of duty to one's neighbor. "Who is my neighbor?" asked Lord Atkin and answered it by giving an extended definition of the word, so as to take in all who could reasonably be foreseen as being affected by one's action. Reading Christian scripture according to its spirit, he thus established a principle of prime importance in modern law in regard to product liability.

The principle underlying that case lies at the heart of the discussions in this chapter, for this chapter pleads for more appreciation of the ever-widening circle of persons who now come within the scriptural description of neighbors, to whom we owe a duty. "The second most important commandment is like it: 'Love your neighbor as you love yourself.' On these two commandments [love of God being the first] hang all the Law and the Prophets" (Matthew 22:40, KJV). A teaching considered by Jesus to be so fundamental must be interpreted according to its spirit and its practical dimensions in the contemporary world.

Also to be stressed is the individual's responsibility, however slight, for all that goes on in the community of which he or she forms an integral part. If there is crime in the community, or ignorance, or selfishness, the individual who is part of that community and partakes of its communal life must—in view of that—take a share of the blame for that lapse. He or she is not entirely free of guilt or responsibility for the deviant conduct of its members, for that deviant conduct is in some way a reflection of the individual's own attitudes and perhaps lack of concern.

Kahlil Gibran put this notion well:

> And as a single leaf turns not yellow
> but with the silent knowledge of the whole tree,
> So the wrongdoer cannot do wrong
> without the hidden will of you all....
> And when one of you falls down

> he falls for those behind him,
> a caution against the stumbling stone.
> Ay, and he falls for those ahead of him,
> who, though faster and surer of foot, yet
> removed not the stumbling stone.[7]

The unjust and the just, the good and the wicked, cannot be seen as separated from each other in watertight compartments. There is some share of blame in not warning wayfarers of the stone one has eluded or in not putting it out of the way. Failure to do so may not be a sin, but it is a trespass, a shortcoming that represents a departure from the highest standards of righteous behavior. If we are to be judged by the standards we ourselves practice, we cannot expect that we shall be treated, when our turn comes to fall, any better than we treated those who fell because of our failure to give warning or take action.

This notion has applicability also to the community of sovereign nations. Nations that are lapsing into conduct unbecoming a member of the world community often do so for lack of warning signals from the rest, for lack of understanding, lack of concern, and, indeed, sometimes from deliberate traps laid for them by other members of the world community. National behavior, like individual behavior, cannot ignore this principle. Moreover, the international order in which we shall live in the next century will be an order of active cooperation among states, replacing the concept, dominant till our age, of a world order based on passive tolerance of the existence of other nations. All the more, therefore, must the international order of the future pay heed to this principle.

The universal concepts set out in the Lord's Prayer cannot be disregarded as being irrelevant to the conduct of nations, for the conduct of nations is in the last analysis the conduct of the individuals who comprise it.

The Concept of Social Sin

There is such a notion as social sin recognized in Church theology—that is, blameworthy conduct committed by a group of which one is a member. The Labor Day Statement of 1976 of the Canadian Catholic Bishops entitled "From Words to Action" defines social sin in terms of institutional oppression. Focusing attention on the injustices in Canadian society, the document calls for a rereading of the scriptures from the viewpoint of the poor, a consideration of the problems of the disadvantaged peoples of the country, and a careful analysis of the socio-economic causes of injustice and oppression.[8] We may well be members of a group responsible for these causes.

If this reading of Christian duty be correct, social sin constitutes a trespass for which we should seek forgiveness. We cannot merely seek forgiveness without doing that which lies in our own power to prevent a continuance of the group trespass to which we are a party—or else the Prayer lacks symmetry and meaning. To pray the Lord's Prayer requires that, while praying it and acknowledging the trespass or shortcoming involved in social sin, we should do our best to avoid the continuance of such oppression to which we are a party through our membership of the group.[9]

One does not have to go so far as to examine to what extent the Church itself as part of the dominant culture has become a symbol of legitimation for the conditions of oppression.[10] It is not my purpose to venture into that area, for this study does *not* concern itself with questions of church responsibility. It concerns itself only with the individual who prays the Lord's Prayer; and it seeks to convey a broader understanding of that which is prayed, according to normal principles of interpretation.

It is true few individuals are given the opportunity to induce social change by their own unaided action. However, a large number showing concern individually can achieve dramatic results—as in the case of apartheid. All that is pointed out here is that a sincere praying of the Lord's Prayer requires that the individual who is seeking forgiveness of his or her trespasses should be conscious of the shortcomings in social responsibility of the community to which that individual belongs. Should he or she, as a participating member of that society, be unconcerned with the social iniquity in question, that individual is a party to that social wrong and cannot ask forgiveness without a corresponding individual effort to end that iniquity. Indifference to inequality, poverty, and basic deprivation of human necessities has never been an attitude sanctioned by Christian ethics, and least of all by the teachings of Christ as encapsulated in the Lord's Prayer.

The U.S. Bishops' *Pastoral Letter on Catholic Social Teaching and the U.S. Economy* issued by the American bishops in reliance on John Paul II's *Laborem Exercens* (which received quick support from the Canadian bishops) is another example of a pastoral document that calls for a heightened sensitivity toward these concerns. It demands the creation of institutions that guarantee economic rights such as the rights to food, shelter, health, and work (paras. 79–80); and the bishops propose that the market economy operate within a national plan aimed at the service of the common good and controlled by the democratic process (paras. 315–7).

That responsible episcopal bodies should issue such calls underlines the importance of the fact that the individual's responsibility reaches out beyond purely individual actions to the actions of the group of which the individual forms a part.

As expressed in John Paul's *Laborem Exercens*:

> For instance, the highly industrialized countries, and even more the businesses that direct on a large scale the means of industrial production (the companies referred to as multi-national or trans-national) fixed the highest possible prices for their products, while trying at the same time to fix the lowest possible prices for raw materials or semi-manufactured goods. This is one of the causes of an ever-increasing disproportion between national incomes. The gap between most of the richest countries and the poorest ones is not diminishing or being stabilized, but is increasing more and more to the detriment of the poor countries.

The result is human suffering, destabilization, and possible threats to international peace. If the pope's words are well-based—and there is no reason to think otherwise—there is cause for reflection by every Christian who utters the Lord's Prayer as to whether acquiescence in such a situation does not constitute a trespass. If it does, and the individual does nothing about it, can such individuals validly pray for a forgiveness of their trespasses?

Beyond Legal Accountability

The fact that a vast area of moral wrongdoing lies outside the pale of legal accountability generates a comfortable feeling that no wrong is being done. Herein lies a hidden temptation of vast significance in our time.

A few examples follow, illustrative of the numerous areas that the law cannot reach, however deep the moral issues involved.

Human relationships

The law cannot reach the sphere of love and affection at which human relationships function. The law can order a father to provide his child with basic support but cannot order him to give affection.

Science and technology

Modern technology is moving so fast that the law has not the time to assess its impact upon society and respond with regulatory measures. Every sphere of technology can probably offer instances (as we'll see in Chapter 10). This vast area of possible wrongdoing, which the law cannot reach, can only be reached through tapping the moral sense of each individual. That moral sense will respond in many cases, when it is appropriately alerted. It does not respond now because in most cases it has not been alerted to the problem.

Failure to assist those in distress

Modern legal systems stress principles of individual autonomy and abstention from interference in the affairs of others. Yet this principle can be carried too far. Thus, in the English common law, a person committed no offense by passing by an eighty-year-old person drowning in a puddle of water, without extending a helping hand. Systems of morality cannot possibly take such a limited view. Few would dispute that moral blame attaches in such a situation, and indeed many a legal system does attach culpability to such a person. Such reflections reemphasize the truism that the yardstick of "trespass" is certainly not the failure to perform a legal duty.

Conversely, where there is a *legal* obligation, it may not always be moral to comply with it. An illustration from the period of wartime Germany will make this clear. A law of Hitler's regime required all persons to bring to the notice of the authorities disrespectful statements made regarding the Führer. A wife desiring to be rid of her husband registered a complaint with the authorities of such a statement made in the privacy of the home. The husband was taken up on this and rather than being sentenced to death was sent to the perilous Eastern front. Here was conduct perfectly in conformity with law, but totally in conflict with morality—as was demonstrated when the postwar German courts upheld the husband's complaint of wrongful conduct by his wife.

These two illustrations underline the chasm that sometimes divides conduct permissible in law and conduct proper in morality. Inaction, without violating the law in the one case, and action in compliance with the law in the other, both attract strong censure from any system of morality worthy of the name.

The fact that particular conduct is not censured by law can lull a person into a false sense of moral righteousness. This temptation can be better resisted when it is more clearly realized that one can act in complete compliance with the law and yet be guilty of a series of trespasses in terms of the Prayer.

Trespass beyond the reach of legal proof

In the forum of the conscience, nothing stands between wrongdoing and guilt. The forum of the conscience requires no witnesses and no legal proof, contrasting strongly in this regard with the forum of the law. All the stumbling blocks to legal justice do not operate in the forum of the conscience— *in foro conscientiae*, as the canon lawyers would express it. Justice goes into operation unimpaired and at once.

Important Perspectives From Other Traditions

In keeping with the universalistic theme of this work, it would be useful to take a glimpse at some other cultural traditions for their approaches to concepts of morality and duty.

African customary law: the community of humans

We begin with some perspectives from the rich cultural traditions of Africa, concerning which there is an increasing awareness in contemporary legal scholarship that:

legal systems in other parts of the world may well be enriched by drawing on some of the insights and alternative approaches afforded by African law.[11]

DRAKE COMMUNITY LIBRARY
930 Park St. Grinnell, Iowa.
PATRON: Fritz, Karol J.
02/24/17 10:12AM

You have these items checked out

The Lord's prayer : bridge to   DUE: 03/17/17
326610019315

Thank you for supporting YOUR LIBRARY
Call 236-2661 to renew
grinnell lib ia.us

Among these insights and alternative approaches is the concept, often referred to by Archbishop Desmond Tutu in his sermons, that the community of humans is threefold: those who went before us; those who share with us our present time on earth; and those who are yet to come. Together they constitute the human family to whom duties are owed. Concern for humanity, therefore, presupposes concern for all three. Duties such as honoring the dead and preserving the earth for the future all spring from this basic concept. Such a perspective underlines the principle that willful damage to the environment is a trespass. To talk of duty only in terms of sin obscures these perspectives.

By enlarging in this fashion the circle of those to whom we owe a duty, the question is also brought into focus of how we would react had we been the generation adversely affected—the victim. Would we forgive a previous generation that had, for its selfish advantage, irreversibly poisoned our land, water, and atmosphere for many generations to come?

Islam: the notion of vertical relationships

Some philosophies—for example, the Islamic—look upon all duties as those which exist in a person's vertical relationship with God. Attend with devotion to those duties and the "rights" due to you from your fellow human beings fall automatically into place. Obeying God's injunctions results in a proper attention to all our horizontal relationships among human beings *inter se*.

Hence, in human rights discourse, we see the contrast between anthropocentric (man-centered) and theocentric (God-centered) views of human rights. Whereas the Islamic view of rights was theocentric, modern human rights discourse in the Western tradition concentrated on anthropocentric rights—principally civil and political rights. These rights were acquired by human beings vis-à-vis other human beings who held authority over them. They were wrested historically through bitter political struggles, thus obscuring the importance of duties. But as every right is accompanied by a duty, emphasizing the right without like emphasis on the duty is a rather lopsided view. Moreover, the emphasis on civil and political rights obscures also another set of rights: economic, cultural, and social rights.

Another Islamic concept is the concept of "bidding unto good," that is, the positive duty imposed by law upon all citizens to assist those who are in danger or distress.

Buddhism: the noble eightfold path

If we are engaged in a search for standards of righteous or ethical conduct, the vast analytical literature of Buddhism can afford us much guidance. Buddhism has analyzed the concept of ethical conduct in fine detail and laid down a "noble eightfold path" of conduct for the righteous. The component elements of such conduct are: right vision or understanding; right thoughts; right speech; right action; right livelihood; right effort; right mindfulness; and right concentration. A lapse from the requisite standards in any of these areas would constitute a lapse in righteous conduct. Such lapses are not necessarily sins in the sense in which the term is commonly understood, but constitute a falling away from the standards of nobler conduct that Buddhism postulates.

Each of these heads of conduct has been the subject of minute analysis by the commentators who have taken it to a degree of sophistication perhaps unmatched in commentaries that concentrate purely on sin and offenses. Buddhist scriptures make fine analyses of the conduct that constitutes right understanding, for example, and the distinction between this concept and right thoughts, right mindfulness, and right concentration. These heads, which relate to the mental discipline of the individual, also exert an impact on his or her relations with others. For example, right concentration would seek to discard passionate desires and unwholesome thoughts such as ill will.[12] For a rounded understanding of the full implications of ethical conduct, it is useful that one be aware of such analyses in other religions. These seldom reach the Christian, however anxious he may be to attain the highest standards of conduct.

One is reminded in this context of Aristotle's analysis of right conduct. An act must be performed at the right time, in the right manner, and to the right extent. If, for example, one is giving assistance to a supplicant, one is not indulging in right conduct if one gives it in extravagant quantity; or at the wrong time after his need has passed; or in the wrong manner, as when one gives with a supercilious attitude; or of the wrong kind, as when one gives the sort of assistance that will cause more harm than good.

On the larger scale contemplated by the eightfold path of Buddhism, there are many more indicia that must be given due consideration in determining the righteous nature of a piece of conduct.

Hinduism: the concept of dharma, or the law of righteousness

Hinduism has an all-embracing word for righteousness: *dharma*. The word has so many connotations as to defy definition. A vast body of juristic writings has sought over the centuries to expound its meaning. For practical purposes it may be summarized as requiring the good Hindu to follow the law of righteousness in every facet of his or her conduct. A person must not merely refrain from sin, but must live righteously in the fullest implications of that word.

In the words of the Indian savant, Sri Aurobindo:

Truth, honor, loyalty, fidelity, courage, chastity, love, long-suffering, self-sacrifice, harmlessness, forgiveness, compassion, benevolence, beneficence are its common themes, are in its view the very stuff of a right human life, the essence of Man's *Dharma*.[13]

So it must be with Christianity.

Truly Christian conduct, such as Christ enjoined, is suffused with love. "Love thy neighbor as thyself"; "And now I give you a new commandment: love one another" (John 13:34). One of the most beautiful expositions of love in the scriptures of any religion is Paul's exposition in the First Letter to the Corinthians (13:2-7):

I may have all the faith needed to move mountains—but if I have no love, I am nothing. I may give away everything I have and even give up my body to be burnt—but if I have no love, this does me no good.

Love is patient and kind; it is not jealous or conceited or proud; love is not ill-mannered or selfish or irritable; love does not keep a record of wrongs; love is not happy with evil, but is happy with the truth. Love never gives up; and its faith, hope, and patience never fail.

If this is what love means, even its most elementary manifestations must go beyond mere abstention from sin. They must enter the arena of affirmative action in pursuance of this basic principle. Anything less than such affirmative action is a shortcoming in Christian conduct. Mere abstention from sin connotes a negative. The Christian life is resoundingly positive.

CHAPTER 7

"AND LEAD US NOT INTO TEMPTATION"

This clause has been described as the most intense of the Prayer's petitions.[1] Unlike the first two petitions, which relate to sustenance for the present and forgiveness for the past, it looks forward into the unknown future—a future beset by dangers both physical and moral, dangers against which protection is required because of the weakness of the body and the frailty of the mind. There is, moreover, a deep humility that underlies it, for it recognizes human frailty and inadequacy, and the need for strength and assistance if these are to be overcome.

There is an implied moral note that rings through the clause, for clearly protection cannot be requested under the Prayer by a supplicant who rejects the values and standards laid down by that same Prayer. It is only a mind attuned to the values underlying the Prayer that is on the right wavelength to receive its benefits.

If there is to be protection against temptation, there must be an initial resolve to order one's conduct according to the appropriate moral values. The petition thus operates in a twofold manner: strengthening the moral fiber of the supplicant and gathering strength from the divinity in that same endeavor.

As with trespasses, so also with temptations: The scope of the concept has altered vastly with the vast alteration in human society since the time of Jesus. This magnification can only be described as phenomenal. For twenty centuries it was interpreted within the comparatively narrow confines of such conduct as sexual misbehavior, theft, lying, cheating, assault, murder, pride, and hypocrisy. Today's interpretations must take account of modern technology, the sophistication of corporate law, the pervasiveness of the media, the interknit nature of global society, and the power and distant reach of accumulated capital. In the interpretation of the word "temptation" the practical effects of such changes upon the meaning of temptation have not perhaps been adequately considered.

The interpretation of "temptation" thus falls into step with our interpretation of "trespasses" in the previous chapter, where it was pointed out that the expanding power now available to human beings begets expanding obligations. It demonstrates also how the different sections of the Prayer dovetail with one another. In praying "and lead us not into temptation," we are seeking protection against being led into conduct that does not conform to the norms of Christian righteousness. We are seeking protection against being led into trespasses of all descriptions. We are asking for help against the temptation to trespass. (Hence, after this chapter, the two petitions will be treated as one integrally related theme.)

The reading of this particular clause of the Prayer presents, perhaps more acutely than any other in the Prayer, the problems posed by translation upon translation. In the first place, we do not know exactly the flavor of the particular Aramaic expressions that Jesus used when he spoke of temptation. Second, the English word "temptation" is a translation from the Greek word *peirasmos*, which, as William Barclay reminds us,[2] had as many as six different meanings, including a deliberate seduction, a tempting of Providence, and a testing of truth or quality. It is unlikely that all these specific flavors of meaning would have been carried by the original Aramaic word used by Jesus. Conversely, it is most likely that the word he used carried other meanings as well. We must therefore understand the word in the spirit of the Prayer.

The word "temptation" appears in some of the earliest and most famous English versions of the New Testament—the translations of John Wycliffe, William Tyndale, and John Knox. Some modern versions of the Prayer substitute the words "Do not put us to the test" in place of "Lead us not into temptation." Such a version suggests that we are seeking to be spared from being tempted, rather than that we are seeking strength to resist temptation. Since temptation will always beset humans, this approach seems to me to sidetrack the problem of moral decision in the exercise of one's own free will—which is the essence of this portion of the Prayer.

The Greek word *peirasmos* also conveys the idea of continuity. One is being put to the test or tempted throughout one's life, not only at moments of crisis. This continuous process is part of life and applies in little matters as well as great.

"Lead us not"

The expression "lead us not" has puzzled interpreters, for God cannot be seen in any event as *leading* anyone into temptation. The phrase could mean "do not allow us to enter into temptation" and "do not let us yield to temptation."[3] It is also strange to suppose that human life can be freed of temptation. Any such meaning that the words in translation may suggest must therefore be rejected.

Saint Augustine draws a distinction between actually falling victim to temptation and being brought within the ambit or power of temptation.[4] Temptation will necessarily come, and when it comes we are to ask for help to resist it. We are always within its *ambit*, but we must not be in its *control*. We ask God not to allow us to fall into temptation. Dionysius of Alexandria's interpretation was similar: "That means, let us not fall into temptation."[5]

Another way perhaps of regarding it is through the well-known Platonic simile likening the soul to a charioteer driving two steeds, one representing the spiritual and the other the sensual element in man. It is the charioteer's responsibility to prevent the latter from pulling the chariot in the direction it chooses.[6] We thus avoid being led into temptation by keeping it in check. Strength is needed to do this, and the Prayer asks for that strength without which the charioteer may be unable to remain in control. "But every man is tempted when he is drawn away of his own lust and is enticed" (James 1:14, KJV).

A comparable sentence from the *Upanishads* of Hinduism reads, "Lead us beyond all pain and grief *along the path of righteousness*."[7] This positive aspect, quite clearly inherent in the notion of guidance, is often missed in recitals of the Prayer. As already noted, the social virtues of Christian conduct include the affirmative practice of virtue, not merely the negative abstention from evil. In a world desperately crying out for help for the afflicted and downtrodden, there is great danger of missing an important aspect of this prayer for Divine guidance, through a concentration on the mere avoidance of evil. Just as the true Christian is not one who merely abstains from evil, the true world citizen of the future will need to do more than merely abstain from evil. Affirmative action in the cause of justice and righteousness is an important part of the deliverance sought by reciters of the Prayer. We are asking not merely to be guarded from evil, but also to be guided along the path of righteousness of conduct.

"Into"

The preposition "into" is not without significance. Various meanings are possible here. The word "into" could mean "toward" or "in the direction of." We thus ask that we be diverted away from the route toward temptation.

Another interpretation, supported by those who work through the Greek word *eis* and the similar Hebrew word *lidhe,* conveys a more intense and graphic picture. The Greek and Hebrew words relied upon carry the connotation of "into the hands of" or "into the power of."[8] We are then acknowledging the enormous power of temptation to take us into its grip. It can envelop us and trap us as a carnivorous plant traps its prey. It lies waiting quietly, inviting the unwary to come within its reach. We need protection against this, for we realize the power of evil and our helplessness to face it unaided.

One could, of course, analyze this further. Temptation is not evil in itself. Even the greatest, Jesus included, have been exposed to temptation. Temptation is but the bait through which one is drawn into evil. When we ask not to be delivered into the hands of temptation, we are in effect asking not to be delivered into the hands of the evil that lies behind temptation. Temptation is one step before the portals of evil, and we ask for protection at this earlier stage before we enter that threshold.

The Ever-Present Nature of Temptation

Being on one's guard against temptation is an important part of the Christian message. The temptation of Adam and Eve illustrates its power at the very beginning of human society; and Jesus himself, at a central stage of his mission, warned his disciples explicitly of this danger when, shortly before his betrayal, he said, "Pray that you will not fall into temptation" (Luke 22:40).

Many commentators have stressed the inevitability of temptation as a necessary accompaniment to the human condition. In Origen's words, "Is not man's life on earth one continuous temptation?"[9] Saint Peter put it more vividly when he observed that Satan, the source of temptation, "roams round like a roaring lion, looking for someone to devour. Be firm in your faith and resist him, because you know that your fellow believers in all the world are going through the same kind of sufferings" (1 Peter 5:8–9).

In short, a reading of the Prayer in light of its social implications offers both a positive and a negative aspect. The temptation to commit a wrong affirmatively is by no means the only evil against which the Prayer asks for protection. The temptation to abstain from interference when a wrong cries out for preventive action is just as strong. Modern life, both national and international, is replete with examples. An extreme example, which modern global conditions have highlighted, is the temptation to sit back with folded arms even when genocide, the worst of all crimes, is being perpetrated. Here is temptation indeed, for it is tempting to sit back in the comfort of one's own safety while the basic principle of human dignity is being torn to shreds.

Recognizing that temptation is an ever-present part of life, the Prayer becomes a call to vigilance and a request for the steady help of God in this continuing struggle.

Even as this book goes to press, the Church of England is debating whether to delete the words "Lead us not into temptation" and substitute "Save us from the time of trial" in a modern version to be introduced in church services in the new millennium. The Church's general synod voted for the change in February 1998, but the prayer change is not final, as it has to go before a revision committee and then be approved again by the general synod.

What is important to remember is that trial and temptation will always attend the human condition and that what we are seeking is guidance and protection to save us from falling victims to them—to be saved *at* the time of trial rather than to be saved *from* the time of trial. We do not want to fall victim to temptation. If we are not to be tempted at all, there is little scope for virtue or free will. That would not be a true picture of the battle with evil which we must face and win, rather than make detours and avoid.

CHAPTER 8

"BUT DELIVER US FROM EVIL"

These words carry forward the Prayer for strength against temptation. Just as much as we do not wish to be authors of wrongdoing, we do not wish to be at the receiving end of wrongdoing, for trespasses and temptations are the cause of infinite evil to others—in fact, the cause of most evils in the world. Pertinent to the theme of trespasses and temptations, we thus see that the Prayer is now pursuing this theme to its inevitable conclusion and thus, in a sense, moving to the other side of the coin. Another way of looking at "but deliver us from evil" is to consider that temptation itself is one of the forms of evil against which we seek protection.

We shall not detain ourselves here with theological discussions as to whether the word "evil" means "evil" in the abstract, or "the Evil One," as in Lucifer or Satan. Rather, it will suffice to observe that most of the evils that beset the human condition in the present age are the result of the work of man.

In Homer's *Odyssey*, Zeus, the king of the gods, rebukes men in these terms:

Look you now, how vainly mortal men do blame the gods! From us they say comes evil, whereas they even of themselves, through the blindness of their own hearts, have sorrows beyond that which is ordained.

Joseph Conrad, who wrote in works such as *The Heart of Darkness* of man's inhumanity to man, saw this in a manner related to the realities of the world scene and of colonialism when he wrote, in *Under Western Eyes*, that "The belief in a supernatural source of evil is not necessary; men alone are quite capable of every wickedness."[1] Looking around the world scene today, one gets the impression of escalating evil in many parts of the world—man-made evils, planned and unplanned, which dwarf some of the atrocities of the past. It was of such that Conrad wrote; and, eighty years later, one can only say that they are still escalating—often escalating at the very hands of those who pray to be delivered from evil.

As already noted, all religions drive home the point that evil comes not from God but from man. Buddhism teaches: "By ourselves is evil done. By ourselves we cease from wrong." And Islam teaches:

> Nothing can be evil on the part of God. For a thing is evil on our part only because we transgress the limit and bound set for us and do what we have no right to do.[2]

Eminent philosophers say much the same, as, for example, Jean Jacques Rousseau in *Emile* (1762): "God makes all things good: man meddles with them and they become evil."

Saint Basil wrote, "Evil is...but a disposition of the soul which is contrary to virtue and comes from a heedless desertion of good"[3]—an idea dramatically echoed by William Law (1686–1761) when he wrote, "Evil can no more be charged upon God than darkness can be charged upon the sun."[4]

The prayer "deliver us from evil" thus requires that we should turn the searchlight upon ourselves and scan the areas of our own wrongdoing as well, when we ask that we be delivered from evil.

The Self-Propagating Power of Evil

Evil, like temptation, feeds upon itself; and the longer protection is delayed, the more difficult it is to ward off. "One evil flows from another," wrote Terence Eunuchus in 160 B.C., and Herman Melville in *Moby Dick*, two thousand years later, repeated the wisdom of the ages when he wrote, "As the most poisonous reptile of the marsh perpetuates his kind...so equally...all miserable events naturally beget their like."

Another version of this is the "slippery slope" argument: Relax from the rigors of the straight and narrow path, place one foot upon the slippery slope, and the downward momentum may be difficult to control.

Applied to evil in practical terms this points to one act of deprivation or dishonesty leading to another to cover it up and yet another, till the exponential growth of wrongdoing acquires a life of its own that one is power-less to resist. This has been said of the armaments industry and could be said of many more such spheres of activity. Thus a course of exploitative conduct, of militarism, of dishonest business dealing, once launched, soon reproduces itself and generates in the doer a mental attitude that begins to take the wrongdoing for granted. Lowering expectations is a powerful way of lowering standards. Moreover, such patterns of conduct become so pow-erful that, at a certain stage, the initiator loses the power to resist them, after which they career unrestrained.

The prayer for protection against evil acquires another dimension when one views it in this light, for it is also a prayer for protection against descent into an evil course of conduct, rather than against particular acts of evildo-ing. The Buddhist scriptures state the proposition in the form that, "Even if the water falls drop by drop it will fill the pot; and the wrongdoer will become full of evil though he gather it little by little."[5]

Saint Cyril of Jerusalem offers a similar figurative description:

Do you know that oftentimes a root has split a rock, when suffered to remain in it? Give no lodgement to the seed of evil, seeing that it will break up your faith.[6]

Attacking the Roots of Evil, Rather Than the Branches

Deliverance from evil does not merely involve deliverance from evil con-sequences while the roots of evil remain. The roots of evil may consist in certain attitudes that will keep producing their evil consequences even though the latter are lopped away. As the eminent philosopher Henry David Thoreau observed in his classic work *Walden* (1854), "There are a thousand hacking at the branches of evil to one who is striking at the root."

This aspect has special pertinence to many of the global problems of our time, of which poverty and starvation are the preeminent examples. Relief operations that seek to alleviate poverty, however well intentioned, are at-tacks upon the branches of evil only. They do not penetrate the root, which may be unfair trade practices or exploitative commodity contracts heavily weighted against weaker contracting parties. As long as these latter evils flourish, their fruit and branches will continue to appear—even though the branches may be lopped off from time to time.

The perpetrators often do not see such evil. They may be members of a vast commercial conglomerate, not seeing in their little sphere of operation the overall scheme of damage to a small economy that the conglomerate is destroying. Otherwise they would probably not be party to the scheme. Instead, they do their own particular job with devotion and care. The same could apply to workers in the armaments industry, as, for example, those engaged in the myriad separate operations that go into the creation of a nuclear weapon. It is necessary that workers step back from their daily routines to try to take in the overall impact of a great operation to which they contribute only a small and seemingly insignificant part. It will not be sufficient for the worker merely to say that the responsibility for the ultimate product depends upon the overall directors of the scheme, and not on the individual worker. That would be a facile method of falling into the clutches of evil. The less one inquires about the end result of one's work, the less sensitive one becomes. It is true that "No man is clever enough to know all the evil he does."[7] Yet it is one's responsibility to inquire about the results of one's actions.

Evil to Oneself, Evil to Others

There is a communal appeal in this part of the Prayer as well, for one prays not only that evil does not befall oneself, but also that evil does not befall others. The Prayer says deliver *us* from evil, not "deliver *me* from evil." It is a prayer "for the deliverance of the whole human family,"[8] and it "brings before the Father all the distress of the world."[9] Just as it is selfish to pray for *my* daily bread as opposed to *our* daily bread, it is selfish also to pray that *I* alone be delivered from evil.

The meaning of *us* in this context is again not the narrow meaning of one's own family or tribe or group, but the human family who together form a group in the universal sweep of the Prayer and in the eyes of the Almighty to whom the Prayer is addressed.

CHAPTER 9

TRESPASSES
AND TEMPTATIONS
OF VIOLENCE

W hat are these trespasses and temptations, against which the Prayer warns us, that fill our path toward the next millennium? Their range has grown phenomenally under the influence of the physical power and the organizational reach made available by the enormous growth of technology, communications, industry, bureaucracies, corporations, military establishments, and power groupings of all kinds. From the comfort of one's office in an affluent city, one can, with little fear of detection and under cover of the law, make profits from the exploitation of undernourished people at the other end of the world whom one neither sees nor knows. When the rewards are enormous, the temptations are correspondingly great. And they will grow dramatically in the next millennium. The immediacy of one victim's suffering can be put as far away as if that victim lived on another planet; a person's conscience is not stricken as it would be when wrongdoer and victim are within sight of each other.

Temptations can be of endless variety, and the categories of temptations are never closed. Their immense variety is such that Jesus himself was exposed to them in the desert for a continuous period of forty days. We are given an indication of three of them: the temptations of wealth and power, as where all the kingdoms of the world were displayed before him; temptations of putting God to the test by creating problems and expecting God to solve them ("throw yourself from this turret and God will protect you"); and temptations of overweening egotism and the purposeless display of power ("command this stone to turn into bread").

Trespasses and temptations can be broad and clear or they may be "subtle ones in which only a passing thought tells on a man's being and actions...."[1]

In our current phase of development, it is the subtle temptations that wreak the greatest havoc.

For present purposes, we have, without any attempt at an exhaustive list, grouped trespasses and temptations under the heads of problems of violence, and technological, economic, attitudinal, social, and ethical problems—which will be examined, in turn, in this and following chapters. We also examine legal protections of moral wrongdoing. In each of these areas temptations open up of a magnitude and nature unknown when the Prayer was formulated.

Genocide

The complacent assumption that our age had graduated out of the barbaric practice of genocide was shattered by the Holocaust, perpetrated by a professedly Christian regime. Yet many regarded this as the solitary exception that proved a general rule: Christian communities do not, but for bizarre aberrations, commit genocide. Such smugness concealed the truth—that genocide has been a very real practice in our century. For example, in this very century, in German South West Africa, a large section of the Herero people were driven into the Omaheke desert in 1904, and the last water holes sealed behind them so that over 20,000 men, women, and children perished in "a waterless oven of sand."[2] A Herero wrote to a German settler, "The missionary says that we are the children of God like our white brothers…but just look at us. Dogs, slaves, worse than baboons on the rocks…that is how you treat us."[3] In Tasmania, not one aboriginal person survived. Events in Yugoslavia in recent years have riveted global attention under the euphemistic description of "ethnic cleansing." The gulf between profession and practice that Jesus expressly warned against when he taught his followers how to pray could not be better illustrated.

Clad in the lounge suits and military uniforms of the twentieth century, the perpetrators of modern genocide stir up racial hatred and incite atrocities with all the virulence of the skin-clad dwellers in some primeval cave. A newspaper picked up at random any day will tell us of current genocidal activity in Europe, Asia, Africa, and South America. Genocide is practiced in a dozen places even as the reader reads these lines. There is, however, another form of current genocide about which the newspapers do not tell us: the genocide quietly practiced away from the glare of publicity, by corporate might, particularly by mining and logging interests that operate in remote forests inhabited by unsophisticated tribes. Exploitation of the rain forests in the Amazon has, to judge from available literature on the subject, resulted in the extermination of several tribes. One writer mentions over twenty tribes thus exterminated, including:

> The Caritianas, whose fief was close to the sources of the Rio Candeias. The Caxarabis of the Rio Abuna. The Querquiriwats who once lived along the banks of the Rio Pimenta Bueno. The Macuraps, who used to haunt the rapids of the Rio Branco. The Mialats, formerly settled on the Rio Leitao. The Mondés, who roamed the upper part of the Rio Pimenta Bueno. The Palmeras, men of the interior of the jungle. The Rama-Ramas, who rode along the Rio Anaris and Machadinho. The Sanamaicas, who used to dominate the streams which flowed into the Rio Pimento Bueno.[4]

Other tribes were decimated—for example, the Cacaas Novas tribe was reduced from 30,000 people to 400 between 1950 and 1968. The alleged methods of genocide there included presents of clothing deliberately infected with germs, gifts of poisoned food, and candy containing arsenic given to children.[5]

The same author asserts that, even at the time of his writing (1971), it was possible for a businessman in the comfort of an affluent metropolitan center, acting in combination with a bank associated with the enterprise, to plan the extermination of a tribe which inconvenienced a mining or tree-felling concern. In the 1990s, we hear assertions of similar atrocities in certain Asian rain forests. The interests concerned are often powerful enough to throw a media blanket around their activities and, indeed, to buy the complicity of officials. In the result, a world order which is rightly concerned with the problem of vanishing species of flora and fauna turns a blind eye on vanishing tribes of humans.

If even a hundredth part of such accusations is true, it is more than sufficient to displace any complacency resulting from the supposition that modern civilization has left genocide behind it. Recent experience has underlined the lesson that genocidal movements can flare up in almost any community, and that once the genocidal fires have been lit, it is difficult to control the flames. Communities not attuned to their duty to resist even its incipient expressions are like dry grass waiting to explode in flames if a chance spark should come in its direction. The grass needs to be watered before the spark strikes it.

Torture

As you read these words, someone somewhere is about to face his torturer. Since torture is practiced by people of all religions, that torturer may well be a Christian who has recited the Lord's Prayer this very week, if not this very day. The tortures he will perpetrate on his victim are more refined by far than the medieval rack and thumbscrew.

The Secretary General of Amnesty International once described the wave of torture now sweeping the world as an epidemic. It eclipses the reign of terror of Nero and is a very real feature of the political landscape in the closing years of a century that has seen the greatest advances in our understanding of the human mind—how best it can be tormented and how best its resistance can be broken.

Torture has been institutionalized as an accepted method of handling political opponents, and is regularly practiced in dozens of countries across the globe. It is practiced by officials in many of the world's prisons and detention camps, in police stations and in political investigation bureaus. It is practiced by private individuals as an incident of kidnap and rape. All the cries of human rights activists are voices in the wilderness. The carnival of torture goes on.

At a time when torture was a normal instrument of the judicial process throughout Europe, the great Italian lawyer Cesare Beccaria showed what one concerned individual could do, by publishing a treatise in 1764 arguing that torture should be abolished. Under his influence ordinances outlawing the practice were passed in Russia in 1767, Portugal in 1776, Sweden in 1786, and Austria in 1789. If one dedicated individual, actuated by humanitarian principles, could achieve so much, what could not be achieved by the untold thousands galvanized into action by the Prayer to which they are committed?

Although, as the eighteenth century closed, it seemed as if the stage was being set for the retreat of torture from the civilized world, it seems, as the twentieth century closes, that it is making a frontal advance on the way back to uninhibited acceptance. Implements of torture have become commercial goods, advertised by their manufacturers in glossy sales booklets dispatched to potential international customers. Expertise in the art of torture is a commodity that is exported, for torture experts are hired by governments to train their torturers. As the century closes we witness this grotesque scenario in which many of the participants are Christians.

The brotherhood and common humanity of torturer and victim have receded into the background, and human beings have become objects no different from mice in the hands of a vivisectionist. Even as they assert their religious faith, as some of them do from time to time, the torturers perfect their implements of torture. By the time you finish reading this page, a few dozen victims have probably been dealt with to the satisfaction of the torturer and his superiors, and lie broken in spirit and body on some desolate prison floor.

The Escalation of Violence

Violence has attended the course of human affairs from the dawn of history. The clash of arms, the wails of widows and orphans, the flames of homes and cities put to the invader's torch were familiar sounds and sights in almost every preceding century. But as we enter the twenty-first, some sinister new twists are being added to the old spirals of violence. Some that may be readily identified are the increase in individual violence, the increase in gang violence, and the increase in domestic and international terrorism.

In the United States alone, two hundred million guns are in the hands of the civilian population, and one and a half million more are added annually to that total. There are several thousand deaths from firearms annually. The widespread unrest of our times has resulted in private citizens arming themselves to the teeth in many countries. The individual thus armed can hold his neighborhood and the community to ransom—and indeed does so from time to time in lurid incidents that grip international television audiences.

Armaments interests aim also at the international spread of arms, for selling arms to the Third World is big business and, as guns are sold to one country, more guns are needed in another to fight those guns. The great powers compete with one another to sell arms to the Third World, justifying their action on the grounds that, if they did not, some other Power would. It is even openly argued, for the purpose of winning public support for such practices, that such sales put bread on the tables of one's own workers, rather than on those of foreign workers whose countries might supply such arms. Of course, the daily bread the Lord's Prayer requests cannot be bread secured by the sale of instruments of death.

Organized gangs can, mafia-style, terrorize a given occupation or neighborhood, exacting tribute in what has become lucrative business, on a scale not known before. They can sometimes hold governments to ransom. Terrorism—sometimes state-funded, sometimes encouraged by the armaments industry, sometimes in alliance with the narcotics trade—spreads its wings globally with a power beyond the wildest dreams of the Barbary Corsairs of the past. Hijackings have become a feature of our times.

These flames are fanned by a psychology of violence, which is being built into the mind-frame of our age. Violence is taken for granted. It is seen as a matter of course by all age groups, for our television sets present it as part of their daily fare. And so resistance to it is blunted, for the commonplace does not excite. Even the slow extermination of an entire nation leaves its global audience passive and paralyzed.

Is there a possible explanation or answer offered by the Good Samaritan concept? In 1964, when a young lady, Miss Catherine Genovese, was done to death in Queens, New York, in the presence of thirty-seven bystanders who looked on without lifting a finger to protect her, a wave of soul-searching spread across the United States. Where did the fault lie, which permitted callous violence to flourish while the world looked on? Was the spirit of the Good Samaritan completely dead in the bustling city of New York? That incident provoked numerous seminars on the legal, moral, and social aspects of good Samaritanism. Lawyers, psychiatrists, sociologists, journalists, and philosophers met at the University of Chicago Law School to discuss the problem. A book was published entitled *The Good Samaritan and the Law*,[6] which contained studies on the subject. The finger of blame was pointed in many directions. The fault lay with law and its procedures, with the schools, with apathy, lack of concern for others, sensitivities blunted by exposure to frequent violence, and the lack of concern shown by those who should lead the community, including lawyers and teachers.

Moreover, organized crime further obstructs the processes of worldly justice in many countries. It does not stop at instilling terror into the minds of potential witnesses. In more than one country, government prosecutors, and even judges themselves, are threatened and in fact murdered at the behest of organized crime, when an inquiry is pending. The average civilian witness lacks even the protection such officials enjoy and consequently exhibits an understandable reluctance to come forward to give evidence.

On the world scene, we are witnessing the Genovese incident in macrocosm. Blame cannot be attributed to any one group alone. Only a mass sensitization to the values of peace and individual duty can prevent these flames from burning out of control in the next century. The Lord's Prayer affords a powerful means of accomplishing this.

The Glorification of Violence

The glorification of the cult of violence is a powerful promoter of violence. International crime often comes dressed as patriotism, and the educational system itself tends to glorify violence. The child in school is taught that armies of conquest have "covered themselves with glory"—when in simple terms they have killed large numbers of defenseless people, annexed the lands of others, and shown callousness to captive populations. As Tolstoy caustically observed of Napoleon in *War and Peace*:

> He conquered everyone everywhere, that is, he killed a great many people because he was a very great genius. And for some reason he went off to kill Africans, and killed them so well,…that when he returned to France, he ordered everyone to obey him. And everyone obeyed him.[7]

In the same vein, when Japan was introduced into the "civilized group of nations" after its successful wars against China and Russia, a Japanese diplomat remarked, "We show ourselves at least your equals in scientific butchery, and at once we are admitted to your Council tables as civilized men."[8] Disguise it as we may, the truth, as we close the twentieth century, is that military strength is still the best argument at the conference table. When cultured diplomats speak in gentle tones of bargaining from a position of strength, they are referring, more often than not, to raw physical power rather than to the moral strength of their arguments. Such are the values that command respect and attention.

Blaise Pascal observed in *Pensées*, "Can anything be more ridiculous than that a man has a right to kill me because he dwells on the other side of the water, and because his prince has a quarrel with mine, although I have none with him?"

Can anything be more ridiculous than that this continues to be so in an age which has universally proclaimed its commitment to "the dignity and worth of the human person."[9]

From the schoolroom to the national and international world, tribute is paid to strength and the ability to triumph through violence. So long as the world admires naked force and pays obeisance to those who command it, these phenomena will continue. It is only by striking at its root that the cult of violence can be challenged.

Narco-Terrorism

There are strong political overtones to the narcotics trade. In the past, it has generated wars, as for example, the Opium War. In the building of great empires, it has been looked upon as a substantial source of imperial revenue. In today's world, there is an alliance between narcotics and terrorism, for traffic in drugs is often used as the means of financing terrorist activities. There is a direct link between narcotics and the arms trade. Narcotics barons build up empires of fear around themselves and hold entire populations under their sway.

One can think of few activities more diametrically opposed to the notion of attempting to create God's kingdom on earth. A trade that derives wealth from the crippling of the human personality, and then proceeds to use that wealth for the destruction of life, must surely be as close as one can get to the forces of evil against which the Prayer seeks protection.

Narcotics and narco-terrorism can be handled only by concerted international action. Human rights principles of dignity and health, as well as the fundamental norm of peace, are considerations that render international and national action imperative.

Narcotics is as great a world problem today as the slave trade was in the nineteenth century, and is seemingly as well entrenched. It has been described, in a detailed study of the subject, as "a deadly symbiosis that tears at the vitals of Western civilization."[10] The world has yet to marshal its moral resources adequately to meet this new threat to human dignity, even as it successfully rallied its moral resources to outlaw slavery.

Sex Crimes

The world was taken aback recently to hear that rape had been used as an instrument of war. This has, of course, happened before, with a view to undermining the resistance of a captured people who have been bonded together by membership of a common race or tribe. Rape on an organized scale can produce a mixed progeny which undermines this bond. Yet it was an emotional shock to hear of it in the closing years of this century. Force, terror, the shattering of human dignity, the exploitation of the weak, the lack of forgiveness, the furtherance of hate, the transgression of the basic commandments—all these, which are anathema to the Prayer, are woven into such an act. That it should even enter into the range of possibilities as we close this century must send shock waves through the moral fiber of the world community.

But sex crimes have many more manifestations, just as insidious. The prostitution of children for sex, child pornography, sex tourism, the proliferation of individual acts of sexual crime, murders for sex—these are the daily fare reported in the media.

In 1989, the government of Norway reported to the United Nations Working Group on Contemporary Forms of Slavery that one million children are sold, kidnapped, or in other ways forced on the world's sex market every year,[11] and child sex slaves are bought in certain markets for prices that may be as low as twenty dollars.[12] Child slaves, once purchased, are led away and rarely seen by their family again. They are whipped and beaten if they do not submit to the wishes of their owner's clientele.[13]

World tourism runs to tens of millions of people a year, and it is estimated that in some Asian countries sex tourists comprise as many as ten percent of this number.[14] The First World Congress Against Commercial Sexual Exploitation of Children, held in Stockholm in 1996, made several recommendations for national action against this evil, but the eradication of child prostitution faces many hurdles.

Kidnapping

Kidnapping for ransom or for political objectives has become commonplace. In some countries, parents sending their children to school are unsure that they will return without falling into the clutches of kidnappers demanding a ransom. Sometimes two groups, each claiming to be the child's kidnapper, confront the confused parents with demands for ransom for the same child, and the parent does not know with whom to deal.

Paramilitary groups indulge also in political kidnappings and extortions, issuing threatening communiqués and assuming the role of death squads. High-ranking officials, and even cabinet ministers, are taken hostage for the reinforcement of political demands.

Reports such as these have recently surfaced from more than one Christian country. The force of the state can hardly hold such movements in check. It is in the forum of the individual conscience that the decision can be made whether or not to yield to the temptation of resorting to such means of extortion.

The Victims of Violence

Modern legal systems, by and large, tend to concentrate on the punishment of criminals, but not on the rehabilitation of the victims. They and their families have had their lives shattered by the criminal act to such an extent that they are unable to pick up the pieces unaided. Just as the state has set up powerful departments for tracking down and punishing the offender, it needs to spend no less effort on the rehabilitation of the victim. The temptation to relax, in the belief that justice has been done when the offender has been tracked down and punished, leads to obscuring a deep moral duty lying upon the community and its members. Punishment of the offender is only one half of justice. The other half is rehabilitation of the victim , to which society often turns a blind eye.

The potential racists, arms dealers, torturers, terrorists, and drug barons of the twenty-first century are in our schools today. They are not yet racists, arms dealers, drug barons, or torturers but are in the process of becoming so, conditioned by the callousness they see around them. The message reaching them through the intellectual currents of the age is the irrelevance of religion to the practical problems of their time. They pull up the drawbridge and seal off their minds. Those minds can be reached by a meaningful interpretation of religion that makes sense to them, by being integrated into the practical problems they see all around them. Clothed in this garb, religion can penetrate into minds otherwise resistant to its abstractions and apparent irrelevance.

Of course, not all minds will be reached in this way, but enough to enable religions to play a more meaningful role in contributing to peace and tranquillity. To douse the firestorms waiting to be ignited as the twenty-first century gets into its stride, we need to resort to the reservoirs of moral principle available to us.

CHAPTER 10

TECHNOLOGICAL TRESPASSES AND TEMPTATIONS

The Arms Race

The use of the highest form of scientific knowledge[1] for the basest of all purposes—the premeditated extermination of human beings—must raise grave questions regarding the power, ethics and direction of the scientific enterprise.

Thomas Merton, in *Faith and Violence*, captured the concerns underlying these problems when he wrote of the armaments industry:

Modern technological mass murder is abstract, corporate, business-like, cool, free of guilt feelings, and therefore a thousand times more deadly and effective than the eruption of individual violence. It is this polite, massively organized, white-collar murder machine which threatens the world with destruction, and not the violence of a few desperate teenagers in the slums. But our antiquated Christian theology myopically focuses on individual violence and does not see this. Our antiquated moral theology shudders at the phantasm of mugging or a killing on our doorstep. But it blesses and canonizes the antiseptic violence of a corporately-organized murder, because corporate murder is respectable, efficient, clean, and above all, because corporate murder is profitable.[2]

The point Merton makes is valid. The citizen who involves himself in a brawl after a few drinks at the local tavern is hauled before the law, but not the millionaire arms dealer who sells death in bulk. Rather, he is honored by the towns where he holds his arms fair, and the major decision-makers of the country are his honored guests.[3] The firearms displayed at the fair are openly extolled by their manufacturers for their accuracy in killing their human targets at an ever-increasing range. The antiquated theology that Merton refers to has clouded the perceptions of these activities in the eyes of the many Christian people who thus endorse this festival of death. A proper interpretation of the "temptation" referred to in the Prayer should help to drop the scales from our eyes and enable us to see these activities as they really stand in the scale of morality. The armaments industry has displayed great skill in blotting out our perceptions of the brutalities involved. Even as the world is appalled by the brutalities of genocidal wars, the arms merchants continue to supply the warring parties with weapons. Arms sales to the Third World bring a rich harvest of billions of dollars a year to the arms-producing countries and, indeed, form an important part of even some of the strongest economies.

Truly, morality has a doubly onerous task to discharge here, for existing legal doctrines and structures rather curiously leave the armaments industry completely on the right side of the law. This constitutes a blind spot in international law and human rights.[4]

So powerful is the arms industry, and so all-pervading its influence, that even in the 1960s it was seen as seeping into nearly every aspect of society and culture,[5] and President Eisenhower himself, in his Farewell Address in 1961, warned that, "In the councils of government we must guard against the acquisition of unwarranted influence, whether sought or unsought, by the military-industrial complex."

When one considers also that the arms race avidly consumes earth resources that should feed the hungry and clothe the naked, it is not difficult to determine where Christian duty lies and that the arms trade is a continuing trespass against that duty. From major weapons that can cause the death of millions, to the little land mine, of which 110 million are now planted in sixty countries across the world, each capable of blowing off the feet of those who tread on them, the arms trade makes profit. Yet there are many categories of peace-loving citizens who do in fact unwittingly give it their support. They may be shareholders in large corporations that profit from the arms industry, without giving much thought to the fact that their humble investment dollar helps in the manufacture of instruments of death. They may passively approve the support the industry receives from politicians and the government because it generates jobs and prosperity. They may be employees in the industry itself, justifying it to themselves on the basis of their special training, or their lack of perception that they are actually manufacturing weapons of mass destruction, because they make only a small and innocuous looking component of them. They may refrain from inquiring into the end result of their work.

The twentieth century presents its temptations concealed under heavy wraps, thus imposing a specially onerous duty of vigilance. The temptation to inaction is an important part of the temptation the Prayer warns against. It is a very attractive temptation, especially if the facts are complex, the requisite information difficult to achieve, and the resulting conduct inconvenient. However, these could be the acid tests of sincerity in the recital of the Prayer.

President Eisenhower's unrivaled experience of military matters makes it impossible to discount his words. In a speech before the American Society of Newspaper Editors on April 16, 1953, he drew a direct connection between human hardship and military spending. The following quotation from that speech is cast in stone above Eisenhower's tomb in Abilene:

> Every gun that is made, every warship launched, every rocket fired signifies, in the final sense, a theft from those who hunger and are not fed, those who are cold and are not clothed. This world in arms is not spending money alone. It is spending the sweat of its laborers, the genius of its scientists, the hopes of its children....This is not a way of life at all, in any true sense. Under the cloud of threatening war, it is humanity hanging from a cross of iron.

Of course the plea will be made that armaments are essential for national defense, but a large part of the armaments industry goes well beyond this. A world in which homelessness, starvation, and grinding poverty are the lot of hundreds of millions, still sees trillions of dollars being pumped into armaments. A visitor from another planet would stare in disbelief at the reasoning processes involved.

A quarter century after Eisenhower's statement, there was another famous statement linking food and armaments. The words were those of Pope John Paul II in his first encyclical, *Redemptor Hominis* of March 4, 1979.

Recalling the passage from Matthew, "I was hungry and you gave me no food...," the pope said:

> These words become charged with even stronger warning, when we think that, instead of bread and cultural aid, the new States and nations awakening to independent life are being offered, sometimes in abundance, modern weapons and means of destruction placed at the service of armed conflicts and wars that are not so much a requirement for defending their just rights and their sovereignty but rather a form of chauvinism, imperialism, and neocolonialism of one kind or another. We all know well that the areas of misery and hunger on our globe could have been made fertile in a short time, if the gigantic investments for armaments at the service of war and destruction had been changed into investments for food at the service of life.[6]

Biomedical Technology

This area has perhaps more potential than almost any other to cut the ground under the feet of the concept of human dignity, which is a fundamental message of the Prayer.

We are entering a bewildering new era in which the fundamentals of humanness are being eroded by dazzling new technologies. Organs can be transplanted; fertilized ova are grown in rented wombs; gender can be preselected; DNA of all living creatures can be sliced up and recombined; mutations can be induced; the genes of humans and animals can be blended; children can be conceived from sperm of men long deceased; selective breeding can become big business; cloning technologies have traveled up the evolutionary ladder from frogs to sheep, and one wonders whether and where they will stop. The human body has become an article of property.[7] The weapons at the command of science stupefy the imagination, and "playing God" offers an area of temptation inconceivable to any prior generation. Recombinant DNA technology enables the scientist to take the DNA of one organism and splice it on to another, creating a living thing that is absolutely new. This breathtaking power in the wrong hands can lead to nightmarish results and poses the gravest moral issues.[8]

A multibillion dollar genome project is underway to map every one of the 100,000 human genes by the year 2005. The stupendous nature of this undertaking can be glimpsed from the fact that each of the one hundred trillion cells in the human body contains a nucleus with forty-six chromosomes arranged in twenty-three pairs. Each chromosome is filled with tightly coiled strands of DNA, each of which acts like a biological computer program containing three billion bits of information. Shaped like a spiral staircase, each strand is a molecular ladder three billion rungs long.[9] This hitherto impenetrable field is being confidently invaded by modern science.

While the Bible spoke of the human body as one and entire, with limbs, mind, and heart serving different functions, we can now take a reductionist view of the entire organism, as consisting of myriad building blocks that we may have the power to revamp and rearrange. Though the resulting knowledge will have the immense advantage of possible curative use, it opens a Pandora's box of problems affecting human dignity and the integrity of the human personality.

Genetic engineers will be able to use this knowledge to manipulate genes and change living structures. When they reach this stage with human genes, the structuring of humans with preselected properties will enter the realm of possibility. As combinations become possible of human and animal life, a man-mouse chimera, for example, can well be put on the drawing board. As the frontiers of cloning research draw ever closer to the human body, the issue has attracted so much concern that the President of the United States has endorsed a bill barring human cloning for five years, and has stressed the need "to continue the national dialogue on cloning."[10]

New techniques, such as amniocentesis, enable us to determine within a few weeks of conception the sex, qualities, and defects of the embryo. Fetuses revealed as carrying some comparatively minor defect may be exposed to routine abortion. Prior knowledge of the sex of the unborn child has already led to massive abuses. As with all branches of science, the benign and the malignant will emerge from the selfsame test tube. In the absence of a legal code to provide guidelines, moral concepts must be summoned to assist in constructing an ethical structure before it is too late in the day to set one in place.

In another department of biomedical science—the field of *in vitro* fertilization—other developments affecting the human personality are well advanced. The day a test-tube baby can be grown to full maturity outside the womb, there will be pandemonium in the world of the law, for we will not know when that entity attains the status of a human. When decantation, not birth, will mark the commencement of human personality, we will not know when and whether human life in a test tube can be terminated for defects resulting from laboratory procedures. Should the new entity undergo a probationary period of observation before it receives a certificate of humanness? On what criteria should that certificate be issued, to mark the entry into the community of a brand-new human being? Should fetus farms be permitted, where fetuses can be cultivated for special characteristics?

On the organ transplant scene, can cadavers be kept pulsating when the brain is pronounced dead, so that organs may be harvested from a cadaver bank? Can the poor of the world be used as a reservoir for the supply of organs for the rich? The sale of an organ such as a kidney for a sum of around 10,000 dollars could bring affluence to an entire family in a poor country—and "brokers" are already arranging such deals.

Law cannot answer these questions; the moral sense of the community must be the arbiter. The field is complex, the answers not easy. Yet there is at least a framework of principles that can keep us from going far astray. Human dignity, equality, the right to recognition as a person, the right to health, and the integrity of one's personality are principles contained in the Lord's Prayer. If we keep within these principles when approaching a solution, we have at least the assurance that the ground is not caving in under our feet.

Environmental Degradation

This book cannot stress enough that there should be no inconsistency between one's own conduct and one's recitals, or requests, when uttering the Prayer. Else the recitation of the Prayer lacks sincerity and, hence, value. The inconsistency is obvious, but not often perceived.

For the first time we shall greet a new century as a race endowed with the ability to destroy the entire life-support system of the planet. Humanity entered the twentieth century with the belief that the environment was powerful enough to absorb all the shocks and abuses inflicted on it by man. The oceans, the atmosphere, and the land were of infinite dimensions as compared with the work of humans and, consequently, nothing that puny man could do was capable of causing lasting damage. Human activity could be expanded without limit—a world-view that supported an ever-expansionist view of economic and industrial activity. That confidence no longer holds. For the first time we are weighed down by the consciousness that planet Earth, our common home, is fragile and that man-made wounds can damage it beyond repair. The ultimate destiny of the race—indeed, of our global home—lies in our hands. Law, whether national or international, cannot alter this, but can only nibble indecisively at the problem. Here, again, a more comprehensive spread of principles is needed — which can only come from moral imperatives.

In the meantime, living species die out by the hour, vast fertile areas are being totally denuded of top soil,[11] the ocean habitat of our food sources is being contaminated, rain forests are felled at the rate of twenty hectares per minute, 20,000 to 25,000 plant life species are threatened with extinction, thousands of tons of carbon dioxide pumped into the atmosphere are raising global temperatures, the ozone layer is further damaged rather than repaired, and nuclear contamination is scattered so far and wide in the oceans as to pollute them for a minimum of twenty thousand years. A better blueprint for the destruction of the environment could not be devised. No one knows when the proverbial straw will be added to break the camel's back.

A major international report,[12] released in October 1996, listed a quarter of the world's mammal species (1,096 out of 4,600 known species), and a third of the 275 primate species, as facing the risk of extinction. The Interior Secretary is reported to have observed of this report that it is "probably the most thorough scientific assessment of the world's wildlife ever undertaken," and that, "Unless people of all nations make extraordinary efforts, we face a looming natural catastrophe of almost biblical proportions."[13] The reference to biblical proportions reminds us of a vivid passage from scripture that anticipates our latest scientific information:

> …another angel coming up from the east…called out in a loud voice to the four angels to whom God had given the power to damage the earth and the sea. The angel said, "Do not harm the earth, the sea, or the trees….The first angel blew his trumpet. A third of the earth was burnt up, a third of the trees, and every blade of green grass….Then the second angel blew his trumpet….a third of the living creatures in the sea died, and a third of the ships were destroyed….Then the third angel blew his trumpet….A third of the water turned bitter, and many people died from drinking the water because it had turned bitter…. Then the fourth angel blew his trumpet. A third of the sun was struck, and a third of the moon, and a third of the stars…there was no light during a third of the day and a third of the night….Then the fifth angel blew his trumpet…the sunlight and the air were darkened….The rest

of mankind, all those who had not been killed by these plagues, did not turn away from what they themselves had made. They did not stop worshipping…the idols of gold, silver, bronze, stone and wood….[14]

The cause of all these catastrophes is thus stated to be the work of humanity's own hands, and the motive suggested seems to be the pursuit of the things of this world—gold and silver—rather than the higher values. The correspondence between the latest scientific information and this passage from scripture is eerie indeed.

The World Environment Conference held in 1992 in Rio de Janeiro failed to achieve many of its targets. We head into the twenty-first century as continuing polluters of the planet and continuing predators of its nonrenewable resources. Each person in the developed world has been likened to a robot gobbling up thirty kilograms of raw steel a day, and drinking a barrel of oil every week. Though steel is its staple diet, the robot also consumes sundry accompaniments of copper, aluminum, lead, tin, zinc, and plastics. It breathes out noxious fumes and produces at least two kilos of garbage every day.[15] At such rates of consumption, the pressure placed by the average person in North America on the environment is almost twenty times the pressure placed by a person in India or China, and sixty to seventy times more than a person in Bangladesh. If the whole world were to do the same, the entire ecosystem would collapse. Quoting these figures, Gro Harlem Brundtland, the Premier of Norway, has written, "Indeed, were all 5.5 billion people on the planet to consume at Western levels, we would need ten worlds, not one, to satisfy all our needs."[16]

Is there here a level of waste of nonrenewable earth resources and a level of pollution that are the direct results of self-centered attitudes? Is there pursuit of individual self-interest at the expense of the common good? The values that give us the answer are to be found in the Lord's Prayer—a prayer that speaks not in terms of superabundance of material needs, but only in terms of daily bread. We must resist the temptation to get the best for ourselves and dump the problem on our grandchildren.

Food Technology

Technology has in our time acquired a dominant role in the whole enterprise of global food production. Fertilizers, pesticides, food processing technology, development of new strains and hybrids—all of these require expensive and sophisticated technology. No farmer in the rich or poor world can do without them. Since extensive capital is needed to command the technology, those commanding the capital and the technology are in a position to dictate their prices, lay down terms to poorer countries, and control markets. Global food supplies are very much in their hands. Enormous profits are to be made in what is now described as "agribusiness." This area, as the ones previously discussed, cannot be controlled by laws. Moral watchfulness is required.[17]

"Species patents" over such products as genetically engineered cotton and soybeans, the patenting of soil samples, and such scientific activities raise a host of moral and ethical issues. The flow of crop germplasm from the developing to the developed world has been estimated as extending to four to five billion dollars (U.S.) a year. By the end of 1994, the problem had become so serious that the Consultative Group on International Agricultural Research (CGIAR) and the UN Food and Agriculture Organization (FAO) had to sign an agreement placing approximately forty percent of the world's invaluable seed collections under United Nations control. The term "bio-piracy" is gaining currency in this context and calls for vigilance and the application of ethical principles to a totally new area of activity, in which it is so easy to yield to temptation.

Likewise, the Third World farmer has become dependent on pesticides and must continue to purchase them, even though prices may be progressively increased. Fixing those prices becomes a matter of ethics and conscience; but when one has a monopoly over the product, there is great temptation to fix them at extortionate levels.

Cybernetics

The computer has opened out vast new avenues of hard-to-detect crime. Law and legal regulation can scarcely police this area either, so we are thrown back upon our moral resources—the moral strength of each individual to resist this easy source of temptation.

So great is the danger that it was described a quarter century ago, in a work on computer crime, in terms that "the computer offers a sitting target to crooks, enemies, and hostile fanatics, and presents the alarming possibility that society could be robbed blind *without even knowing it*."[18] Those dangers have multiplied with the amazing growth of the computer since then.

New temptations have thus been brought to the doorstep of every citizen, and the vast traffic in stolen and counterfeit credit cards is evidence of massive yielding to this new temptation.

The news media are already full of the ways in which pornography can be purveyed on the cybernetic highways, making it very difficult to police. In light of children's easy accessibility to cyberspace, traditional parental supervision of the moral temptations to which they are exposed is extremely difficult.

Illicit transfers of funds—"cyberpayments" as they are called—are another abuse. Internet users are already using this device for illegal and unregulated payments of millions of dollars across the globe for all sorts of criminal activities, including the laundering of criminally acquired money (which is dealt with in the next chapter of this book). No longer is it necessary to fill suitcases with one-hundred-dollar bills and send them across continents by secretly hired couriers. A private laptop computer can do the job, and the size of the transaction is no impediment.

The forms of computer crime are too numerous to detail and constitute crime of an enormous new magnitude. They are a current and potential source of spreading human misery on a global scale. They are a particularly attractive temptation because they are so easy to perform and so difficult to detect. And, once again, they cannot be particularly itemized in a code of conduct. They come within the general moral guidelines outlined in the Prayer.

Computerized Invasions of Privacy

Personal privacy, a long-cherished attribute of human dignity, is under grievous threat in the computer age. It is integral to the right to privacy that the individual should have the ability to control the circulation of information relating to himself or herself. When that control is gone, the individual becomes subservient to the people and institutions that can manipulate that information.[19]

The individual has now lost control over those who have access to his or her informational profile, and has lost control over the accuracy of that profile. Laser technology makes it possible to store a twenty-page dossier on every American on a single piece of tape.

Through the flow of data across borders, information about an individual can in an instant be transmitted into another jurisdiction beyond the reach of the national privacy laws protecting that individual. Comprehensive information about an individual's credit ratings or personal details, wherever he or she resides, can be flashed upon a computer screen in a corporate board room in New York, Paris, Tokyo, or London. Moreover, computerized information-handling is a "low visibility" operation, and an individual may never know that he or she is the subject of a file. Senator Sam J. Ervin, Jr., the then-chairman of the United States Senate Subcommittee on Constitutional Rights, in his Foreword to the book on *The Assault on Privacy,* written twenty-five years ago, expressed the hope that it would "bestir all Americans to demand an end to the abuses of computer technology before the light of liberty is extinguished in our land."[20]

Moreover, it is now possible for any individual to address any other individual on the computer networks, under cover of total anonymity. This is an altogether new species of temptation created by the age of computers.

Such is the order of danger implicit in this new technology, if the conscience of its users is not alerted to their social responsibilities.

To conclude this brief survey of some of the temptations to which modern technology exposes all of humankind, we refer to two statements that go back a generation in time—a generation during which, if the warnings contained in these statements had been heeded, much could have been achieved. On the contrary, we have moved further along the path of danger they visualized—one from the perspectives of government, and one from the perspectives of science.

Robert S. McNamara, Defense Secretary, in an address of September 18, 1967, to the editors of United Press International, San Francisco, observed:

...technology has now circumscribed us all with a conceivable horizon of horror that could dwarf any catastrophe that has befallen man in his more than a million years on earth.[21]

The Russell-Einstein Manifesto, signed by Bertrand Russell and Albert Einstein, and some of the world's leading scientists, observed:

...We appeal, as human beings, to human beings: Remember your humanity, and forget the rest. If you can do so, the way lies open to a new Paradise; if you cannot, there lies before you the risk of universal death.

CHAPTER 11

ECONOMIC TRESPASSES AND TEMPTATIONS

C urrent philosophies of monetarism are bidding fair to turning the whole world into a market stall. The worth or goodness of an action tends to be judged by its economic value, and the end is seen as justifying the means. The iron rules of the marketplace are to be trusted to make the right decisions for society, whether in one's own country or in the most distant, where perhaps hunger and starvation are prowling at the door. We live in a world where, according to the latest figures released by the Food and Agriculture Organization (FAO), 841 million people go to sleep hungry every night. Tennyson's lament regarding Victorian England, over a century ago—"Too much we make our ledgers Gods"—seems to ring even more true in our time than in his. Here is a great area of trespasses and temptations where the guiding light of the Prayer can save the world enormous privation and global tension.

The Prayer becomes specially relevant in the light of Jesus' express teaching regarding the evils of subordinating oneself to the pressures for economic gain. Serving Mammon often conflicts with serving God. The moneychangers in the temple aroused the highest level of Jesus' indignation. If Jesus' conduct and teaching are an index to our understanding of the Prayer, the warning against temptation must surely apply very heavily and specifically in the area of economic trespasses and temptations.

The Polarization of Rich and Poor

Concern for the weak and the suffering has always been considered a mark of true faith. The basis of judgment on Judgment Day, as narrated by Matthew (25:31–46), is the extent to which those who appear at the seat of Judgment have or have not helped the hungry, the friendless, the naked, the sick, and the oppressed.

This key message of the gospels, as embodied in the Prayer, is being steadily undermined by the polarization of rich and poor, a result of the widening gap between them. While on the global scene the rich world and the poor world drift apart, both materially and ideologically, every country sees within itself a division into two cities—the city of the rich and the city of the poor. This tendency, discernible by the thoughtful observer in the rich world, is startlingly apparent to all in the poor world.

Frantz Fanon, in his classic work *The Wretched of the Earth*, described such a world as a "world cut in two" across which a cold war raged, fueled by a helpless sort of envy. In the poor countries, one group, a very small minority, lives a gilded existence, moving around from one center of affluence to another. Oblivious of the sufferings of the people in the areas of privation situated between their gilded enclosures, they ride in limousines to and from their air-conditioned offices, sumptuous hotels, and exclusive clubs. They travel abroad when they will, to merge with their counterparts of the rich world, with whom they readily identify. Their interests straddle national boundaries, and they find themselves closer to the foreign rich than to the local poor. The latter find themselves a common object of exploitation—by fellow citizen and foreign entrepreneur alike. They feel ground between two millstones too heavy for them to resist. Meanwhile, the pursuit of affluence by those already privileged becomes an end in itself, obscures the Prayer's message of helping one's neighbor, feeding the hungry, and clothing the naked. Asia, Africa, Latin America are rife with this phenomenon.

High living and extravagance in islands of economic power stand in contradiction to a surrounding sea of hunger, disease, and illiteracy. The poverty-stricken millions who view the world of wealth from across oceans or continents are not, in this age of instant communication, any further away from the world of affluence than a beggar in the outer darkness, viewing through an ornate window the festivities in a chandeliered ballroom. It is a situation of immediacy, one that breeds anger and envy. On the domestic front, this spawns revolution; internationally, it breeds tension in the global village to which we all belong. The grapes of wrath grow everywhere. The scenario we have painted is a long way removed from the togetherness of the Lord's Prayer—for togetherness in the sense of the Prayer is not merely togetherness in prayer, but also togetherness in seeking *our* daily bread, togetherness in *our* wants and in *our* abundance. Sections of the world's population cannot long live in peace across this great divide.

True, many members of this privileged group are essentially well-meaning. They do not directly see the suffering outside their group, for distance often obscures visibility. Their vision is also obscured by the philosophy of individualism and *laissez faire*, which gives them a theoretical justification for their conduct, limiting their inquiries into their own responsibility for the deprivations outside their circle. Yet they are sowing the seeds of dissension through a neglect of the social orientation toward their obligations—which the Lord's Prayer would view as obligatory.

So widespread is this problem that some thinkers liken it to apartheid and have designated it "Global apartheid."[1] Such writers pile up evidence from the political, economic, military, racial, cultural, social, and legal spheres to support their thesis that global society is thus being effectively divided on apartheid lines. The evidence is impressive and is mounting. Apartheid or separation in any form is directly contradictory to the first principles of the Prayer.

At the United Nations' World Summit on Food held in Rome in November 1995, Pope John Paul II drew attention to the urgency of Christ's words "I was hungry and you gave me no food" and observed that "Believers must feel compelled in conscience to reduce the differences between North and South, and to build just and honest relations on every level—social, economic, cultural and ethical—of human life on this earth."

The Director General of the Food and Agricultural Organization noted that FAO had been entrusted with the task of helping the world's 841 million hungry, yet its budget had been cut to "less than what nine developed countries spend on dog and cat food in six days, and less than five percent of what the inhabitants of just one developed country spend on slimming products every year." The Rome declaration affirmed people's right to food and pledged participants to a commitment to end hunger and, by 2015, to halve the number of the world's hungry. Yet this is but a declaration, with the implementing action far away, in the same manner as the Prayer's declarations are solemnly pronounced, with implementing action indefinitely deferred.

Over a quarter century ago the author of a widely read work on the human future observed, "We still incline to believe that if the U.S. 'standard of living' is thirty times that of Bengal, Americans are thirty times as happy as Bengalis."[2] Yet demands on the ecosystem are stepped up to raise that standard even further.

It is a useful indication of global concern with this problem that while the United Nations-recommended level of aid to help countries with the highest levels of hunger and poverty is 0.07% of GDP, the contribution of some of the most affluent countries has fallen far short of this mark. Such a level is scarcely compatible with a pledge that "thy will be done on earth as it is in heaven," when God's will in regard to those who are hungry, naked, or oppressed is so clearly stated. It is helpful to remember that there is no sector of the global community whose economic future is cast in gold. Every sector is dependent upon every other. The rich world is dependent on the poor world, no less than the poor world is dependent on the rich.

Legacies of Colonialism

For centuries the pulpits of Christianity have thundered against theft. Quite rightly, the individual was reminded that he must respect the property of others and that the consistent teaching of the Church has been that one must not unjustly enrich oneself at the expense of another—whether by the use of cunning or by the use of force.

Yet over the centuries a great veil of blindness hung over history's most massive expropriation of the property of others through deception and naked force. That expropriation took the form of colonization. With rare exceptions, such as Japan, China, and Thailand, it blanketed all of Asia, Africa, and Latin America in the nineteenth century. The forcible occupation of other peoples' territories, the subjugation, downgrading, decimation, and sometimes even the extinction of those peoples, all proceeded under the forms of law and with scarcely any protest or opposition from either law or religion. For the mainly Christian colonial powers thus extending their dominions, it was as though the warnings against trespass and temptation in the Lord's Prayer did not exist. Fortunately, that dark chapter in history has nearly turned its last page. Though now virtually abolished in law, its after-effects reverberate in every corner of the former colonial world.

Atrocities were perpetrated in many parts of the colonial world on a scale that will not be understood by the present generation. The literature on this is immense and covers every colonial regime. A document that helps to catch the enormity of these atrocities, and would send waves of horror through the reader, is Mark Twain's *King Leopold's Soliloquy*,[3] in relation to the Belgian Congo. Mark Twain, when first requested in 1902 to lend his pen for the cause of the Congo people, had refused; but by 1904 his conscience would no longer permit him to stay aloof from the need to arouse the world to the Congo atrocities.

The Lord's Prayer teaches humility, fair dealing toward others, and equality. It is now widely accepted that colonialism breached all these values fundamentally. Consequently, colonialism has, by common consent, been relegated to the trash heap of regimes that violate basic morality. The colonialism of military conquest, so highly respectable in the nineteenth century, has few defenders at this point in the ongoing stream of history, but the twenty-first century will need to consider the trail of suffering it has left behind.

At the same time, it is vitally important that those who have been the victims should approach the problems in a spirit of forgiveness. With goodwill and frankness on both sides, the scars can be healed; but unless the problem is addressed in the spirit of reconciliation, goodwill, and forgiveness taught by the Prayer, it will be a threat to peace and order in the next century.

This is no time for recrimination, but a time for taking stock. It is essential that the past, however iniquitous, be forgiven—and that is a powerful message of the Prayer. Yet, in the process of stock-taking for the present and planning for the future, the facts must first be known, if the wave of reaction against colonialism is to be understood. The legacies of colonialism are a real factor not to be ignored.

No consideration of the world of today can divorce itself entirely from the after-effects of this historical phenomenon, or ignore the lesson that the major colonizing powers—all Christian (with the exception of the Ottoman Empire and Japan)—saw no incompatibility between such activity and their Christian beliefs or, indeed, with the Lord's Prayer, which the colonial authorities constantly recited in their legislatures and on public occasions.

Also, where possible, some form of affirmative action needs to be actively considered, and this demands a clearer view of the extent of the damage. In Canada, for example, a 41,000-page forty-million-dollar Report of the Royal Commission on Aboriginal People released in November 1996 details how more than 800,000 Indians were left largely destitute, deprived of their land and resources, and placed under immense pressure to assimilate into Western culture. In Australia, the landmark decision of the High Court in the *Mabo* case[4] is another example of attempts to face this problem fairly and squarely.

The New Colonialism

While colonialism would now be seen as incompatible with the Prayer's governing principles of equality and dignity, other forms of oppression are arising that tend to be obscured from the vision of those who perpetrate them. The effects of such oppression on victim territories and populations are no less severe, for they cause privation and loss of human dignity to millions.

It is true the colonialist no longer rides, whip in hand, through other people's territory, extracting tribute and respect from a cowed-down population. Yet, a new colonialism threatens imperceptibly to turn the clock back and reintroduce a regime of subjection, this time through the purse, rather than the sword. Because the new colonialism flourishes largely unseen, it does not present to the public gaze the deprivation of human rights and the denials of freedom that it threatens to carry into the new century. Its effects, nonetheless, can be just as telling.

Pope Paul VI foresaw this danger and warned against it in his encyclical *Justice in the World*. The pope observed:

> If the developing nations and regions do not attain liberation through development, there is a real danger that the conditions of life created specially by colonial domination may evolve into a new form of colonialism in which the developing nations will be the victims of the interplay of international economic forces.

Vast numbers of well-meaning people throughout the world are contributing to this danger through their inactivity and unconcern, while at the same time often deriving advantage from it. This new type of temptation is peculiar to our time. We need moral assistance to be able to perceive it. And when we do, we will recognize its violation of the fundamental principles of equality and dignity that are central to the Lord's Prayer and no longer shut our eyes to an important reality of the world around us.

We have the advantage that in the age of the new colonialism, unlike the age of the old colonialism, the churches of the world are aware of the danger and are seeking to warn their followers against it. Quotations can be offered from the pronouncements of many churches, but it would perhaps suffice to offer an illustrative quotation from Vatican II, showing how deeply sensitive that council was to the problem. "We are at the moment of history," the council observed,

When the developments of economic life could diminish social inequalities, if that development were guided and coordinated in a reasonable and human way. Yet all too often it serves only to intensify
inequalities. In some places it even results in a decline in the social
status of the weak and in contempt for the poor....The contrast between the economically more advanced countries and other countries
is becoming more serious day by day and the very peace of the world
can be jeopardized...Hence numerous reforms are needed at the socio-
economic level, along with universal changes in ideas and attitudes.[5]

Moreover, development must not be used as a means for imposing on
poor nations the cultural patterns of the rich. Here, again, the encyclicals
sound a note of warning, for John XXIII, in *Mater et Magistra,* drew attention to the individual characteristics all countries possess by reason of their
cultural heritage.

Now, when economically developed countries assist the poorer ones,
they not only should have regard for those characteristics and respect
them, but should take care lest in aiding those nations, they seek to
impose their way of life upon them.[6]

The main cause of the new colonialism is the widening gap of the poor
and the rich nations, owing to the former's lack of bargaining power in
exchanges of their goods for those of the industrialized world. President
Nyerere of Tanzania, interviewed many years ago in the United Nations
Development Program film *Five Minutes to Midnight,* said that, if two tons
of sisal were needed to buy what one ton of sisal bought before, the advantage of that extra ton must be pocketed by someone, somewhere.[7]

As observed by the American jurist William Seagle, in a panoramic survey of the development of the law, "The problem of distributing the world's
supplies of raw material must be solved before there can be any stability in
international relations."[8] This was the cause of colonialism and conflict in
the nineteenth and twentieth centuries. The forms of colonialism have gone,
but the problem remains completely unsolved; and the new colonialism
stems from the same problem, though it takes on a different garb.

In Asia, Africa, and Latin America the problem grows more acute by the
day. More effort, more fertilizer, more land goes into the production of
their commodities in an attempt merely to keep the balance even. But, how-

ever hard a runner may race on foot, the gap between him and the motorized vehicle keeps widening.

The classic theory of contract law in the nineteenth century stipulated that when two parties made a contract the terms are binding, however unequal the bargaining power of the parties, and however unfair the resulting contract. That theory has been overturned in all domestic jurisdictions, and throughout the world it is recognized that unfair terms extorted from a weaker contracting party are not necessarily binding, and that the weaker party needs some protection. However, the international marketplace where the world's primary commodities are bought and sold does not recognize such a principle. It is a free-for-all where the richest dictate their terms and the poor are often driven to the wall.[9]

Where can the poorer bargaining party turn? A vicious spiral begins, with a loan from a world-lending institution being seen as the only answer. It often comes with strings attached. Various conditions are laid down regarding the economic policies of the borrowing country. These policies often require a curtailment of welfare schemes, a free movement of capital, free entry of foreign enterprises, free repatriation of profits. All of these, justifiable when viewed in isolation, can amount in their totality to an increased weight upon the poor of the poor country, and an increasing volume of dictation from outside.

As with the old colonialism, a new class of allies of external power arises within the country. The rich at home become the allies of the rich abroad, even as, in the past, many rose to high advancement through supporting the colonial power. The internal gap between rich and poor widens in the same way as the external gap.

In extreme instances—as we've noted already—the poor in Latin America, Asia, and Africa are sometimes driven to selling their organs to the rich world for organ transplants, and to selling their children whom they cannot support, thereby permitting them to be the victims of child labor or sexual exploitation.

The arguments in support of free contract and free trade are claimed by those depending on them to be theoretically unassailable. The practical results, however, are devastating. Somewhere, somehow, the basic principles of equality and dignity are belied. One cannot pray the Lord's Prayer with sincerity, while turning a blind eye to this problem.

Herein lie the seeds of future conflict. Instability within the country breeds dictatorships. Those dictatorships tend to receive the support of foreign countries as they give protection to invested capital. The dictatorships are resisted internally. Those resisting are condemned as revolutionary and suppressed, often with the help of the external country supporting the dictatorship. The violence rises in another ascending spiral, and the stage is set for a conflict with international overtones. The old problems of colonialism surge through into the new dispensation, unnoticed because the process is more subtle than conquest by the sword.

One cannot address the problems of the twenty-first century without coming to grips with this new colonialism in all its aspects. The great wars of the twentieth century were largely the consequence of the old colonialism. The conflicts of the twenty-first century could well be the results of the new.

On whose shoulders lies the blame? The twenty-first century will need to ask this hard question of all its citizens who live a lifestyle that may be described as even moderately affluent, for it is the crushing pressure of their cumulative demands that compels the market forces to act the way they do. Hemmed in by a narrow national consciousness, the world's average citizen sees the problems outside his or her doorstep as the problems of someone else—problems so remote that they impose no direct personal responsibility. But the Lord's Prayer reiterates the directness of this responsibility that comes from the togetherness of the human family, which uninhibited monetarism is splitting asunder.

Corporate Wrongdoing

Corporate wrongdoing, decided upon in the elegant board rooms of the affluent world, can cause starvation, malnutrition, or infant mortality in a distant Third World country. The list of possible acts is vast and varied. Obvious examples are the dumping of shoddy goods, environmental pollution, the release of untested chemicals, the use of dangerous equipment without necessary safeguards, the sale of armaments, the installation of substandard nuclear reactors, the dumping of radioactive waste, the depression of commodity prices, the deliberate inducement of the smoking habit among the younger generation. The list is unending. The decision-makers do not see directly the effects of their acts; and their conscience, not pricked by immediate realities, exercises little restraint upon further incursions into iniquity.

The corporations bargain with poor nations, not only from a position of economic superiority, but also from a position of superiority in information power. In today's world, information is a potential source of power and if, in relation to international contracts, one side has a vastly superior store of information against the other, it enjoys a considerable bargaining advantage.

All these circumstances in combination give such corporations a vast amount of leverage in trading with the poorer countries. That leverage, not surprisingly, is used to forge a contract that is often of such advantage to the multinational as to be grossly unfair to the poorer country. Since their *raison d'être* is profit, not altruism, any leverage they can use to maximize that profit is rarely left unused.

Multinational corporations, many of them more economically powerful than three-quarters of the nation-states of the world, are thus among the most powerful new actors on the global scene. With the turnover of some of them exceeding the value of the entire economic activity of countries like Belgium or Switzerland, Australia or Spain, their power—and therefore their capacity for good or evil—is phenomenal. Even as early as 1972, of the one hundred largest economic units in the world, fifty were nation-states and fifty were multinational companies.[10] This proportion keeps altering significantly to the further benefit of the multinationals, who have overtaken in size even the medium-size state economies, such as those of Spain and Australia.[11]

Yet their accountability to the national or the international community is minimal. Legal regulation, whether national or international, is hopelessly unable to police them and never will be able so to do. Ralph Nader[12] brought to public notice the vast array of abuses that flourish within the framework of a corporate law that presents a fine appearance on paper.

There is all too often a conviction that private morality is to be discarded as one enters the doors of the corporate board room, for, in that sanctum of economic power, the profit motive reigns supreme. It deserves to be more generally realized that since the huge arenas of their activity cannot be reached by law, the potential for wrongdoing is immense unless moral considerations are activated. To say that morality can never restrain business is negative thinking, for many of these corporations are headed by well-meaning individuals, just as tens of thousands of their shareholders are well-meaning. An urgent reminder is required of the moral and/or religious obligations attendant on unpoliced economic might. No one would argue that there are no such moral obligations. The problem is the difficulty of bringing them into the practical arena.

When the world's first multinational (the Dutch East India Company) commenced its far-flung enterprise in the seventeenth century, the Dutch Reformed Church stood over it as a spiritual constable of its market capitalism.[13] We do not have such constables today, but we do not lack moral standards that most individuals accept, if shown to be applicable. There are sufficient guidelines for commercial rectitude in the words of the Lord's Prayer.

How, though, do moral considerations, such as those enshrined in the Lord's Prayer, effectively come to bear in this hard and powerful world of corporate might? One answer is that much can be achieved through the vigilance of shareholders, if they can be stirred out of their attitudes of nearly total unconcern. Individual shareholders, if sensitized to this question, would see the wrongness of enjoying the return on their investments, irrespective of whether it is made out of armaments, or felling rain forests in some tropical country, or spreading the habit of smoking among the world's children, or exploiting the practice of apartheid.

Another is a greater emphasis on evolving an ethical code for business, which is dealt with in chapter 14.

A third is the evolution of the notion of the responsible company—the idea that a company, whose size renders it virtually an actor in the public domain, has a social responsibility to the public.[14] The underlying notion is that companies use public resources, receive public protection, and have become public institutions in their own right. They therefore carry a social responsibility. Their responsibility does not begin and end with making profits for their shareholders.

From an immense range of possible illustrations, we offer here one homely illustration to show how strongly a moral argument could be put up on all these three fronts. The acts in question violate all possible ethical codes, ignore the principle of social responsibility, and will demonstrate to the conscientious small shareholder the impossibility of reconciling with the Lord's Prayer the return he or she receives upon their investment dollar.

A *Reader's Digest* investigation, "Teaching the World to Smoke,"[15] covered twenty countries on four continents. According to this study, vast numbers of children are being lured into nicotine addiction by cigarette makers· and while domestic U.S. sales have dropped for eight years in a row, sales overseas have more than trebled since 1985. Despite the World Health Organization's estimates that tobacco will prematurely kill 200 million people who are now children, and despite thousands of medical studies demonstrating the hazards of tobacco smoking, and its linkage to cancers of the mouth, lung, esophagus, kidney, pancreas, bladder and cervix, tobacco interests are alleged to be spending more than $170 million every year giving away cigarettes, many of them to teenagers.[16] According to this *Reader's Digest* study, free cigarette packets are handed out at discos and concerts, with a focus on the cigarette as part of an affluent lifestyle. There are even gifts, for example, sunglasses, given to those who accept an offer to light up on the spot.

The temptation to overlook the health damage caused is compounded by the fact that in the United States alone the industry provides around 250,000 full-time jobs and contributes more than $4 billion to the positive side of the trade ledgers in terms of balance of trade.[17] So great is the temptation that officials tend to argue the issue of prising open markets in Asia, in terms of free trade, and economic fairness, while public health advocates see it as a moral issue.

If one were to point out that in the nineteenth century trading companies opened up "smoking schools" in the South Pacific islands to entice the inhabitants into the smoking habit so that they could trade tobacco for South Pacific products, the modern reader would be aghast. If told their method was

> To establish smoking schools in districts which the traders wished to penetrate, at which pipes and tobacco were handed out to the islanders free of charge so as to encourage them to demand a quickly consumable article of trade, though less success was had at first in making the islanders feel the need for European clothes[18]

the modern reader would probably bristle with indignation, asking how such conduct could be reconciled with basic morality. Yet the same enticement takes place today on a much vaster scale.

Price Fixing

This looks attractive at the corporate end where the hardships it causes are not seen, but apart from its illegality, it is also a violation of basic ethical and moral principles. It is a cornering of the market by suppliers, giving the consumers no option but to purchase at the stipulated prices. It is profiteering. It can, where it is related to food production, amount to a denial to others of their daily bread. This has been brought to the forefront in recent times in the context of price fixing by agribusinesses whose products are required throughout the world, and who thus play a significant role in denying "daily bread" to the poor of this world. Chemicals used for food production or for livestock food additives are other illustrations of this pernicious practice that in America has recently attracted high publicity with fines running to millions of dollars.

The extent of the damage such practices cause to global food supply can be estimated when one considers that sales of these products run to several hundreds of millions of dollars. Even a single animal food additive has been known to command a six-hundred-million-dollar market.[19]

Money Laundering

The business of money laundering has grown by leaps and bounds in recent years. This line of business, worth $85 billion in 1986, has in 1996, according to the International Monetary Fund, grown to around $500 billion. Global criminal operators use money laundering to disguise the black money made in drug trafficking, child pornography, illicit arms deals, international prostitution rings, and the like. The money involved exceeds the combined value of international trade in petroleum, steel, pharmaceuticals, meat, fruit, wheat, and sugar.

Money laundering involves workers in banking, telecommunications, and service institutions of all kinds. It is a new business culture that has grown to a high level of sophistication with the possibility of instant electronic transfer of millions in a manner that is increasingly difficult to detect. Tens of thousands of well-meaning persons are drawn into the net, for the "clean" money that results, generates jobs, and even helps governments to such an extent that they invite "black money" for laundering. "Safe havens" with governmental guarantees proliferate.

To quote a recent article on the subject by an Undersecretary General of the United Nations:

> States which look the other way as the proceeds of human suffering are funnelled into their treasuries should be universally recognised for what they are: aiders and abetters of international criminals.... Transnational crime is a new geopolitical force, undermining governments and wrecking economies. If the world community does not act decisively—and soon—to stem this deluge, it will be too late.[20]

A United Nations Convention of 1988 called for urgent attention to the problem of money laundering to prevent the spread of organized crime and requiring governments to make money laundering a criminal offense. Yet more than a third of the United Nations' 185 member states have yet to become parties to the treaty.

The will to resist this new method of spreading the tentacles of international crime needs to be strengthened. As we've noted elsewhere, it is very easy to be tempted into not seeing the peril on account of its distance and its complexity, and to be attracted by the quick returns it yields. Resistance to it comes directly within the simple rules of conduct the Prayer prescribes.

Using Aid as a Means of Enriching the Donor

Foreign aid to needy countries is admirable, and is one of the highest examples of the practice of Christian duty. Yet there is a strong temptation to use it as a means of self-enrichment of the donor. This seems at first sight a contradiction in terms, but a great volume of factual and statistical material has shown that in many an instance aid operates precisely in this manner.

Aid is often tied to requirements that recipient states should purchase goods from the donor, and the resulting profits of this trade can more than offset the value of the aid donated. Aid can be tied to strategic considerations, requiring the recipient to exchange its independent foreign policy for acceptance of the foreign policy and interests of the donor state.[21] The threat of suspension of aid, particularly food aid, can be used as a powerful political weapon.[22] Even emergency relief aid, for which the 1996 world budget was eight billion dollars, is big business that can be a lucrative source of income, with many countries anxious to increase their share of the aid business.[23]

Aid is often offered with the best of motives, and the public of the donor countries needs to interest itself in ensuring that it is kept true to its high ideal. They must resist the temptation to assume that merely because it is described as foreign aid it is necessarily altruistic.

Exploitation of Cheap Labor

An easy means of inflating trading profits is the exploitation of cheap labor, particularly child labor, in countries of the poor world. A strong temptation exists for businesses of the industrialized world to indulge in such practices, encouraged by the fact that many governments of the developing world tend to turn a blind eye to them.

Some trading groups in the Western world have sought to self-regulate themselves in this respect by adopting a charter of fair trade practices, incorporating minimum standards laid down by the International Labor Organization, covering areas such as child labor and working conditions. The Fair Trade Foundation, backed by charities such as Oxfam and Christian Aid, has taken a leadership role in this regard. Such guidelines are useful aids to resisting the temptation to make easy profits in this manner.

Viewing Development in Purely Economic Terms

Many modern temptations are disguised by the glitter attending the concept of development. Development is often thought of in purely economic and material terms. However, development considered solely in such terms can screen one's vision of the denials of human values involved in this process. The true purpose of development is, of course, not merely to increase levels of production, but to use this only as a means to increase human welfare and happiness. The end must not be confused with the means. This has been powerfully formulated in the encyclical *Populorum Progressio*, wherein Pope Paul VI described man as the *raison d'être* for every development program.

> This is true, since every program, made to increase production, has in the last analysis no other *raison d'etre* than the service of man. Such programs should reduce inequalities, fight discrimination, free man from various types of servitude and enable him to be the instrument of his own material betterment, of his own moral progress and of his spiritual growth.[24]

Pope John Paul II, in his *Sollicitudo rei socialis*,[25] observes that authentic development, which lies between the excesses of superdevelopment and the deficiencies of underdevelopment, is inherently moral in character and, as he views the issue, truly moral individuals must act to see to it that genuine development is realized.[26] He described development as the new name for peace.[27] If Christianity's ideal is peace on earth, and if in the context of today development is synonymous with peace, it is difficult to see how the duty to concern oneself with this problem is not a basic Christian duty, the neglect of which is a trespass within the meaning of the Prayer. The Christian duty of concern for others is not thus easily satisfied.

CHAPTER 12

ATTITUDINAL TRESPASSES
AND TEMPTATIONS

The world's malaise is caused not only by acts of external violence, but also by acts of internal violence, against which Jesus uttered such powerful warnings throughout his ministry. Attitudes toward other people and groups often nurture the seeds of future wars and dissensions. One can sin with the mind without so much as lifting one's little finger in violence. As Martin Luther King, Jr. observed, "Nonviolence means not only external physical violence, but also internal violence of the spirit. You not only refuse to shoot a man, but you refuse to hate him."

This chapter deals briefly with some of these internal acts of violence, which are endemic in our time.

Racism

Racism is the parent and fervent ally of genocide. It flows strongly among the deep political currents of our age. It is anathema to the Prayer.

We need not look far, wherever in the world we may be, to see the specter of racism rising gaunt and severe over the ruins of once happy communities that it has destroyed. Issuing from some dark corner of the subconscious mind, racism is linked to the view that land and jobs should be preserved exclusively for one's own kith and kin. The territorial instinct, selfishness, greed to reserve for oneself what has to be shared with others, false feelings of superiority, ignorance of other cultures: All of these combine to produce the phenomenon of racism. Each one of these is in direct contradiction of the teachings of the Lord's Prayer. Yet religion and Christianity itself are today used to fan the flames of racism.

With racism on the rampage, no home is safe. As the twentieth century draws to a close, it shows us how racism can turn neighbors living in amity for generations into assassins, school friends sharing childhood memories into each other's murderers, disciplined soldiers into organized rapists. Expressions such as "ethnic cleansing" gain currency and no longer cause shock and horror. Feelings of revenge rise in ascending spirals as one atrocity begets and justifies another. The hatreds escalate until one or the other antagonist is destroyed. Asia, Africa, and Europe are all throwing up this phenomenon in an evermore acute form as we approach the close of the century.

In the twentieth century, unabashed racism reached its apogee in Hitler's *Mein Kampf*, which has only to be read to realize how far a school of thought claiming to function within the framework of Christianity could travel down the road toward racism. The following extract is not far in the text from a discussion of Protestantism:

> ...[T]here is only one most sacred human right, and this right is at the same time the most sacred obligation, namely: to see to it that the blood is preserved pure, so that, by the preservation of the best human material, a possibility is given for a more noble development of these human beings."[1]

No comment is necessary, except that such a book held a place of honor in the literature of a Christian society, in the memories of people yet alive. Even closer to our time is South African Christian literature approving of racial discrimination. For example, *Human Relations and the South African Scene in the Light of Scripture,* a document justifying apartheid in the light of scripture, issued by the Dutch Reformed Church in October 1974, with the approval of the General Synod, cites Galatians 3:28: "there can be neither Jew nor Greek, there can be neither bond nor free, there can be no male or female: for ye are all one in Jesus Christ," and makes the comment:

> To read in these passages a mandate for social integration between peoples would be to abuse them. It is obviously the purpose of these verses to emphasise the all-prevailing importance of the new unity in Christ, but not to deny the existence of individual and diverse communities.[2]

Such passages lead one to wonder how often the Lord's Prayer was formally intoned in the churches of Nazi Germany and apartheid-ridden South Africa by exponents of Nazism and apartheid. A curious feature of racism, thus demonstrated, is that it can sink its roots even into religion, deriving therefrom a spurious nourishment for its teachings of intolerance.

As countries are torn apart by feuding tribes, larger groupings external to the country support the contending groups and tend to get drawn into the conflict, attracted to it by ties of consanguinity or common culture. The conflict spreads, and the armaments involved increase to levels wholly disproportionate to the scale of the original conflict. Regional conflicts can be set in motion that are even capable of endangering global peace. As racial conflicts proliferate on every continent, the peace of the twenty-first century is placed in jeopardy.

It's important to address the mental attitudes that give rise to racism. The baser instincts, the selfishness, the arrogance, the greed, the ignorance, the pseudo-piety that lie at its root can only be extirpated by a different sense of values. In the words of Tom Paine, "an army of principles will penetrate where an army of soldiers cannot."

The North/South Ideological Cleavage

The very first word of the Prayer emphasizes the unity of humanity. A new factor, even more potent than racism as a divisive force, is splitting the human family into two camps that are growing further apart by the day. Separated by vastly different lifestyles and levels of economic, military, and political power, each becomes increasingly intolerant of the other's viewpoint. Even as the power differential becomes entrenched, so is the attitude of separation that it breeds.

As noted in the last chapter, the widening material gap between the rich and the poor nations has been considerably reinforced by a conceptual difference in their approach to basic questions of progress. The affluent sectors are not attuned to hear or perceive the sufferings of those on the other side of the great economic divide. As a result, "the still, sad music of humanity," as it occurs among the bulk of the world's population, passes unheard and unheeded.

In *The Greening of America* Charles Reich described the philosophy widely prevalent in the developed world as "Consciousness II"[3]—the consciousness that believes in science, technology, organization, and planning as prime values. It is a consciousness far removed from what he described as "Consciousness I"—the dream of the founding fathers of America who had an idealistic view of what man could be in the new community—a dream envisioning a society based upon individual dignity that made each person an equal being in a spiritual sense,[4] rather than being "subject to the impersonal lordship of an economic and technological system."[5]

Well-meaning though this "Consciousness II" might be, it fosters world cleavage and disturbs the prospects for a lasting peace for humanity.

Some modern Western philosophers, such as Henry Adams and Lewis Mumford, have long crusaded against the false assumptions of the superior values of technological civilization, which are fast leading the world to crisis and breakdown. Mumford spoke of the "pentagon of power"[6] consisting of progress, profit, productivity, property, and publicity, which, if continued unhindered in their operations, could produce an ecological, cultural, and personal desert. These can cause the destruction of our planet unless philosophy, education, and all other available means can be used to recreate attitudes that will place human dignity rather than materialistic values at the center of society. This is the essence of the teachings of the great religions. Christianity stresses inner development rather than material advancement. "My kingdom is not of this world," said Jesus.

This is precisely what many of the basic Third World philosophies teach. The Buddhist theory of development, for example, to which many Western readers were introduced by E. F. Schumacher in his *Small Is Beautiful*, stresses how important it is that technology and machines should serve rather than control human beings, and the importance of avoiding excessive greed and excessive giantism. The concentration is on human development, and the four steps recommended to that end are the Buddhist teachings of kindness to others, empathy with and compassion for others in their suffering, joy at the success and happiness of others, and the cultivation of a balanced attitude of mind in the face of prosperity or adversity, success or failure. These values prevail over worldly success and material progress.[7]

This message, strongly carried by the Lord's Prayer, must cause us to ask whether the current philosophy of development is geared instead to opposite values. Are those values many steps removed from the Lord's Prayer, and is this a factor deepening the current cleavage between the developed and the developing sectors of the world? Are we thus sowing the seeds of future conflict? Does one of the answers lie in what one of the outstanding peace researchers of our time, Johan Galtung, describes as "inter-civilizational dialogue?"[8]

Considerations of self-interest that are the cause of the great ideological divide have far-reaching implications, for they even undermine the foundations of the one great global institution that can lead us to global peace. In the past, they led to the failure of the League of Nations. If, in the words of one commentator, "the League had died long before its official funeral in 1946,"[9] a principal cause was that the race for national wealth, power, and armaments continued after World War I in the same manner as before it. That race has continued after World War II, as well, with the result that the United Nations today has its own infirmities, as the League had before it. Both instances indicate that the causes need attention, rather than the organization itself. With the failure of the League of Nations, there was a collapse of the last bulwark against World War II. The world cannot afford a similar failure again.

Parochialism and Ignorance

Universalism and respect for others are values deeply written into the Prayer. The human family is one, bonded together by a common acceptance of its total dependence on the Infinite. If all are brothers and sisters to one another, it is everybody's concern to know of the traditions, the joys, and the sufferings of others. Yet, paradoxically, in an age when information about other cultures is more easily obtained and disseminated than ever before, parochialism continues to be the order of the day almost universally.

Needless to say, our attitudes are the product of our environment. Although it is said that the walls of the nation-state are being increasingly penetrated by the forces of universalism—as in the field of human rights—we are still walled in very much within our nation-states.

Shortly after World War II, the American author Emery Reves wrote a work, *The Anatomy of Peace,* which caused a stir among intellectuals and student groups at the time. Thousands of special discussion groups across the world considered and discussed Reves's work, and students appealed to their counterparts on other continents to pay heed to these ideas. Reves wrote basically of the outmoded nature of the concept of national sovereignty. The nation-state, he said, was a modern Bastille that imprisoned its people's minds by narrow concepts of loyalty. It clouded their vision concerning the global problems on which alone their survival depends. The selfsame event, viewed by populations in Moscow, London, New York, Cape Town, or New Delhi, would appear in altogether different lights. Any reasonable person, viewing it with the nationalist spectacles provided in each of these different centers, would have a different view of the problem, some of them diametrically opposed, but all eminently reasonable in the light of the experience available to each.

The essential problem is lack of communication and, with it, lack of understanding. The end result is estrangement of mankind from itself.

We tend to see matters only within our own cultural and historical framework for sheer ignorance of others' traditions and ways of thought. Some philosophers see the social and political crisis of the twentieth century as a real intellectual crisis, caused by a narrowness of popular attitude, which is intensified by a narrowness of teaching even in institutions of higher education. For example, Allan Bloom's *The Closing of the American Mind*[10] argues that higher education has failed democracy and impoverished the souls of today's students by producing young people lacking in an understanding of the past or a vision of the future, and living in an impoverished present. In a sweeping analysis of the intellectual currents of this century, this study concludes that today's higher education fails to arouse or nurture the self-knowledge that has always been the basis for serious, humane learning.

If higher education lacks this breadth-giving quality, the same is even more true of elementary and secondary education, where there is a failure to impart information on other cultures, histories, and traditions. The resulting insularity of outlook permits a vision of global problems only from the standpoint of narrow, national self-interest. The Islamic world, the Hindu world, the Buddhist world, the world of African, Polynesian, and Amerindian culture: All these are a closed book to the bulk of the world's Christian population. The reverse ignorance, likewise, can be abysmal.

Ignorance of other cultures and traditions can sometimes reach epic proportions, even among the most educated people of a given culture. To quote one instance, Lord Macaulay, one of the best informed Englishmen of the nineteenth century and a member of the Governor-General's Council of India, wrote in 1835, "a single shelf of a good European library was worth the whole native literature of India and Arabia."[11] William Archer, a well-known drama critic of the day, pronounced that the whole life and culture of India, her philosophy, religion, poetry, painting, sculpture, *Upanishads, Mahabharata*, and *Ramayana* was one mass of barbarism.[12]

One wonders whether, one-and-a-half centuries later, such insensitivity toward other cultures, born of ignorance, has been dissipated, or whether indeed our education systems are such that it still persists. H. G. Wells observed that the future of humanity depends upon a race between education and catastrophe. In this race, education may well be losing ground.

One of the basic messages coming through in the Lord's Prayer is the message of universalism and a trampling down of the barriers that separate person from person—ignorance and the parochialism born of it being among the foremost of those barriers.

Unbridled Individualism

The world seems set to move into the twenty-first century on a note of unbridled individualism. The message of the Lord's Prayer is a socially oriented message, viewing the individual in his or her social context, rather than as an entity pursuing individual self-interest unrelated to social duty.

Individual self-interest pursued as an end in itself divorces the individual from his or her social context and from the fabric of social obligations. It is within the milieu of that intermeshing fabric that the individual has his being. To take him or her away from it and treat the individual as a monolith standing alone in space and time is to tear that fabric. A few tears can be withstood; but many of them, some of a major nature, tear that fabric to tatters.

If one were to take a rounded view of human rights, one would have to note that, while individual rights are important—such as the right of free contract which is so important to the individualist theory—the rights of society and the group are equally important. Social, economic, and cultural rights are just as vital as the legal and political rights of the individual.

As stressed elsewhere in this book, excessive concentration on individual *rights* also obscures the concept of *duties*, which is so essential to a rounded view of the human rights concept. In fact, the concentration on rights to the exclusion of duties has been one of the principal grounds of criticism of the human rights concept as it has evolved in recent times. Third World societies traditionally stressed duties rather than rights—duties that arose toward a group by reason of one's membership in that group. Indeed, in some traditional societies, the concept of duty so much overshadowed the notion of rights that there was no word in their vocabulary directly corresponding to "rights." A proper view of the position of the individual in a social group must necessarily pay due regard to both aspects, not concentrating exclusively on one or the other. The Lord's Prayer is resonant with the concept of duty: duty toward God, duty toward society, duty toward one's neighbor, duty toward oneself.

From the earliest times, philosophers have discussed the effect upon society of individuals functioning in pursuit of their own self-interest, as contrasted with their functioning as members of a social team. Philosophers such as Thomas Hobbes have painted a picture of life as being nasty, brutish, and short in an era when each fended for himself.

Most of the world's societies evolved with a group orientation, for outside the group survival in the face of harsh natural forces was not easy. Within the group there was protection and companionship. We perhaps delude ourselves by believing that modern life is vastly different. Without dependence on our respective groups, survival is indeed not possible. It is self-evident that individuals living in a community, as opposed, for example, to the solitary hermit on a deserted island, cannot themselves grow their own food, tailor their clothes, medicate themselves, or educate their children.[13] These require a communal effort. For all our pretensions of individual greatness, the Genghis Khans, the Napoleons, and the Hitlers of this world, if stranded alone in a primeval forest, would be but quivering, helpless creatures. Like primitive man, his modern counterpart cannot exist in a social vacuum, but depends upon the community to which he belongs. Ancient wisdom knew this well, and the Lord's Prayer enshrines this truth.

Today many seek to take advantage of the community on which they depend, without making a corresponding contribution in return. The philosophy of individualism, daily proclaimed by powerful political leaders and the media, and demonstrably giving to ambitious individuals considerably more power than they would enjoy under any society-oriented philosophy, entrenches itself daily, driving further away from reality the social obligations ingrained in the Prayer.

Unbridled individualism is often defended in the name of equality. Its defenders argue that once the principle of equality is tampered with by assisting the weaker party (as in contracts between parties of grossly unequal bargaining power), the floodgates are opened and equality is destroyed. This is a specious argument. The Lord's Prayer itself enshrines equality, but it also enshrines social obligations. Equality does not mean lip service to equality where true equality does not exist, or equality in the sense of unbridled individualism, but equality in a social context.

An added strand of harshness is contributed toward individualist attitudes through the support given to individualism by Darwinian theories of the survival of the fittest. The merciless law of the jungle is thus imported into human conduct as though it affords a rationale and justification for conduct divorced from considerations of morality. Many a fiercely competitive businessman and politician justifies his success to himself on this basis. Moreover, states themselves have functioned on this philosophy in the past, with consequences only too painfully apparent to all. Such a totally amoral approach is too far removed from the basic philosophy of the Prayer to need any elaboration here.

As discussed in an earlier chapter, individualism also produces the effect of leaving everyone to fend for himself or herself, and of abandoning one's duty to assist, even where assistance is possible. The recent English case of a two-year-old child being abducted by two youths, and being led to its murder through a populated area, may perhaps be partly explained by this individualistic attitude of not concerning oneself with others through fear of being seen as interfering.

Monetarism

Individualism is strongly helped forward by monetarism: the philosophy that the pursuit of wealth and profit is a desirable end in itself. Many philosophical justifications are invoked in support. Wealth, once accumulated, percolates through the entire community and is good for its economic well-being. Commerce is an essential part of civilization. Monetarism was even looked upon at one stage as a justification for empires, as when Joseph Chamberlain, the British statesman, asserted that the colonial powers, as custodians of the tropics, were "trustees of civilization for the commerce of the world."[14] Consequently, the merchant, the miner, and the manufacturer did not enter the tropics on sufferance as "interlopers" or "greedy capitalists," but as fulfilling the mandate of civilization.[15]

Henry Ford articulated this attitude with specific reference to morality when he asserted, "We now know that anything which is economically right is also morally right; there can be no conflict between good economics and good morals."[16]

A leading economic historian has pointed out that the Church was slow, in the early days of economic expansion, to emphasize the relevance to such activity of the teaching that all people are brothers to each other:

It [the Church] had insisted that all men were brethren. But it did not occur to it to point out that, as a result of the new economic imperialism which was beginning to develop in the seventeenth century, the brethren of the English merchant were the Africans whom he kidnapped for slavery in America, or the American Indians whom he stripped of their lands, or the Indian craftsmen from whom he bought muslins and silks at starvation prices.[17]

That comment, written of a much earlier age in the expansion of mercantilism, rings just as true today. In the pursuit of purely mercantilist values in our age, there is danger of the same error being repeated.

Monetarism aims at the acquisition of profit, whatever the merchandise sold and whatever its damaging impact upon the recipient. Markets must be expanded—whether the goods in question be cigarettes or nuclear reactors, implements of torture, or weapons of death. Monetarism pursues its objects globally on a dramatically expanding scale, free, because of its vast power, of the restraints that governments or the international community can impose upon it. All around us we see the higher values of global culture being asphyxiated by monetarism. It will probably be the most powerful global force that the twentieth century will release into the twenty-first.

Monetarism and the exaltation of wealth as an end in itself are a reflection of the individualistic spirit of the age. This spirit is even taught in the educational system, and stands in stark contrast to the brotherhood notion implicit in the Prayer. Pope Paul VI put his finger on this problem when he observed:

The method of education very frequently still in use in the world today encourages narrow individualism. Part of the human family lives immersed in a mentality which exalts possessions.[18]

Complacency and Moral Paralysis

Reference has been made more than once in the preceding pages to the ways in which complacency in the face of evil—as in the case of slavery or apartheid—becomes as blameful as the actual perpetration of that evil. Of all the forces we need to contend against in the next century, complacency will be one of the most powerful.

The theologian Father Thomas Merton, who has written extensively on spiritual and social themes, put this very forcefully when he wrote:

The awful problem of our time is not so much the dreams, the monsters, which may take shape and consume us, but the moral paralysis in our souls which leaves us immobile, inert, passive, tongue-tied, ready and even willing to succumb.[19]

Many factors contribute to that moral paralysis: closing one's mind to obvious injustice; failure to equip oneself with the necessary information; feelings of frustration; convictions of the futility of individual action; readiness to receive the benefits that flow from injustice; reluctance to stir oneself out of a comfortable mode of life. None of these will bear scrutiny, for acts of omission can be just as culpable in morality and law as acts of commission. Trespasses in terms of the Prayer are not limited to acts of commission alone, as acts of omission can often produce results just as grievous. As a result we see whole communities walking past injustice and washing their hands like Pontius Pilate.

Wrongs can be committed directly, as by wielding the whip on a slave, or indirectly, as by watching without protest when the whip is wielded by another, and by reaping the benefits of slavery. If the one is not permitted by the code of conduct encapsulated in the Prayer, neither is the other. Each is equally a "trespass." By remaining mute in the face of evil, one is encouraging the evildoer to further wrongdoing toward others. Such an individual is drawing a selfish distinction between wrongdoing to oneself (to which one reacts) and wrongdoing toward others (to which one does not react). This constitutes a failure to recognize the unitary nature of wrongdoing, splitting it down the center on the basis of an untenable distinction.

This leaves a lopsided picture of moral duty, for

- the wrongdoer is given the impression that he is free to extend his wrongdoing toward others without being inhibited by our reaction; there is an implied or tacit approval of his wrongdoing;
- it is a thin line that separates such conduct from active encouragement of wrongdoing;
- acceptance of any act of wrongdoing is a tacit acceptance also of the principle underlying that act. Such acceptance damages one's own rights;
- the individual is ignoring the damage to society that generally follows from the principle underlying the said act;
- the individual is demonstrating a level of exclusively self-oriented concern or selfishness, which is contrary to the spirit of the Prayer;

- even from the standpoint of sheer self-interest, today's unprotesting observer of wrongdoing could well be tomorrow's victim.

In short, a wrong is done to others by encouraging further wrongdoing, and a wrong is done to oneself by permitting the denigration of the essential human dignity common to wrongdoers and oneself. The Prayer draws no distinction between wrongs to oneself and wrongs to others. What is wrong is wrong, irrespective of the identity of the victim. To draw a self-interested distinction between wrongs depending on whether one is or is not directly involved is contrary to the universal concerns embodied in the Prayer.

Religious Intolerance

History is littered with the bodies of those who have suffered torture and death because their views on matters religious did not accord with the interpretations of others who thought they alone had the key to God's pronouncements on matters of religious truth.

The practice of reviling other religions as being creatures of falsehood, and the resulting practice of intolerance of other religions, follows from too little contemplation of the hallowedness of God in all its amplitude of meaning. It presupposes that God *as seen by the individual in question* is the sole truth and confines God within the limited framework of that individual's understanding, oblivious that one's own perception of God may be cast in too narrow or dogmatic a mold. To show disrespect for God as seen by other religions, or to show disrespect for other religions themselves, is the ultimate demonstration of one's own narrowness of perception. There is little room for such attitudes in the era of respectful coexistence that will be indispensable in the twenty-first century. We can do no better than to bear in mind the statement of Jesus himself that, "In my Father's house are many mansions" (John 14:2, KJV).

There is food for thought, and an enrichment of one's own conception of God as Truth, in the realization that the Hindu sees God in many forms and the Buddhist is enjoined to show proper respect for all religions, for to show disrespect to other religions is to show disrespect to one's own. They are all paths to truth as seen by their adherents, whose profession of them is to be respected as a manifestation of their own yearning for the highest ideals rather than their contentment with the mundane. The famous Edict of Toleration of the Emperor Asoka of India, issued twenty-three centuries ago, must rank as one of the great human rights documents of all time. It stated:

> ...the sects of other people all deserve reverence for one reason or another. By thus acting a man exalts his own sect, and at the same time does honor to the sects of other people. By acting contrariwise, a man hurts his own sect, and does disservice to the sects of other people.[20]

So also in Zoroastrianism, the Zend-Avesta teaches: "I worship you in every religion that teaches your laws and praises your glory."[21]

Such considerations reflect modern human rights doctrine in relation to religious tolerance and freedom of religion, and to the constitutional provisions in many countries based upon the same principle. All of these owe their origin to philosophical recognitions that no individual, group, or sect has a monopoly of religious truth—a recognition that temporal, and indeed religious, powers long delayed in accepting until they were forced to do so by revolution and bloodshed.

Throughout history, the view that there are "lesser breeds without the law"—a view sadly prevalent in some quarters to this very day—has exacted an enormous toll in the form of human suffering. Religious intolerance is not, of course, confined to intolerance of other religions. It extends also to divisions within one's own religion, and even to differences of interpretation of scriptural texts.

Pedantry

An attitude very closely related to religious intolerance is pedantry: the conceit that we alone are the possessors of truth, and an intolerance of contrary views. It was initially the result of religious bigotry, but now persists in various forms—all of them expressions of pride and self-centeredness. The attitude that one's own interpretation of scripture alone was authentic quite easily spills over into nonreligious realms.

Illustrations are not difficult to find. Firmianus Lactantius (c. 260–c. 340), an early Doctor of the Church and one of its great early writers, typified this attitude when he wrote:

Is it possible that man can be so absurd as to believe that there are crops and trees on the other side of the earth that hang downward, and that men have their feet higher than their heads? If you ask them how they defend these monstrosities, why things do not fall away from the earth on that side, they reply that the nature of things is such that heavy bodies tend toward the center, like the spokes of a wheel, while light bodies, as clouds, smoke and fire tend from the center towards the heavens on all sides. Now, I am really at a loss what to say of those who, when once they have gone wrong, steadily persevere in their folly and defend one absurd opinion by another.

Citing this passage in his outstanding book *The Story of Law*,[22] the distinguished American lawyer John M. Zane observed:

If this Christian Father, an enlightened man for his age, with access to correct knowledge, was sunk in this self-satisfied stupidity, what must have been the Stygian darkness of the degraded and bigoted multitude?

The Doctors of the Church easily slipped into the thought frame that they were the supreme exponents of truth, with scarcely a realization that they had passed from the realm of doctrine into a totally extraneous field. That temptation still exists at all levels today, with many little people seeking to establish little empires of authority around the area of their supposed expertise.

Such attitudes of omniscience have been a cause of much persecution and human rights denials in the past, and such bigotry has not died down in the present age. The attitude of the Church to Galileo and Copernicus regarding the earth's position with respect to the sun, or in relation to Darwinian theory regarding the origin of species, are later examples of this line of thought. On both of these the original positions of the Church have had to be modified centuries later, proving thereby the need for more tolerant attitudes.

It is a humbling experience to contrast these early attitudes of religious omniscience with the theory expounded in the earliest days of Islam when a distinction was drawn between theological truth and the truths revealed by natural science. This is well illustrated by the tradition in Islam known as the tradition of the pollination.

The Prophet Mohammed, it is said, once observed people pollinating date palms and made some observations from which they concluded that he doubted the correctness of their procedure. Out of respect for him they changed their practice that year, whereupon the yield dropped. They took this information to him stating that they had suffered a poor yield in consequence. His reply was, "I am only a man. When I bid you anything relating to the affairs of your religion, receive it, and when I give you anything as my opinion, I am only a man."[23]

This telling demarcation of the different spheres of knowledge and authority of the religious and the secular was often invoked in the history of knowledge in Islam to indicate the boundaries between the two areas. Another tradition relative to the importance of the independent pursuit of knowledge is in a saying of the Prophet Mohammed that the ink of the scholar is holier than the blood of the martyr.

All religions, of course, at different stages of their development have thrown up schools of theologians who do not recognize this distinction—and Islam is no exception—but these early traditions perhaps account for the independent pursuit of knowledge in the world of Islam when the lights of learning were going out in Christian Europe, in what has been described as the Dark Ages. Perhaps the explosion of scientific knowledge in the early centuries of Islam was due to traditions such as these and to the exhortations to the faithful to go as far afield as China, if need be, in search of knowledge. They were a factor enabling the Islamic world to keep alive during this difficult period what Bertrand Russell has described as "the apparatus of civilisation"[24]—whether it was logic or metaphysics, chemistry or algebra, astronomy or medicine, sociology or political science.

Intolerance of other views inhibits the growth of knowledge. There are many species of intolerance now abroad. Each, in its own way, leads to an area of obscurity and darkness where instead there could be light. The twenty-first century cannot afford another dark age in any area of knowledge, however small. That would be a negation of the commitment to truth that is affirmed through affirming the hallowedness of God. As Confucius put it, "Those who know the truth are not equal to those who love it."[25] The lover of truth may have less knowledge than the knower of truth, but is more to be respected. He or she comes closer to God and to sincerity in uttering the phrase "hallowed be thy name," for he or she is saying, among other things, "hallowed be God as an embodiment of truth."

National Glorification

Patriotism is a virtue, but it can be carried to excess—to the point that one can see no wrong in the actions of one's own country, insofar as concerns its relations with other countries. Every nation has shortcomings in this regard, and the more ready its citizens are to perceive these, the more quickly they would be corrected, and its prestige and influence enhanced. Xenophobic attitudes are widely prevalent in many countries today, generating much international tension, instead of the goodwill that the Prayer prescribes.

Many of these attitudes are the result of indoctrination in schools of a spirit of national glorification. The history of any country must be seen in global context and not in isolation. The Lord's Prayer is set in the context of the human family as a whole, and not in the limited context of the nation-state.

Arrogance and Superciliousness

Many of the attitudinal trespasses discussed in this chapter stem from one principal root cause: pride in the cultural, racial, military, intellectual, or other perceived superiority of one's own group or nation. This is largely born of ignorance. One is weighing a known against a total unknown, and in the ocean of one's ignorance there is never a doubt regarding the superiority of one's own. Again, this points to the imperative need for greater understanding of other cultures.

The following expression of this superiority was uttered at the highest levels of the law: in a judicial opinion of the Privy Council, which was for long the highest court of appeal in the British Empire, in the case of *Re Southern Rhodesia.*

The Privy Council said:

> The estimation of the rights of Aboriginal tribes is always inherently difficult. Some tribes are so low in the scale of social organisation that their usages and conceptions of rights and duties are not to be reconciled with the institutions or the legal ideas of civilised society. Such a gulf cannot be bridged. It would be idle to impute to such people some shadow of the rights known to our law and then to transmute it into the substance of transferable rights of property as we know them.[26]

In moral terms, the indignities committed on these peoples were compounded by the fact that such expressions of ignorance were used as the argument for depriving the people concerned of their rights. Superciliousness and arrogance must indeed rank very high in the hierarchy of trespasses against which the Prayer warns us.

These examples prompt the general reflection that the Prayer seeks an attitude of oneness between each human being and all others—what could be called the "we attitude," rather than the "I-it attitude." The Prayer is heavily laden with the "we attitude." If such complete identification takes place, all of the problems discussed in this chapter automatically disappear. If one cannot identify completely in this fashion—and indeed this is difficult—the minimum standard the Prayer requires is that one must treat every human being as possessed of the same God-given human dignity as oneself, or what may be described as the "I-thou attitude." What often tends to happen, however, is that one's attitude toward others, especially those not belonging to one's group, is not a "we attitude," nor even an "I-thou attitude," but an "I-it" attitude. Others are depersonalized and reduced to objects out there that do not concern me, except to the extent they impinge on me or can be used as things. This is an attitudinal contradiction of the entire message of the Prayer.

To treat fellow human beings with the dignity due to them is to show respect also to the supreme source whence that dignity derives—the Father of all, whom we address in the Prayer. In the words of *I and Thou*, Martin Buber's classic treatment of the religious and social dimensions of the human personality, "Every particular Thou is a glimpse through to the eternal Thou."[27]

CHAPTER 13

SOCIAL TRESPASSES
AND TEMPTATIONS

This chapter deals with a variety of social problems stemming from conduct directly contradictory to the principles of equality, dignity, inalienability of rights, brotherhood and sisterhood, nondiscrimination, and universalism implicit in the Prayer. Every person who, even by inaction, encourages or tolerates the situation that produces the following conditions, is in violation of the Prayer and cannot therefore be said to recite it sincerely.

Slavery

One of the greatest indignities to which a human being can be subjected is to be treated as an object of property rather than a person in his or her own right. Nevertheless, that is the condition in which many individuals find themselves today—and to an extent most people of the world don't realize.

According to the Slavery Convention of 1926, a slave is a person in a position where "any or all of the powers attaching to the rights of ownership are exercised" over him. Slavery has been the subject of concerted condemnation in a number of international documents dating back as far as 1815. Later documents include the General Act of Berlin (1885) and of Brussels (1890); the Geneva Convention (1926) and Protocol (1953); the Supplementary Convention on the Abolition of Slavery, the Slave Trade, and Institutions and Practices Similar to Slavery (1956); and the Convention for the Suppression of the Traffic in Persons and of the Exploitation of the Prostitution of Others (1951). Yet the practice of slavery persists.

So current is the question that the Commission of Human Rights appointed a Working Group on Contemporary Forms of Slavery, which reported extensively on such topics as the slave trade, the sale of children, and debt bondage.[1] It showed that there are several countries where men, women, and children are in fact still bought and sold. Further, it revealed, they are exposed to brutal treatment, physical punishment of a severe nature, and confinement in places where they can best serve the interests of their "owner."

The Working Group pointed to the wide prevalence of practices akin to slavery, such as indentured labor, exploitation of child labor, prostitution, and sex slavery. The indentured labor system, which has survived into modern times, is simply slavery under another name. An indentured laborer is one who has entered into a form of bondage that ties him to a particular employer and employment and exposes him to severe punishment, if not imprisonment, if he leaves that service without his employer's permission. In effect, the indentured laborer is chained by law to his master's service much in the same manner as the slaves of the past were chained in irons.

A distinguished past member of the International Court, Judge Manfred Lachs, in an article published shortly before his death, entitled "Slavery: The Past and the Present,"[2] drew attention to the fact that bondage on tropical plantations, indentured labor and other kinds of servitude still existed in total violation of several international documents. He wrote, "Very frequently governments and the public seem to forget or ignore them...." Judge Lachs observed that the greatest danger of the continuance of these prohibited practices lay in connivance.

The tendency to turn a blind eye to slavery and slavery-like practices is not new. It was so locked into the social landscape of previous historical eras that even some of the most enlightened people did not see it as an aberration. Aristotle, who contributed so much to the philosophy of individual development, did not protest against the institution of slavery so prevalent in Greece. Jefferson, who was the author of the ringing phrases on individual freedom that have echoed around the world through the Declaration of Independence, owned around two hundred slaves, and even sold some of them in the slave market. When William Wilberforce sought, in 1787, to have slavery abolished by Act of Parliament, his bill was rejected, and he had to have it reintroduced every year from 1792 until 1805 when it was eventually passed. That Wilberforce had to make his "annual motion for the Abolition of the Slave Trade" was due to apathy and lack of concern of hundreds of worthy people in an entirely Christian Parliament,[3] who were not prepared to look into the evidence. Indeed, despite the Act, slavery continued in the British colonies for another quarter century.

The world could today be described as being in a similar frame of mind if it refuses to look into the evidence, which is there for all to see. Contemporary slavery flourishes by default. The Lord's Prayer, thoughtfully recited, should jolt us out of any tendency to complacency in this regard.

Child Abuse

Perhaps the worst victims of contemporary slavery are those who are of a tender age. They are scarcely in a position to resist the procedures that *de facto* enslave them. It may be that dire hardship forces their parents to part with them for a payment, passing them into the hands of unscrupulous employers who thereafter subject them to a form of virtual slavery.

Children are a particular object of Christian affection, if the Prayer is to be interpreted in the light of Christ's own conduct and the special attention he paid to children. The love that pervades the Prayer flows out in a special way to children. Conduct that does nothing in protest against rampant child abuse is a flat contradiction of the Prayer's message of love and affirmative action.

The Report of the Special Rapporteur (Vitit Muntabhorn) on the Rights of the Child, submitted in accordance with Resolution 1993/82 of the Commission of Human Rights, makes harrowing reading. Among the matters dealt with are the internationalization of the sale of children, cutbacks in social services leading to child prostitution, bonded labor and pornography, conscription of child soldiers at gunpoint, the channeling of thousands of children into a market for organ transplants in Europe, child bondage, child marriages in which children are kept in near slavery, the organized killings of street children, and the use of child prostitution for promoting the marketing of sex tourism.[4] Pedophiles and sex tourists abuse children in exotic holiday locations on sex tours organized by travel agents in affluent world capitals, and recent court cases, both in Asia and in Europe, have highlighted this form of human rights abuse.

The Working Group on Contemporary Forms of Slavery has stated in its report[5] that, according to one estimate, nearly 300 million children, both in the developed and developing world, were subjected to exploitation through hard labor and debt bondage. The Commission on Human Rights has requested the Secretary-General of the United Nations to stimulate the creation of effective reporting mechanisms so that these abuses can be brought to the attention of the world's public. Reference should be made in this connection to the 1990 Convention on the Rights of the Child.

The sale of children occurs *de facto* on a considerable scale and has to be checked and limited by international action. The sale of children from the former eastern bloc to western Europe is reportedly on the increase as a comparatively new factor, in addition to the earlier trafficking in children between the poor world and the rich world. Here again the average world citizen can play his or her part in ensuring that the necessary pressure is brought to bear at national and international levels to end these practices. Only concerned citizen action can effect a clampdown on questionable intercountry adoptions and impose strict surveillance on those that have taken place. The International Labor Organization has also taken very strong action to end abuses of child labor.

The problem of child soldiers has been the subject of study by the UN Working Group on Contemporary Forms of Slavery, which estimates that around 200,000 children under the age of fifteen are in military service, despite the protocols to the 1977 Geneva Conventions that fix the lowest age for military service at fifteen. Children could be recruited into armed service either compulsorily or because they themselves opt for it as a way out of absolute destitution or starvation.

At the time of this writing, reports are coming to hand of the systematic elimination of child vagrants on the streets in certain parts of the world. Hired assassins for this "social cleansing" destroy these "disposables" for a reported fee of $400 per head. The children roam the streets through no fault of their own. They are an inconvenience to vested business and other interests. The concept of human dignity is not strong enough to stand between them and their liquidation, even though Christianity is the religion that prevails in the areas in question.

Migrant Workers

There is a natural tendency for labor to seek markets in which it commands better wages; and the more prosperous economies tend to require such migrant labor. The result has been a vast migration of labor to the more affluent countries, which have benefited immensely. When hard times come, that labor, once a useful asset, is looked upon as a liability. Various kinds of discrimination, both open and subtle, begin to make life a misery for those migrants in their adopted home. They become second-rate citizens. Violence is unleashed against them, and even riots ensue. Tensions arise between their home country and the host state. Ethnic and cultural differences are emphasized as justifications for rejecting them. But the rights of those people in their host countries are a matter of universal concern, for they involve basic human rights.

This situation spawns a vast crop of problems bearing on human dignity and equality. Are the migrants entitled to equal treatment with the indigenous labor of their host countries? Should they be encouraged to retain their own culture in the country of their adoption? Does the host state have a special duty to see to such matters as the adequacy of their housing and the education of their children?

Many of these workers are in a situation where their roots with their own countries have been severed through their prolonged stay in the host country. The latter is their only home, and they have nowhere else to turn. They are in effect chained to the country and to their inferior status in very much the same manner as feudal labor was chained to both an inferior status and the land.

The resulting position of inequality is very often the cumulative result of numerous petty acts of discrimination practiced across the length and breadth of the host community. They are easily preventible if a little more concern is shown toward one's neighbor, as the Lord's Prayer demands. An accumulation of little acts of unkindness makes up a climate of rejection, just as an accumulation of little "unremembered acts of kindness and of love" makes in their totality a climate of acceptance. Great acts and sacrifices are not called for, but even the little acts are often not forthcoming. No Christian could claim such conduct to be in accordance with the standards postulated by the Lord's Prayer.

Refugees

The sad plight of unprecedented numbers of refugees is yet another problem of our time. Today's wars and internal persecutions result in streams of refugees turning up at national boundaries with their pitiful possessions, their infants in arms, and their memories of loved ones lost in the violence or during their arduous journey. They arrive in other countries in such great numbers that the host countries are often quite unequal to the task of handling them. Many of them, such as the "boat people," lose their lives at sea in their bid for freedom. Those who are successful in setting foot in another country enter into a legal vacuum, with no one to protect their basic human rights. They are often held in detention in closed prison camps, with no access to lawyers or visitors, and under the constant surveillance of search-lights or television monitors. An article in the *New York Times* some years ago described such people as wallowing in a "legalistic and bureaucratic mess which has enveloped them."[6]

This is not a modern problem. A well-known historical example is the fleeing of French Huguenots to England, Prussia, and Holland after the revocation of the Edict of Nantes in 1685. But its unprecedented scale makes it a truly global problem today, with refugees numbering millions. Persons fleeing the Nazi persecution were a dramatic example. Rwanda is a more recent one. If tribalistic wars proliferate, as well they may, these numbers will multiply.

The global scale of the problem has necessitated the appointment of a United Nations High Commissioner for Refugees, but such officials can-not alleviate the sad lot of refugees without goodwill and simple charity on the part of the host country. Laws cannot achieve this. Moral and religious standards can. Especially Christianity, with its poignant tradition of a child born in a stable with nowhere else to lay its head, must cause Christian communities to pay special attention to their plight.

Moreover, a new species of environmental refugee is expected to present new problems in the next century. Chernobyls can cause people to flee the territories they have occupied for generations. Rising water levels of the oceans, resulting from global warming, may submerge low-lying islands in the Pacific and elsewhere. Earthquake disasters, even in developed coun-tries, such as the Los Angeles earthquake of January 1994 or the Kobe earthquake of January 1995, show the extent to which a national disaster can stretch the resources of even an affluent and well-organized state. There needs to be a global readiness to cope with these new problems.

The 1951 Convention and the 1967 Protocol relating to the Status of Refugees prescribe required standards of treatment and the criteria of en-titlement. Space doesn't permit details here, but it will suffice to observe that the absolute discretion of states to control the entry of foreign nation-als has been significantly limited by these developments in international law.[7] However, laws can have only a minuscule effect unless supplemented by social conduct and attitudes such as the Prayer enjoins.

Women

Male dominance of society has been taken for granted in most cultures throughout recorded history.

The twentieth century saw the first stirrings of a global awareness that here was a deep-seated problem awaiting international attention. The twenty-first century will be the first wherein male dominance will no longer be axiomatic.

The full participation of women in government could soften national tendencies toward war and aggressiveness. As wives and mothers, their restraining influence on the politics of militarism must be great. Had half the world's rulers been women at the time of World War I and World War II, the twentieth century may well have taken a different course. What we do know is that forty centuries of male-dominated governments have produced an unending succession of military confrontations. Perhaps a gender mix at the highest levels could produce a change. When Mrs. Sirimavo Bandanaraike of Sri Lanka became the world's first woman prime minister, the news attracted worldwide attention. Since then what was once a phenomenon has been so often repeated as to attract scarcely a mention. Bangladesh, India, Israel, Norway, Pakistan, the Philippines, Turkey, the United Kingdom—these are only the beginning of a long line that will become a commonplace of the twenty-first century. That would be in accordance with the total lack of distinction between the position and rights of male and female in the Prayer.

Without speculation on the impact of women on governments, it will be sufficient to outline some conditions which, in this closing phase of the present century, place half of humanity under disadvantages and discriminations that are no part of the equality of all humans underlying the Prayer.

The areas of discrimination currently affecting the female half of the world's population make a sorry list. Justice cannot reign on earth when continuing injustice is perpetrated on half its population.

The problems are such as to attract the concerned attention of the United Nations, which has passed a series of declarations on the subject. Ranging from broad policy pronouncements such as Declaration 37/63 of December 3, 1982, on the Participation of Women in Promoting International Peace and Cooperation, and Resolution 42/64 of November 30, 1987, on the Integration of Women in Society, these deal with such specific concerns as child marriage and adolescent childbearing, nutritional taboos and differential feeding patterns, untrained birth attendants, female circumcision and genital mutilation, taboos preventing women from controlling their own fertility, the increase in gender-specific violence, inequality in legal capacity, economic status, and political participation. All these problems await attention. It is not for different sectors of the world population to say that a problem remote from themselves does not concern them.

The Convention on the Elimination of all Forms of Discrimination against Women, proclaimed by the General Assembly on December 18, 1979, which entered into force on September 3, 1981, imposes positive duties on states to pursue actively the objectives it sets forth; this is an obligation in international law. As the next century gets underway, these problems will no longer be capable of being swept under the carpet. They will cry out for active attention, which will not be forthcoming without heightened public concern.

Another factor needing attention will be the control of the medical technology that now enables preselection of gender. Used indiscriminately, this could lead to a vast imbalance in the next century between male and female populations, owing to the belief prevalent in many societies that males are more conducive to a family's economic advancement and social protection. This new technology will need to be subjected to an ethical code based on the equality of all human beings.

The Children of Conflict

As the great international wars are replaced by internecine conflicts within nations, vast numbers of children are growing up in a situation that must make no sense to their hearts and minds. There is need of much healing to repair the damaged psychology of the children of conflict. Christian sympathy and understanding must go out to these innocent victims of conflicts.

When yesterday's neighbor becomes today's assassin and kills the child's parents, brothers, or sisters in cold blood before its very eyes, that child, should it survive, must carry through life a bitter view of humanity and of its own obligations toward its fellow human beings. When in a state of declared war an enemy nation wreaks havoc on one's own, the child's mind, though repelled by the brutality, can yet fit it within its pattern of understanding. The internecine situation, on the other hand, leaves the child uncertain in its own country of the rights of the citizen or the sanctity of life.

In the hidden recesses of the child's subconscious mind there will remain forever the blood-soaked vision of inhumanities that warp all sense of values. The child will probably carry into adulthood, and throughout its life, the seeds of hatred; and the rest of the world, not seeing the warped vision through which that child saw its unfolding world, will expect from that child as from any other the same attitudes of love and concern for one's fellow citizens as it expects from one who has grown up in a sheltered childhood.

Here are the seeds of future conflicts, more acute than those that gave them birth, to which the twenty-first century is heir. There are millions of such children the world over. Born into divisiveness, witnesses to violence, heirs to longstanding hatreds, theirs are minds which must be carefully approached and tactfully weaned away from the experiences of terror. This is a wholly neglected world problem, to be approached in the special spirit of love toward children that Jesus taught throughout his ministry. If the Prayer is a message of love, the world's children are specially entitled to its benefits; and of the world's children, the children of conflict are entitled to that love in a particularly special manner.

Love, sympathy, and education are the routes by which such minds, shaped by violence in the past and attuned to violence in the future, can be approached. Crippled logic and raw emotion will direct them naturally in the direction of violence. In such a process of education, religion can play a practical and not inconsiderable role.

Prisoners

There is a strong tendency on the part of many a self-righteous citizen to treat prisoners as the outcasts of society. Not incorrectly has it been observed that an index of the civilization of a society is the way in which it treats its prisoners. "Something was dead in each of us/And that which was dead was Hope," wrote Oscar Wilde after his brief sojourn in prison. Not all are gifted as Wilde was with the ability to describe their forlorn condition, but no doubt they all feel the same.

Prisons all over the world contain many a person who has been the victim of circumstances. Many prisoners have indeed been very neglectful of their obligations toward society, and some have exhibited a degree of viciousness and unconcern for human suffering that cannot but arouse strong indignation.

Yet society exists for all its constituent members, and just as no one of them is excluded from the mercy of God, so also no one of them is to be treated as less than a human being. There is so much of ill in the best of us, and so much of good in the worst of us that we are obliged to accord to them every assistance toward reshaping their future, and enabling them to rejoin society as equal members on the conclusion of their term of imprisonment.

Moreover, while in prison they are entitled to the basic human rights to health, humane conditions of accommodation, and treatment with due regard to their basic dignity as human beings.

One only needs to consider in this context Jesus' own observation about the visiting of people in prison as an act of kindness to God himself (Matthew 25:35,40).

Giantism

Productivity demands rigid organization. Rigid organization demands a maximization of the cost-benefit ratio calculated in monetary terms. Such maximization is best furthered when duplication of services is eliminated. Duplication is minimized with the coalescence of a multitude of separate organizations that can then use the same basic support services.

Everywhere the small-scale economic, industrial, administrative, military, and academic unit is being swallowed up by larger operators in the field. The individual values that could shine through in the small organizational unit are being submerged in the giantism of the new unit, which treats each individual as a digit in its books rather than as a human personality.

A double denigration thus takes place of the higher values—the human factor is reduced in importance, and the economic cost-benefit ratio is elevated.

The Degradation of the Family Unit

Broken homes and families have become a major part of the social scenery of our age. Children grow to maturity, torn between conflicting loyalties to warring parents, never having known the stability of a settled home. They know little of the love that by very definition should surge through the concept of the Christian family. As adults they will transmit to their successors the values and impressions they receive.

Respect for elders is on the decline, and assisting relatives in need, especially those outside the nuclear family, is a dying concept. Drug problems among the young, and teenage pregnancies are on the increase. Except in a very small minority of cases, the home is no longer the center where values and discipline are imparted to the growing child.

The breakup of the family unit drives each member to rely upon his or her resources, thus further entrenching individualism in an excessively individualistic world. The broken home, a result of the shifting moral currents of our age, is an enormous departure from the spirit of togetherness and collectiveness that is so heavily emphasized in the Prayer.

These are a few instances, selected at random, from the social trespasses and temptations that beset our age. They do not often hit the headlines, but form a complex of hatreds and tensions seething beneath the surface of even apparently peaceful societies. Each of them is a categorical rejection of the ringing plea of togetherness that echoes through the Prayer. If they are denied attention in that spirit of togetherness, they will leave significant sections of the community to wallow in the bitterness of discrimination, and slash deep scars into the human landscape of the twenty-first century.

CHAPTER 14

ETHICAL TRESPASSES AND TEMPTATIONS— THE UBIQUITY OF ETHICAL ISSUES

In every walk of life the progress made by modern technology and by the growth in size of the human enterprise is forcing ethical issues to surface in a manner never known before. Decisions bristling with moral issues need to be made in nearly every activity and at nearly every level. Many of these, as will be seen from this chapter, touch the meaning of life itself.

In the past, doctors bound themselves to some basic ethical fundamentals by a Hippocratic oath and lawyers by an ethical code, designed largely to protect the image and standing of their professions. Both these codes were rudimentary, but outside of them, no codes were known. Scientists, engineers, accountants, university teachers, and manufacturers, to name a few, were thrown entirely on their own moral resources, with little to guide them in making value judgments on the issues they faced. In the areas of medical and legal ethics, doctors and lawyers decided issues for themselves without any recognition of a need for assistance from other disciplines.

All this has changed fundamentally. As the physicist's particular skill is requisitioned for the manufacture of instruments of death in the armaments industry, or to devise methods of increasing the agony of the weapon's victim (as with the modern refinements of missiles to splinter them into a thousand razor sharp fragments upon entering the body), questions of conscience arise. As chemical or biological weapons enlarge the circle of their victims and enhance their lethal efficacy, the chemist or biologist must fall back upon his or her moral code. As genetic engineers splice up DNA and construct out of it a made-to-measure creature, questions surface about the

ethics of "playing God" and tinkering with life. As the doctor addresses
the problems of euthanasia, or the withdrawal of life support systems, or
the destruction of surplus embryos created for *in vitro* fertilization, or the
fathering of a child by a person long dead, moral issues surface by the
score. The engineer, called upon to construct a nuclear reactor or a dam
that will alter the ecological balance in an entire province, would have to
consider the project's environmental impact. Ever since physics plunged us
into the age of the atom, nuclear scientists, working continuously on the
edge of environmental and ecological disaster, need the strongest of moral
codes.

A manufacturer releasing a product is constantly balancing the need for
public safety against the inducement to cut corners and save costs. A phar-
maceutical company or food manufacturer is constantly debating how much
information should be given to the public on its product's labels. In all
these areas, the law is unable to police the many opportunities and temptations that exist for making profits at the expense of the public. The actor
can only fall back upon morality—his or her own moral code if he or she
has one, or his or her religious principles if he or she believes in them.

Religion and religious inspiration enter the scientists' laboratories, the
hospital wards, the board rooms of the industrialists, and the committee
rooms of the universities—though officially the doors are shut to them. But
just as the spiritually elevated are recorded in many scriptures as being able
to enter rooms through walls of stone, so also are ethical issues penetrating
these mundane places of decision making.

The prevalence of these issues on a global scale has prompted concerned
philosophers to contemplate the need for a code of ethics, even on a global
scale, a minimum ethic that is absolutely necessary for human survival,
comprising basic moral principles on which the great religious traditions
agree. The Parliament of the World's Religions in Chicago, in 1993, proposed a Declaration toward a Global Ethic. Hans Küng, the Swiss theologian, takes the idea further and suggests that religions, governments, and
corporations should agree on such a basic code of ethics.[1]

In the political and bureaucratic arena as well, ethical issues are surfacing as never before, and commissions of inquiry, such as the Nolan
Committee in the United Kingdom, are examining the shortfall in ethical
standards that is currently invading every sphere of public life.

Mere compliance with the law is not ethical conduct, but this has become, all too often, the standard by which proper conduct is to be judged.

We need to go far beyond this, into the area of moral propriety, and this is where the guiding values of religion assume immense practical importance.

Business Ethics

In an earlier section we looked at corporate power and the need for vigilance on the part of individual shareholders. This discussion deals with the need for a generally accepted code of ethics for the board room itself—a task in which some insights from the Lord's Prayer could be of assistance.

Some business codes have indeed been formulated and have worked with success. For example, at the height of apartheid the Sullivan Code, formulated by Rev. Leon Sullivan, was instrumental in persuading twelve of the largest firms operating in South Africa to accept a set of principles ending segregation and job discrimination. Similar codes were formulated by the European Economic Community and the Canadian government. More such guidelines are required in all spheres of business, especially when it comes to what might be described as "tooth and claw" competition for resources, labor, and markets.

Current ethical attitudes

The current corporate ethic is geared to maximization of profits. If improvement of the human condition results from such action, this coincidence between individual profit and public welfare is hailed with satisfaction. If it does not, and there is a contest between private advantage and public good, public welfare must yield to private gain. Stated another way, the choice between extending their own dominion and extending the dominion of fair play and justice cannot be resolved in the absence of an ethic in the world's corporate board rooms.

It seems almost fashionable in the business world to proclaim a code of conduct that is the direct antithesis of a code of ethics. For example, it is often said that "the social responsibility of business is to increase its profits."[2] We see around us "economic man" engaged in the mechanical and soulless pursuit of profits, rather than in a fully human activity. Our age is developing a mythology compounded by the acceptance of such notions as that business is a "game" and a brutal "game" at that; that "it is a jungle out there"; that business is a "battle"; and that capitalism is "a great machine" that functions automatically as machines do. Hobbes' state of nature and

Darwin's survival of the fittest are other notions woven into this belief system, which results in an ethic of "each man for himself." By their continued propagation, these images breed an acceptance of them and of the inevitability of the lack of ethics in the business world. In the picturesque language of one writer, such attitudes make a bonfire of the virtues in the world of business.[3] Indeed, the current trend goes further and causes vices to parade as virtues. In short, the code of business is often based not merely upon a neglect of the Christian values encapsulated in the Prayer, but upon the positive adoption in the board room of a set of values that expressly negates the values in the Prayer.

There is a place in business for an attitude beyond selfishness and for an ethic beyond the making of money. There is a responsibility to society that grows with the scale of one's business and can result in the wide acceptance of the notion of the "responsible company"—the company that accepts its social responsibility to the community out of which it makes its profits. Basic business virtues such as fairness, compassion, and justice can breed that more acceptable code of ethics which tends to be trampled underfoot in the business world.[4]

In the words of a sensitive study on the subject:

> …[J]ustice in the corporation cannot be separated from the personal virtues of caring and compassion, loyalty, and one's sense of honor—and, of course, the six parameters of the Aristotelian viewpoint, a sense of community, a demand for excellence, a sense of belonging and responsibility, a keen sense of one's own integrity, a penchant for good judgment, and a view of the whole instead of a narrow focus on one's own little world and interests.[5]

The social and political impact of the modern corporation

The urgency of such ethical codes becomes evident when we consider the social and political impact of the modern corporation. Today's corporation is different from the street corner business of the past. Its conduct is a matter of public concern—not a private matter, as was the case with the small-time grocer or cobbler down the street. The prosperity of a whole town or region may depend upon the corporation. The law and order instruments of the state spend substantial sums of money guarding its millions of dollars worth of property and its several office and factory sites.

Although the executive president of a country is seen to wield great political power, much of that power is subject to pressures exerted by economic interests. On the other hand, while the executive president of a large multinational corporation is not seen as wielding political power, his or her economic power is strong enough in many areas to impose pressure in some vital fields of political power. Moreover, when the economic sector wields political power, it offers a classic case of power without representation and therefore power without accountability.

So great is this power that some have likened the heads of great multinational corporations to the kings and popes of former times.[6]

Political power in the hands of commerce is dangerous unless it is subject to restraints. Adam Smith, the apostle of free trade, himself observed, in *Wealth of Nations*, that, "the government by an exclusive company of merchants is perhaps the worst of all governments for any country whatever." And Edmund Burke, speaking in the House of Commons on December 1, 1773 on the powers of the East India Company in India, observed, "Magna Charta is a charter to restrain power and to destroy monopoly. The East India Charter is a charter to establish monopoly and create power….This bill, and those connected with it, are intended to form the Magna Charta of Hindustan." Such observations are pertinent to the appropriate degree, depending on the extent of political power wielded by business. If that power is considerable, so is the danger to the principles of democracy.

The basis of ethical codes

One of the important aspects to be borne in mind in formulating an ethical code is the concept "Who is my neighbor?" which was brought into relief in the Good Samaritan episode, regarded by many as Jesus' own illustration of the duties prescribed by the Lord's Prayer. The question here is: Who is the neighbor, affected by its actions, to whom the corporate board room owes a duty? Is it only the shareholders? The tens of thousands of its employees? The millions of consumers of its product? The general public of the country where it operates and whose security apparatus protects its property and investment? Current corporate law thinks only in terms of shareholders. This is thinking only in terms of oneself and is diametrically opposed to the broad social consciousness underlying the Prayer.

It is completely out of tune with social realities for the law still to think in terms of the old concepts of company law that directors are merely trustees for shareholders. The ambit of their responsibilities is far wider, for it is not merely the shareholder who is a neighbor to whom they owe a responsibility. These corporations are social institutions as important to the public generally as many a government department or agency. Their employees run to hundreds of thousands, their products are used by millions, and their decisions affect the availability of community resources. The social responsibilities flowing from this are so great that they have quite outrun antiquated theories of company law, with their concentration on the concept of trusteeship for shareholders. The notion of trusteeship for the community is emerging so strongly that some theorists who earlier held the former view have been weaned away from it by the sheer force of recent developments.

When we realize that these corporations will continue to increase their role in the ordering of the world's economic affairs, we realize what an impact they will also have on political affairs and eventually on world peace.

By and large, corporate business continues its profit-making activity to the limit of what it can do without clashing with the law. How far such a standard falls short of ethical conduct has already been explained. The standard prescribed by the Lord's Prayer—to do unto others as one would be done by—provides a useful guideline around which a code of ethical conduct can be framed. Corporate business, proceeding without self-restraint into the next century, would be sowing the seeds of major international conflicts.

In the fight against some of the grave injustices of the past, as we've seen, the first stage toward positive action was the recognition that a moral issue was involved.[7] It was only thereafter that the necessary political and legal pressure was brought to bear. In regard to global corporate activities, however, we have not as yet reached the stage of general recognition that a moral issue exists. Indeed, whenever the issue is raised, there is straightaway an attempt to dissipate it by reliance on principles of individualism and *laissez faire*. Once the moral issue is recognized, the relevance of the moral wisdom in the Lord's Prayer will immediately be perceived.

Scientific Ethics

A lawyer by profession, I have had the privilege of visiting several university faculties—notably science, engineering, and medicine—over the past twenty-five years and discussing these issues. The reaction twenty-five years ago was one of marked hostility. What right did lawyers have to come into fields that did not belong to them and tell the experts how to behave? The experts saw themselves as concerned human beings with a developed moral sense of their own. Today the reaction in such faculties is markedly different, and there is a warm welcome for the insights available from other disciplines. Doctors, perhaps the most jealous guardians of their territory, routinely welcome the creation of multidisciplinary ethics committees. Nearly every major hospital now has an ethics committee, including theologians, philosophers, and ethicists. Nearly every university has such a committee to oversee the area of human experimentation.

Engineers are beginning to structure ethical codes for themselves. The computer fraternity is doing likewise. Accountants are constantly refining their ethical codes.

In the midst of this wealth of ethical issues, the pragmatic scientist or man or woman of affairs is increasingly realizing his or her limitations. Cramped within the boundaries of definitions and formulae, they feel a compelling need to turn for guidance beyond the boundaries of their disciplines. They are drawn irresistibly to the great moral reservoirs containing the perennial wisdom of our cultural inheritance. Wedded to the nonacceptance of any phenomenon that cannot be perceived, measured, and analyzed, the scientist is now turning to the one source that defies perception, measurement, and analysis.

The absence of ethical codes

Scientists of the utmost intelligence and integrity are often carried away by their devotion to the work they have in hand. When the A4 rockets launched from Peenemünde on October 3, 1942,[8] proved to be a success, a celebration party was held at Peenemunde that evening. When news of the successful explosion of the atomic bomb on Hiroshima was received at Los Alamos laboratory where so much work was done upon it, there was apparently such jubilation that scientists could be seen rushing to telephones to order celebration dinners at nearby restaurants.[9]

By turning up new problems without precedent in the long annals of legal history, modern technology is racing ahead of the legal ability to regulate them.[10] Corporate crime, remote scanning, surveillance techniques, organ transplants, psychological torture, and embryo transplantation offer a few examples. The undermining by science and technology of some of the fundamentals of human rights and dignity often pass unnoticed. Some influential contemporary theologians such as Jacques Ellul, the French political and social scientist, argue that technology has grown into a machine so powerful that no force can stand against it.[11] When law and legal concepts are thus powerless to restrain it, we need to lean more heavily on morality and ethics. Here, as elsewhere, the Lord's Prayer offers guidelines, when it deals with such concepts as human dignity, equality, duties toward society, reciprocity, and standards of living.

The power of the individual scientist

In modern society, especially after the power of scientists was demonstrated in World War II, scientists have acquired a position of great influence in governments and in society. Many of them have become commanding figures in the corridors of power, close advisers to ministers and to heads of government. Vast engineering projects impacting on the environment, major developments in the range and destructiveness of arms, advances in control and surveillance of populations, the construction of nuclear reactors, psychological controls over human behavior—in all of these areas the scientist often has the final word. They all affect society, health, liberty, and lifestyles in the way that governmental decisions do. Yet the scientist is not accountable to the public in the same way that a government official is.

The conscience of the individual scientist

This vast power breeds responsibility. One of the major problems of the next century—a science-dominated century—will be the problem of the scientist's moral and ethical responsibility for the consequences of his work. Does the scientist merely contribute his expertise to a given project and leave to others the responsibility for decisions on its implementation? The same rules of engineering that will construct a church will construct a torture chamber. Can the scientist shut his mind to the purposes for which his expertise is required? Here, again, is scope for the ethic of the Lord's Prayer to make a difference.

It must prick the conscience of Christian communities to note that the social impact of science and the scientist's ethical responsibilities were much neglected subjects until the Second International Congress of the History of Science and Technology, held in London in 1931, focused attention on Marxist perspectives regarding the social purpose of the scientific endeavor. Under the stimulus of this landmark event, interest in the subject was kindled, much literature began to appear on the subject, and Societies for Social Responsibility in Science were founded.[12]

Societies for Social Responsibility in Science in America, Britain, and other countries are doing their best to alert the conscience of scientists, but have not yet been able to obtain a generally accepted code of conduct for all scientists or an adequate input of socially oriented subjects into scientific courses.

The only ethic so far recognized (apart, that is, from rather rudimentary ethical codes of the medical profession and of some organizations of engineers) is loyalty to truth, for the scientist has been taught that he or she must on no account distort the truth in an attempt to prove a hypothesis. In science, misreporting of experiments is the gravest of crimes; but there is no prohibition upon the lending of one's expertise for the most nefarious purposes.

Scientists at the cutting edge of research are among the keenest minds of each generation. There has not been a sufficient attempt even in universities and institutes of technology to build an ethical component into such scientific courses as engineering, physics, or chemistry. In the structuring of ethical codes, some of the moral principles embedded in the major religions would be of great value—principles such as the sanctity and dignity of life, which command acceptance across religious barriers. Most of the scientists of the world are Christian, Jewish, Islamic, Hindu, and Buddhist. Their personal ethical codes are of great importance, and reach areas of their conduct that law can never reach.

It is also possible for Third World societies which, by and large are receivers of technology, to use their traditional cultural values to exercise some discrimination in choosing the technology that they really need, rather than to be passive receivers of all the technology that is thrust on them.[13]

Who is my neighbor?

The extended circle of those affected by the scientist's conduct brings this matter once again within the Good Samaritan principle. The scientist's vision of the overall purpose of his or her work, and those affected by it, is often deliberately obscured. The participant in a limited scientific experiment directed by a superior authority may have no knowledge that the small part he or she plays is meant, together with the efforts of others similarly placed, to fit into the pattern of a project that in its totality he or she would condemn. Some states may well take special pains to screen the individual scientist from a view of the total picture; in effect, the state could use its best brains as innocent tools in a project cutting across the moral fiber of the entire community. Likewise, in those vastly complex commercial organizations that are a feature of modern life, the same considerations apply, for their left hand may not know what their right hand does, and can far less discern what goes on in their controlling minds.

Thus those whose scientific skill went into the making of the first atomic bomb were not all aware of the end to which their overall research was directed. Wernher Von Braun, the father of rocketry, has written:

> With the tight press censorship imposed by Hitler, the abuses of his regime were not nearly as visible to the average German as they were to an outsider who had free access to the international news media. For this reason, I must say, more by way of a statement than as an apology, that I never realized the depth of the abyss of Hitler's regime until very late and particularly after the war, when all those terrible abuses were first published.[14]

The same applies no doubt to other lethal creations, as, for example, weapons used in germ warfare, where the biologist, the doctor, the pathologist, and others may each be employed to work on different aspects of the operation without any one of them realizing the sinister overall purpose for which the work is required. A major problem will be the scientist's responsibility for the foreseeable consequences of his or her work—the concept "Who is my neighbor, who will be affected by my actions?" In the realm of scientific restraints, proceeding from moral and ethical implications, religion obviously affords guidance where law cannot.[15]

Media Ethics

Good faith in the transmission of information

The Prayer demands good faith in one's dealings with others. Good faith demands truthfulness not only in one's direct communication with others, but also in the information one relays about others. One cannot, consistent with the Prayer, distort information about others, purvey information selectively put together so as to misrepresent, or disseminate half-truths. A half-truth presented as the whole truth can become a total lie. Yet, in our age where the power of disseminating information has grown to undreamt-of heights, this is quite often the pattern followed in the propagation of news. Moreover, great news media have acquired increasingly monopolistic controls over international news dissemination and, hence, wield enormous political power free of political responsibility. Although some of them have imposed codes of conduct upon themselves, the dissemination of news is an activity that proceeds largely free of moral restraints.[16]

Quite often the media have little other object but to astonish or amuse, and the compelling needs of these objectives shut out a wider and fairer selection and presentation of information.

From the standpoint of global peace, one of the most alarming problems of this age of information is the way in which the modern electronic information apparatus is often used to entrench ignorance and spread disinformation. This may not be done deliberately, but news dissemination and news selection reflects the attitudes of those who purvey it; and when those attitudes are such as has been referred to in the previous section, and when global news emanates from the developed rather than the developing world, it is only natural that the viewpoint of the developed world is the one projected globally.

A fairer information order

It is through such reports that public opinion is formed. The dangers consequent on such a one-way flow of information prompted the concept of a New World Information and Communication Order which, unfortunately, has not got off the ground. The philosophy underlying such an order has been well formulated in numerous publications, and among the organizations that have highlighted the moral and Christian overtones of this problem is the World Association for Christian Communication. The Association's publication *Communication for All: The Church and the New World Information and Communications Order*,[17] expresses grave concern regarding the consistency of current patterns of global information with Christian standards of truth and fairness.

In default of an observance of these standards, misunderstanding and hatreds arise. These can endanger world peace. One of those misunderstandings endangering peace today is in regard to Islam, one of the great faiths of mankind, which for ten centuries, ever since the time of the Crusaders, has had a bad press in the West. This trend still continues with little effort to understand its elevated teachings and immense contribution to world civilization. Of the calumnies regarding its founder, Thomas Carlyle wrote over a century ago, "The lies which well-meaning zeal has heaped round this man are disgraceful to ourselves only."[18] After the lapse of a century and a half, the description of Carlyle is even more true now than it was when he wrote.

The news presented to the world by the great news media shares certain characteristics—negative events are overreported, positive events are looked upon as uninteresting, reality is presented in a fragmented manner rather than in overall perspective, there is an emphasis on the recent event because it is news and news must be "new."[19] What to report and what to omit is largely a matter of selection by the media giants involved, and many of these selections are made from the perspectives of their financial interests and those of the developed world, thus daily entrenching these attitudes even deeper.

Dominance by the major media

Over a hundred years have passed since the great powers of the day—Britain, Germany, France, and the United States—made arrangements among themselves to divide the world into news regions. By the terms so arranged, Reuters was assigned the British Empire, the Balkans, part of Africa, and the Far East. AFP (Agence France Presse) was given the French colonies, South America, Belgium, Spain and Portugal. The Germans took Scandinavia, Austria, the German part of Switzerland, and all of Russia, and the Associated Press took over the United States, Mexico, Cuba, the Philippines, and the English-speaking part of Canada. All these agencies, with the exception of AP, were heavily dependent for their monopolistic positions on government patronage; hence their reporting up until the First World War was conducted against this background.[20]

The dominance of the major media over the worldwide flow of information has continued and, with the advent of television and the expensive technology involved, has become even more entrenched. Television news packages are distributed by key agencies of the developed world by jet and satellite in tailor-made packages to over a hundred countries. The multinational news agencies thus dominate the selection of information as well. Such news packages can lead to the overthrow of governments, the installation of new regimes, and the perpetuation of dictatorships.

A sample of the news coverage during a given month was summarized as follows by a Latin-American editor:

If this wire file were the only source of enlightenment for the rest of the world, then Latin America would be considered to consist mainly of Cuba. From several countries there was no news at all during the month of analysis. Brazil got a mention once, when it was visited by Prince Philip. Peru was notable for producing short items about an aeroplane crash and a bus wreck. Nothing happened apparently in Chile except that Billy Graham was evangelizing in Santiago. Thus one of these countries only appeared in the cables because it produced two routine disasters, important to people locally concerned, but, considered as information, totally unilluminating to the rest of the world. Two other countries qualified for attention solely because they were visited by eminent persons from two of the four dominant news providing countries.[21]

The social responsibility theory of press freedom

While it is essential that the media enjoy freedom to report the news as they see it, that freedom must be used with responsibility. Herbert Marcuse has pointed out how the theory of free expression has over the generations since the Industrial Revolution turned back upon itself to destroy the rationale on which it was built.[22] Such considerations led to the evolution of what has been described as the social responsibility theory of press freedom, which received high recognition from the United States Commission on Freedom of the Press. Shortly after World War II, the Commission brought out a series of publications aimed at generating greater social responsibility on the part of the media. Much progress has been made, particularly in the United States, in developing this theory. Such reports as *A Free and Responsible Press: A General Report on Mass Communications*,[23] and journalism reviews such as the *Columbia Journalism Review*, have greatly stimulated journalistic awareness of its obligations. Still, the media have a long way to go if they are to discharge the basic social responsibilities lying upon them.

Sensationalism, the glamorizing of crime, dependence on the advertiser, pursuit of profits, the absorption of competitors, and the entrenching of monopolies all drive the media on the course that they have chosen. Such a course is no way to global understanding, nor is it a reflection of the underlying principles of equality, respect for others, and universalism that lie at the core of the Lord's Prayer. James Antonellis recognized the value of applying these principles to the area of media in his work, *A Journalist Looks at the Lord's Prayer.*

Legal Ethics

The legal ethics here referred to are not the narrow professional ethical codes of lawyers that regulate their relationships with one another and that were designed to protect the dignity and exclusiveness of the profession.[24] There are much broader social responsibilities lying upon lawyers than mere loyalty to their profession: There is a duty to give due consideration to the end result of their work. Many examples can be cited from today's legal milieu of lawyers lending their expertise to the perpetration of massive injustice. Corporate wrongdoing, money-laundering, unfair trade practices are all promoted and advanced by lawyers who advise their clients on the maximum benefits they can extract for themselves, regardless of the damage caused to the social interest. Apartheid flourished because lawyers helped to develop and maintain the legal apparatus of apartheid. Dictatorships use the services of lawyers to entrench and justify their rule. Wherever one turns in the fields of major social iniquity, one finds legal talent aiding and abetting its extension. The result is that justice serves some, and not all, sections of the community. This has long been a matter of concern to dedicated lawyers—especially the younger members of the profession.[25]

Just as scientists need to see the overall picture in the light of their individual conscience, so also do lawyers, and it is insufficient to confine oneself to the narrow ethic that one is merely serving one's client. The broader background picture must be taken into account. A lawyer committed to Christian values cannot shut them out under the supposed ethic of serving his or her client. The values encapsulated in the Lord's Prayer are relevant to the lawyer's work at every point. As elsewhere, the question who is one's neighbor, in the sense of being affected by one's work, becomes relevant here.

Among history's most telling examples of legal myopia, which have

caused untold harm to millions, is the help given by succeeding generations of lawyers and judges to slavery and colonialism. These instances are
pregnant with warnings for the future, when new forms of subjection may
take center stage.

Slavery

It is difficult to imagine a more clear-cut contradiction between the realities of slavery and the basic principles of common law, and of Christianity
combined. Yet Christian lawyers for generations turned a blind eye to this
total negation of Christianity.

Legal justifications of colonialism

Lawyers helped in the obfuscation of the real issues involved in colonialism by cloaking it with numerous legal justifications. The appropriation of
others' possessions thus gained respectability through its adoption and endorsement by the most eminent legal scholars and the highest judicial tri-
bunals.

This blind spot causes surprise when the judgments or legal opinions of
even a generation or two ago are reconsidered in the light of the dramatic
new advances that have been made in the field of human rights.

The law tended often to be so technical that lawyers and judges administering it missed out entirely on the human and social impact of the judgments
they delivered—and more particularly, on the impact of their judgments on
peoples distant from them geographically or culturally. Important instances
come to mind in relation to legal attitudes toward the rights of conquered or
aboriginal peoples.

The status of subject peoples

An important early manifestation was the way in which the conquest, confiscation of property, and even decimation of native peoples was considered to be
in full conformity with the law in the age of the Spanish expansion into
Central and South America. The jurists of the establishment constructed
substantial legal arguments justifying the confiscation of the land of non-
Christian peoples, and the decimation of the people themselves.

It required strenuous argument by concerned jurists and theologians such as the Jesuit De Vitoria to advance the point of view, so obvious to us today, that such peoples, being in fact human beings, were entitled to legal protection. What seems all the more surprising at this point in time is that such thinking was possible in a civilization and culture as deeply committed to Christian values as was the Spanish government of the time. In all likelihood, had the notions of equality and human dignity contained in the Lord's Prayer been extracted from the Prayer and brought into the legal argument, the matter would not have proceeded to the unchristian extremes that it reached in the early days of Spanish rule.

Shifting the focus away from early Spanish expansion to later European expansion, we find the same feeling of unconcern toward native peoples manifested in judgments that come down almost to our time.

Indigenous land rights

In the more recent phase of colonial expansion, international lawyers turned their ingenuity to similar ends. Justification of the right of the imperial power to acquire land and territory in the occupation of indigenous peoples from time immemorial was found in the doctrine of *terra nullius*—that property which was not the subject of settled habitation could be taken over by the imperial power in the same manner as any other ownerless property could be acquired by its finder. This doctrine took no account of the fact that many indigenous peoples, for example, the Aborigines of Australia, did not have a settled home and habitation after the European manner, although it was indisputable that they had been in occupation of the territory in question from time immemorial.

We know, for example, that in the Pacific at the time of German and British expansion a battleship would sail alongside a little island, landing a company of marines who fired a few volleys and planted their flag. Contemporary records show how the frightened natives, who had been in occupation as long as human memory extended, ran away into the bush at the sight of the marines and the sound of their guns. Thereupon the land was solemnly proclaimed by the ship's captain as territory belonging to the German emperor or the British sovereign.[26]

Mutual legal recognitions of annexation

Time and again, judicial pronouncements would proclaim that territories acquired in this fashion belonged without a doubt to the sovereign who thus annexed them in the face of all law and morality.

Since it was only a limited circle of powers who thus extended their jurisdictions into the far corners of the globe, it became customary for them to accord mutual recognition to such acts of appropriation, and to extend the courtesies of international law to each other in respect of such territories. They were also able to draw upon conventions and divide among themselves, without any reference to the peoples concerned, the territories of peoples in Africa and Asia. One example was the Congress of Berlin, 1884, which carved up the continent of Africa to suit the metropolitan powers, irrespective of tribal affiliations or territorial occupation. So, also, in 1886 a line was drawn through the Pacific dividing the territories and areas of influence of Britain and Germany without any reference to the peoples concerned. At the close of the century, most of Northern Africa was similarly divided into spheres of influence by treaties of 1898 and 1899. There was a heavy legal input into all of these conventions, but the lawyers of the time do not seem to have questioned the assumptions of their political masters.

Judicial endorsements of annexation

Whenever matters such as these came before the courts, the invariable response of the judicial authority was that such occupation was perfectly lawful, thus giving to these acts of appropriation the support and endorsement of the highest legal authority. The legacy of those early modes of thought is felt even in our time. For example, as recently as 1977, the Banaban islanders appealed for relief to the British courts after their island had been mined out and they were dispossessed of their ancient home. The court referred to the British occupation of Ocean Island in the following terms:

> Jurisdiction over Ocean Island was obtained peacefully and without any overt act of conquest or cession. It became part of the Crown's dominions by virtue of the occupation of the island by the company and the hoisting of the flag on May 5th 1900, coupled with the Crown's licence to the company; and it thereupon became a British settlement under the British Settlements Act 1887. The law officers (Sir Robert

Finlay and Sir Edward Carson) so advised on 16th May 1904, and I think they were right.[27]

Similar judgments were written in the Australian context regarding annexation of the territory of aboriginal peoples without conquest or cession. Such legal justifications were based upon the supposition that aboriginal peoples were not in the habit of settled possession of their lands, but indulged rather in their traditional habit of a "walkabout" every so many years—a tradition due very largely to the necessity of permitting the land to revive for some years after it had been used by the tribe.

Such approaches lent a color of legal justification to acts which, viewed purely in terms of morality, were indefensible, except on arguments that strained credibility—as, for example, that the best use needed to be made of land, or that the European peoples were trustees of civilization, or that the native peoples would be well served if they had enough for their subsistence, whatever might be the value of their possessions, which were thus appropriated by force.

New judicial departures

An epoch-making judgment of the High Court of Australia in *Mabo and others vs. State of Queensland* (1992) is a legal watershed in this area.[28] In that case the High Court examined critically the earlier judgments that had proceeded on the basis that title vested immediately in the British Crown when the British occupied such territory. Justice Brennan referred to the three heads of justification for acquisition under international law, conquest, cession, and the *terra nullius* theory:

Various justifications for the acquisition of sovereignty over the territory of 'backward peoples' were advanced. The benefits of Christianity and European civilisation had been seen as a sufficient justification from medieval times. Another justification for the application of the theory of *terra nullius* to inhabited territory—a justification first advanced by Vattel at the end of the 18th century—was that new territories could be claimed by occupation if the land were uncultivated, for Europeans had a right to bring lands into production if they were left uncultivated by the indigenous inhabitants.[29]

Another technical legal justification was that the new colony immediately received the benefit of the common law. This was a legal euphemism for the reality:

> It would be a curious doctrine to propound today that, when the benefit of the common law was first extended to Her Majesty's indigenous subjects in the Antipodes, its first fruits were to strip them of their right to occupy their ancestral lands.[30]

My purpose here is to show how Christian judges and lawyers, administering a system of law supposedly based on Christian principles, could so far lose sight of the central principles of their faith as enshrined in the Lord's Prayer. They were able, with one stroke of the judicial pen, to confirm the dispossession of people who had occupied land from time immemorial. As a result:

> …[T]he common law itself took from indigenous inhabitants any right to occupy their traditional land, exposed them to deprivation of the religious, cultural and economic sustenance which the land provides, vested the land effectively in the control of the Imperial authorities without any right to compensation and made the indigenous inhabitants intruders in their own homes and mendicants for a place to live. Judged by any civilized standard, such a law is unjust.…[31]

The modern focus on human rights and international law

These examples of legal shortsightedness and active assistance in a course of conduct violating the basic tenets of the Lord's Prayer have great relevance to the problems of the twenty-first century. As the old colonialism fades away and new types of dominance take its place, so much greater is the duty of lawyers to be vigilant about the end result of their work. Even more vigilance is required now, because—as we've already observed—the damaging effects are not clearly evident.

In particular, as we move into the twenty-first century, the lawyer needs to keep in constant focus the possible adverse effect on other people's human rights of any advice he may give to his client. Instances cited in many pages of this book show that the areas of possible abuse are numerous. The problems often come disguised. Lawyers are called in to advise their clients as to how best they can profit from a situation, how best they can evade detection, how best they can launder their gains. The twenty-first century lawyer needs to be on his or her guard. Else the exploitations and deprivations of colonialism that lawyers assisted and justified will be repeated in another milieu under other forms. The practices of commercialism in our age may seem as indefensible to our successors as the practices of colonialism in a previous age seem to ours.

It is to be hoped that injustices of the nature described above will not continue to be entrenched by judicial pronouncements and by legal technicalities. The lesson of legal assistance to colonialism acquires intense relevance for the new forms of domination that subjugate weaker peoples by economic power, rather than the power of the sword. All of this activity takes place free of moral control, today as in the past, because these areas successfully receive tacit, and sometimes express, endorsement from the legal order of the day. As in centuries past, the spotlight of legal ethics continues to focus on micro, rather than macro, conduct. Once again, therefore, the principles of the Lord's Prayer should be kept in constant focus.

Law reform

Translated into practical terms, in the context of the duties of a Christian lawyer, this means not merely that he or she seek after justice but also that he or she seek out and strive to correct the ways in which the law works injustice. Merely applying the law as it stands, while not straining himself or herself to correct it where the law itself operates unjustly, would not be conduct adequate for the lawyer committed to the values encapsulated in the Prayer. In the words of a distinguished Australian judge: "If the law itself is an obstacle to justice, the duty of the Christian lawyer extends to seeking its reform."[32]

Government Ethics

Power magnifies responsibility

To the Christian in any walk of life, the command to do God's will on earth would have deep meaning. Yet the ability to do God's will on earth is magnified severalfold in the hands of those who hold authority in any sphere— social, economic, executive, legislative, or judicial. The particular significance of this invocation for the Christian lawyer and judge needs scarcely to be mentioned. It would be idle for him or her to speak of the hallowedness of God's name while his or her own conduct actually negates one of the prime attributes of that hallowedness. As *Harper's Bible Dictionary* points out: "Justice is demanded of all the people but particularly of the political authorities."[33] They must "See that justice is done—help those who are oppressed, give orphans their rights, and defend widows" (Isaiah 1:17). There is also a special message in Jeremiah for those who are in authority: "Listen to what I, the Lord, am saying. See that justice is done every day. Protect the one who is being cheated from the one who is cheating him. If you don't, the evil you are doing will make my anger burn like a fire that cannot be put out" (Jeremiah 21:11–12).

Bribery

One of the prime obstacles to democratic government, which is manifesting itself in all parts of the world, developing and developed alike, is bribery—the process by which decisions in the interests of society are being converted into decisions in the interests of those who pay the politicians.

Bribery can take various forms, from wining and dining those in power, to paying for their political expenses, to directly depositing money into secret bank accounts. All of these methods are practiced, and each in its way is a subversion of democracy, if democracy means true representation of the wishes and the will of the people.

Some of these methods have become institutionalized to such an extent that they are taken for granted. If eternal vigilance is the price of democracy, the temptation to relax that eternal vigilance is a subversion of democracy.

Democracy is a cherished value highlighted by the Western democracies in their negotiations with the developing world, even to the extent of stipulating it as a condition for the grant of aid. Yet many an industrial venture of the Western world subverts democracy by bribery of Third World politicians for the advancement of its interests, even as their own governments look on. This is especially true in the field of armaments, where such bribery is well documented.[34]

Moreover, there is a great temptation to support governments in the developing world, however repressive they may be, if such governments provide a secure environment for international trade. If democracy be indeed a major value, this is a major inconsistency between profession and practice. The temptation to yield to it is great and, by yielding to it, human misery is perpetuated in a vast sector of the world's population.

Lobbying

Lobbying has become an accepted feature of the political landscape. Interests with the funds to do so maintain permanent lobbies in legislatures. The lobbyists' business is to woo legislators in favor of the policies their clients want governments to accept. Vast industries can spend handsomely on lobbyists and receive very good service from them.

There are various limitations on the means a lobbyist can adopt, but the whole institution makes for inequality when one compares the lobbying facilities available to one cause with those available to a rival, however just the rival's cause may be. For example, pollution and environmental devastation are caused by major industry with ample lobbying funds to spend. Those resisting it are not similarly equipped, and so their influence on individual legislators is considerably less. Moreover, the well-paid lobbyist has honed his professional skills to a fine art.

It is of course the right of every citizen, and of every interest, to approach individual legislators but, in its modern form, the tendency and the temptation to abuse this right, in negation of the principles of democracy and equality, is one that needs to be watched. If not, there is grave damage to the public welfare.

Parliamentary malpractice

Almost the very first step in bringing down God's kingdom on earth is to ensure integrity at the highest levels of the earthly kingdom. It is indeed at the level of the highest legislatures that the process begins—and that is why the Prayer is traditionally recited at the commencement of business in the legislatures of many Christian countries. Yet one hears increasingly of corruption at this very level. Indeed, in the British Parliament, whose reputation as a whole has been among the highest, alleged malpractices recently attracted much public attention—for example, the "cash for questions" accusation that large sums of money are paid by interested parties to members for asking questions in Parliament.

In October 1996, the Speaker of the House of Commons, Miss Boothroyd, told the House:

> While the House has been adjourned very serious allegations have been widely made about the conduct of a number of members. Indeed, the reputation of the House as a whole has been thrown into question....I hope the Committee on Standards and Privileges will find it possible to make an early special report to the House.[35]

There is also a Committee (the Nolan Committee) charged with the responsibility of conducting a close scrutiny of public ethical standards. The Parliamentary Committee on Standards has been appointed to handle complaints about members of Parliament.

The allegation of a lapse in standards in this ancient legislature, which prides itself on its integrity, is cause for similar vigilance in legislatures throughout the world. We do not even begin our journey toward the kingdom visualized by the Prayer without a deep commitment to ending corruption at the highest legislative levels.

The denigration of bureaucracies

Bureaucracies must be obedient to the policy directives of the government of the day. However, once these directives are received, they must be implemented without favoritism and without fear.

There has been a strong trend, however, in many countries to undermine the independence of bureaucracies, and to divert them from their proper path of service to the public onto the path of service to the government of the day. This turns out to be service to the political party and the politicians in power, even to the extent of bending the law to serve their interests. As a result, law and order become subverted, and the rights of the public undermined. Bureaucracies touch the lives of the people at every level, and the transformation of bureaucracies into agencies for the advancement of particular individuals or political groups is one of the greatest and most effective threats to democracy. It is essential to proper government that bureaucracies should not be diverted by considerations of fear or self-advancement from implementing the law in the service of the public. They are servants of the public and not servants of the political authorities of the day. The individual conscience of millions of bureaucrats across the world needs to be mobilized to stop this denigration of basic rights. That same conscience must also be mobilized against susceptibility to bribery, which has now become rampant in many countries.

Every one of the factors discussed thus far increases the turbulence of the waters we must negotiate in the new century. We need to build strong moral supports if we are not to be sucked in by the currents raging all around us. Yet we continue to clutch at straws, believing that the answers can be supplied by the unaided conscience of each individual. There are great logs floating around us, to which we can turn for support, but we let them pass us by. These are the solid moral principles enshrined in humanity's religious inheritance. Without them, we drown in the turbulence.

Whether one is Christian or not, whether one is religious or not, one must accept that these principles commend themselves to one's sense of equity, and also that the large segment of the world's population—which accepts one or another of the major religions—will find practical inspiration and strength for a new approach to these problems by juxtaposing the principles of the Lord's Prayer with the problems of our time.

After this catalogue of temptations, we must now turn to some instances where the law itself seems to encourage and protect moral wrongdoing.

CHAPTER 15

SOME TEMPTATIONS ARISING FROM LEGAL PROTECTION OF MORAL WRONGDOING

The exaltation of an individual's legal rights often results in a disregard of one's social obligations. As a result, a feeling develops that when one is acting within the realm of individual freedom that is protected by law, one is doing no wrong, because one's act is lawful.

To Comply Only With the Letter of the Law

It is very easy to persuade oneself that one is living a good life when one lives in such a manner as to avoid any conflict with the law. However, merely being on the right side of the law is no guarantee of a virtuous life. Some of the most rapacious exploiters of the weak and helpless, and some of the most artful criminals, are adept at being on the right side of the law. They never clash with the criminal law, and can be charged with no legal offense.

Yet they can lead the most unchristian lives because life in accordance with what Christ taught in the Prayer goes far beyond mere compliance with the law.

The legalistic interpretation of laws and compliance with the letter rather than the spirit is anathema to the teaching of Jesus. Indeed, even in regard to the concept of human rights—which has in a sense grown up to neutralize the legalism of the law—there is sometimes a tendency toward reliance on the letter rather than the spirit.

Pope John Paul II in the first encyclical of his reign saw the danger of literalism, even in the field of human rights:

...[T]he Church, aware that the "letter" on its own can kill, while only "the spirit gives life," must continually ask, together with these people of goodwill, whether the Declaration of Human Rights and the acceptance of their "letter" mean everywhere also the actualization of their "spirit." Indeed, well founded fears arise that very often we are still far from this actualization and that at times the spirit of social and public life is painfully opposed to the declared "letter" of human rights.[1]

To Rely on Freedom of Contract

One can, in purported reliance on the principle of free contract, ignore inequality of bargaining power to the extent of driving harsh and unconscionable bargains with those in a weaker economic position.

The law has for centuries turned a blind eye to the stark and obvious fact of bargaining inequality and authorized the sanctity of "free" contract. A contract "freely entered into" was considered binding on both parties, as the integrity of the wills of both parties had to be respected. It thus offered the stronger party a temptation to exploit the weakness of the other, despite the fact that there was no semblance of "free contract" between a millionaire employer and a job applicant with a starving family. Yet, for centuries the law was blind to such realities. For example, in a well-known English case of the last century, a coal miner's widow was prevented from receiving damages for her husband's death in the coal mine resulting from the mine owner's negligence, on the basis that he had, as a prelude to his employment, entered into a contract absolving his employer from all liability even if he, the miner, should suffer injury or death in the service of his employer. That contract of the miner was held to be sacrosanct in pursuance of the principle of free contract, and the courts dared not interfere in that sacrosanct area.

To Rely on Freedom of Expression

A large media company can, in assertion of the right of freedom of expression, stifle the freedom of the smaller media by either swallowing them up or drowning their voice.

Professor Thomas J. Emerson, a noted writer on freedom of expression, has observed:

The basic theory underlying the legal framework [of freedom of expression] has remained substantially unchanged since its development in the seventeenth and eighteenth centuries. But the conditions under which it must be applied have greatly altered. There has been little effort to reappraise legal doctrines and institutions in the light of the new situation.[2]

As a result, the legal and constitutional protection of free expression is being twisted into an instrument for the suppression of fresh ideas and values.[3] The law still turns a blind eye to these examples of the suppression of freedom in the name of freedom of expression.

To Exploit the Concept of Absolute Ownership

Modern concepts of property leave to the owner the absolute right to do with that property what the owner wills. The property could be damaged or destroyed by the owner without any concern for the impact of such actions on others. Crops could be burnt, land devastated by mining, fertile land left fallow, or noxious materials dumped upon it that would contaminate it for the foreseeable future.

It is necessary that there be a social orientation built into the concept of ownership, for modern technology makes available numerous methods, unknown before, of impairing the social usefulness of land.

To Hide Behind the Screen of Corporate Personality

Another huge arena of wrongdoing, though not so readily visible, has opened up owing to the growth of corporate might and the principle of corporate personality. These introduce immense possibilities of abuse of power, with temptations to wrongdoing on a scale never known in prior ages.

A screen of invisibility has been thrown up, shielding from sight those who cause deprivations on a hitherto unprecedented scale, and indeed screening the results of their acts from their own eyes. In his encyclical *Quadragesimo Anno*, Pope Pius XI referred to the increasing ease with which detection can be evaded, for "by hiding under the shelter of a joint name, the worst of injustices and frauds are perpetrated." Sensitivities to wrongdoing have thereby been blunted, and those who are apparently furthest away from criminality are often perpetrators of a harm whose magnitude dwarfs anything known in the past.

Current legal concepts of private enterprise blunt the conscience still further and, in the words of the same encyclical, "Some have become so hardened to the stings of conscience as to hold that they are allowed in any manner whatsoever to increase their profits."

Moreover, under current international and national corporate law, it is possible for the activities of a corporate entity to be masked under hundreds of corporate registrations in a variety of countries, so that the difficulty of detection makes the temptation to corporate wrongdoing under the screen of corporate personality all the more inviting. In fact, in some cases of corporate wrongdoing, even the entire resources of a department of government working full time on the project for some years may be unable to strip away the several interlocking and complex international corporate registrations of a single multinational corporate agency, so as to get to the source of a particular wrongful or illegal act.[4]

This range of trespasses and temptations in our time should make it clear that many of them are concealed through distance, remoteness of responsibility, screens of corporate invisibility, the complex cycles of cause and effect in the international marketplace, and the influence of the media. It is easy to desensitize a person to the effects of his or her wrongdoing when cause and effect are so powerfully screened from each other. A wailing infant on one's doorstep is a more powerful incentive to action than a million starving infants ten thousand miles away in a distant country. It penetrates into one's consciousness far more tellingly, even though one had no hand in the privations of the infant on one's doorstep, and even in cases where it can in fact be demonstrated that one's actions have in fact contributed to the privation of the million children. This is why special vigilance is required, as far as is possible, to ensure that we do not commit trespasses whose effects are not immediately visible to us. Else we could be asked the question, so eloquently asked in the epigraph to a recent film, "Can you hear the sound of dreadful screaming all around, which people usually call silence?"[5]

Indeed, this is a dispiriting catalogue of the temptations that beset our path. The outlook seems dark and gloomy, but there are always gleams of hope that shine through the darkest clouds. Let us look upward to a new beginning, and let us end on a note of hope, for if these temptations can be substantially overcome, humanity is only at the threshold of a magnificent destiny. As Martin Luther King, Jr., observed, on receiving the Nobel Peace Prize:

> When our days become dreary with low-hovering clouds and our nights become darker than a thousand midnights, we will know that we are living in the creative turmoil of a genuine civilization struggling to be born.

PART THREE

A GUIDE TO THE
TWENTY-FIRST
CENTURY

CHAPTER 16

THE RUN-IN TO THE
TWENTY-FIRST CENTURY

P art One outlined the power of the Prayer, and how it can be more effectively harnessed in solving the practical problems of our time. In Part
Two we examined the temptations and trespasses that beset our age, and the
ways in which the Prayer can help humanity from being dragged to its
destruction by those forces. As we face a new century and a new millennium, we need to chart out ways in which the Prayer can serve as a guide in
negotiating the tempestuous waters that lie ahead.

Taking Stock

As the blood-drenched twentieth century draws to its close, we peer from
its upper rungs into the twenty-first, very much in the fashion of a builder
peering from his ladder into an upper storey that he is shortly to construct.
From his vantage point he has a clearer view of the errors below and
the opportunities above. If the builder does not pause to take stock and
correct those errors, they will be repeated, and the twenty-first century
will be a rerun of the wars, the oppressions, the arms races, the genocide,
and the tortures that made a shambles of the twentieth. The difference, if
any, will be in the scale of the inhumanities practiced by humans upon
themselves. These will transcend any we have yet known, for the art of
imposing suffering would have been further refined by the progress of science.

Simply stated, we shall have more of the same, unless individuals, societies, institutions, and nation-states look elsewhere for their guiding principles than to self-interest and materialistic values. As the old adage goes,
tomorrow is decided today; and the shape of the twenty-first century is
being largely determined by us in the twentieth.

The Long Reign of Machiavelli

For centuries, statecraft has openly pursued Machiavellian values. Self-interest was consistently the determining force of government policy despite lofty pretensions to the contrary. The Florentine writer, servant of the Medicis and envoy to the Borgias, has had an influence far transcending his Italian environment. He has, indeed, been for centuries a dominant influence in the boudoirs of the powerful. One can see, in the mind's eye, the portrait of Machiavelli hanging over the corridors of power.

Machiavelli had an Indian intellectual precursor, Kautilya, who, fifteen centuries earlier, in his *Arthasastra*, expounded the virtues of expediency as the guiding code of princes. Though both these writers sharply contradicted their cultural and religious traditions, they have both commanded, over the centuries, the allegiance of some of the most influential figures of each age.

Strength and harshness were virtues, rivals were to be eliminated, policies were to be freed from the need for consistency, people were to be manipulated, promises were to be broken. "[F]oxiness should be well concealed: one must be a great feigner and dissembler…, a skilful deceiver always finds plenty of people who will let themselves be deceived."[1] Military matters were to be the focus of the prince's concern, for "a ruler, then, should have no other objective and no other concern, nor occupy himself with anything except war and its methods and practices…."[2]

Consequently, wars, the greatest demonstration of a ruler's strength, were useful and to be indulged in as instruments of statecraft. They not only elevated the position of the prince, but also cemented national cohesion. It followed that "the prince's only aim, the only art which he should ponder and learn, is the art of war; it is the only art necessary for those who wish to command others."

These are the principles that have guided politics for centuries. They are a far cry from the loftier tone of such works as Cicero's *De Officiis*, advocating a high standard of probity in public affairs—a work whose principles Machiavelli specifically refuted. Figuratively speaking, Machiavelli's *The Prince* has for centuries been lying by the bedside of nearly every ruler, its pages open at some piece of Machiavellian craftiness. To the ears of rulers, its words sound more relevant than those of the Bible. Great empires have been built on the rules of Machiavelli's book by kings and statesmen who privately followed its tenets and publicly recited the Lord's Prayer.

The Clausewitzean Century

War was to become even more respectable in the nineteenth century, for the German philosopher Clausewitz taught that war was a natural extension of diplomacy. "We see, therefore, that War is not merely a political act, but also a real political instrument, a continuation of political commerce, a carrying out of the same by other means."[3] It was a means of state negotiation, perfectly respectable and perfectly normal. It was to be indulged in with no greater reluctance than the polite diplomacy of the conference table. If lives were to be snuffed out and untold suffering inflicted, such considerations should not cloud the clarity of purpose and policy that were the characteristics of good rulership.

> Now, philanthropists may easily imagine there is a skilful method of disarming and overcoming an enemy without causing great bloodshed, and that this is the proper tendency of the Art of War. However plausible this may appear, still it is an error which must be extirpated; for in such dangerous things as War, the errors which proceed from a spirit of benevolence are the worst.[4]

Where did international law stand in this scheme of things? Clausewitz had an answer:

> Self-imposed restrictions, almost imperceptible and hardly worth mentioning, termed usages of International Law, accompany it [war] without essentially impairing its power.[5]

For the century of Napoleon and Bismarck, this made sense. They had shown in their age how the sword could blaze a dazzling trail toward international power and domestic adulation. A scientific age demanded scientific statecraft, free of the fuzziness of sentimental effusions. If war was the path to power and glory, the clearheaded prince must guide himself in that direction undeterred by muddled advisers who saw it as immoral. Clausewitz gained such general recognition that his work "quickly became the 'Bible' of the German officers"[6] and played an influential role in shaping what came to be called the "Dogma of the Battle of Annihilation" which, in its turn, dominated German strategy in the two World Wars.[7] The nineteenth century, which brought the art of war to new perfection, came to be known as the Clausewitzean century. It was in its shadow that the twentieth century saw the light of day. Since there was no change in course between the nineteenth century and the twentieth, the twentieth has itself become a Clausewitzean century. Another Clausewitzean century looms before us if we do not change course and accord priority to the teachings of Jesus Christ over those of such spurious guides as Clausewitz and Machiavelli.

The Cult of Pragmatism

Throughout these centuries, while lip service was regularly paid to Christianity's core teachings of peace and goodwill, these were viewed as irrelevant to the harsh realities of a competitive world. Attitudes of supposed intellectual objectivity played their part in relegating these teachings to the realm of unattainable Utopianism. Practical statesmanship required a matter-of-fact treatment of the stuff of politics, shorn of emotional, religious, and moral overtones. The entire significance of an act or concept was contained within its practical consequences.

In our time, these attitudes have, if at all, been further reinforced. The unarticulated stance of those in authority at every level is that, in our advanced state of social, economic, political, and legal organization, we must outgrow the childish attitudes that religion teaches and buckle down to a realistic approach to the practical problems of our age. The spirit of unbridled commercialism that is abroad, especially in these closing years of the twentieth century, powerfully reinforces this world-view. It is as though the heart is being torn out of humanistic endeavor and a cash box substituted in its place. Moreover, a soulless technology adds new dimensions of power to those who enjoy it.

Such is the temper of our times, and such is the attitude of many in authority. No better assurance can be found of a continuation into the next century of the pillage and rape that in many respects have made this century a big brother of the age of Genghis Khan.

There is a difference, however, that makes this century's record even more sinister. With such figures as Genghis Khan, power strode the stage alone. Today, power has allies whom Genghis Khan could never have known. Technology and monetarism stand by its side, their sharpened tools at its willing service, regardless of the moral issues involved. Power is thus magnified beyond anything known in the past, and as power magnifies, so does its potential for abuse.

The Century of Blighted Hope

Peace was in the air at the opening of this century. Peace societies by the hundreds were strewn across the globe. The great Peace Conference of 1899, the first global assembly of its kind in history, had just concluded at The Hague. The Nobel Peace Prize had been instituted in recognition of the universal yearning for fresh approaches to peace. The path to a better future seemed clear at last. Humanity would at last make its rendezvous with Utopia.

The Great War dashed those hopes. In its opening quarter alone, the new century eclipsed its predecessor in the scale of human slaughter. Yet the spirit of peace was not dead. It rose again, resurgent after the War, with elaborate blueprints for the bright new era of peace which, after the travail and slaughter, seemed to offer the only rational hopes for survival. In the picturesque language of General Smuts at the Peace Conference of Versailles, "The tents have been struck and the great caravan of humanity is once more on the march."

Sadly, even those hopes were blighted. At the Peace Conference, the moves to invest the League of Nations with effective powers to maintain peace were thwarted, and America itself did not join the League—despite the idealism of its president, Woodrow Wilson, who had conceived the idea of the League. The League turned out to be a palace of broken dreams. The plaintive speech of the Belgian delegate at these debates captured the frustration of those times:

> In such circumstances I feel how poor a thing is my eloquence. We need a Demosthenes, a Mirabeau, a Jaurès on this platform. I call upon you to listen to the sound that comes to you from beyond these walls, a great moaning like to that of the sea. It is the voices of the mothers and the wives who are mourning for those whom they have lost. It is the voice that rises from the peoples, the working masses who are weary of the miseries and of the plagues which are striking them and continue to strike them....It is the voice of those who are sleeping buried on the battlefield, who have given their youth and sacrificed hope and joy in order that there might be justice in the world.[8]

Despite such hopes, another world war succeeded hard on the heels of the first, with scarcely any breathing space between. And as if World War II were not enough to drive the lesson home, we have, since its termination in

1945, had a grand procession of little wars, nearly 150 of them, swallowing up around twenty million lives. Since 1945, there have been armed conflicts around the globe every year, with the possible exception of 1968.[9] More detailed estimates such as that of the Tofflers[10] show that in the 2,340 weeks between 1945 and 1990, the world enjoyed a grand total of only three that were truly war-free. In 1990 alone, the Stockholm Institute of Peace Research counted thirty-one armed conflicts in progress. Tribalism, primitive as any in recorded history, has surfaced alarmingly, and expressions such as "ethnic cleansing" have passed into common parlance. Brutality and human rights violations are practiced on such a scale as to tear apart the very concept of humanity. So much for the delusion that we are living in an era of comparative peace after the cataclysm of World War II.

Knowledge Without Wisdom

The twentieth century has seen the greatest explosion of knowledge in the history of humanity. Yet a century so splendid in its creativity has demonstrated that unprecedented violence can flourish in the midst of an unprecedented burgeoning of knowledge. Knowledge comes, but wisdom lingers. The assumption that knowledge and human happiness go hand in hand now lies in ruins. Knowledge without the wisdom to use it leads us nowhere. Masters of an unrivaled body of knowledge, we yet need to turn back in desperation to the wisdom of the ages to teach us how to use it. That wisdom is found encapsulated in the Prayer.

Our global cultures are rich in traditions of peace, but we have turned our back on them. Those traditions, deeply rooted in the great religions, still exercise a powerful grip on the minds and hearts of the present generation, but are crowded out by materialistic values. Flaunted in the marketplaces and the political assemblies of the world, these latter values are often endorsed by the clear-cut and reductionist logic of academia. The bridges between religion and international order have been systematically destroyed, especially over the past four centuries. So great is the separation between them that scholars now seriously ask whether a reconciliation between law and religion is still possible.[11] The same is even more true in the fields of international law and human rights. Can we, as we enter the twenty-first century, attempt to rebuild the bridges or is it already too late? Will this separation between the government of the human family and the traditions of the human family cast a pall over the future?

A Century About to Enter on Its Inheritance

As Thomas Carlyle once observed, the centuries are all the lineal children of one another. The twenty-first century will be the child of the violence-ridden twentieth. Just as the twenty-first century will inherit the achievements of the twentieth, so also will it inherit its racism and its hatreds. These will blaze into the twenty-first century and will not be snuffed out as the chimes of midnight ring out on December 31, 1999. Before we know it, the twenty-first century will have entered upon its inheritance, as the natural heir to all the hatreds and violence of the twentieth.

Born to that inheritance, the twenty-first century will have an even less hopeful beginning on the road to peace than its precursor. This reality offers an index to the magnitude of the task awaiting humanity if it is to steer itself in a different direction as it commences that century. It emphasizes the need for a reversion to the fundamental values of civilization that are often submerged in specious economic, racial, and historical arguments.

The current world order is reinforced by powerful interests that have profited from it. As Winston Churchill has so rightly observed, great reforms offend great interests.[12] Those interests, if they feel threatened, will offer all the resistance they can muster.

As the forthcoming century of last opportunity succeeds the outgoing century of lost opportunity, we need to engage in a real, probing debate on the inadequacies of our current systems for the governance of human conduct. To place our trust once more in principles from which, over and over again, we have only reaped a harvest of violence and disorder is to sow the seeds of our own destruction.

There is an urgent need to mount a race for peace as we enter the twenty-first century. The items outlined in Part Two are major obstacles upon the course. The changes in attitude that will overcome these obstacles must come from within, for, as Mahatma Gandhi said, "We must be the change we wish to see in the world." The Lord's Prayer provides a guide toward that inner change which will produce the outer result. It is a powerful aid and will "unlock hitherto tightly sealed doors of hope and transform our imminent cosmic elegy into a psalm of creative fulfilment."[13]

The Start of a New Historical Era

Against this picture of the run-in to the next century, it is heartening to realize there are many reasons to believe that a new era is opening in human history. This makes it possible for us to make a break with the past that has failed us, and chart out a new course.

Apart from the general problems and trends outlined in the previous and succeeding chapters, there is a new circumstance of recent occurrence on the world scene that needs to be briefly noted. It has much relevance to the subject of this work and offers some new avenues of approach.

The collapse of the Soviet Union was an electric moment in history. The end of the Cold War was a seminal event whose many repercussions on the international scene have yet to be assessed. It gives us brand-new opportunities for charting out the human destiny afresh. It also passes a very heavy responsibility to the sole-surviving superpower, the United States of America. Indeed, although there have been great empires in the past, not one of them had the *global* reach and influence that has today fallen to the United States, a nation thus given the opportunity of playing a significant role in helping to mold the global future. America acts as its citizens would wish it to act, and millions of American citizens, attuned to a more justice-oriented and universalist attitude toward global affairs, can make a most significant impact.

It is already sufficiently clear that the end of the Cold War has brought to the surface a vast array of new factors which, in combination, signal the commencement of a new phase in international relations in which many old assumptions no longer hold true. These include:

1. Increased scope for international action to states in difficulties
2. The emergence of new states on a note of high idealism
3. Failed ideologies
4. A stimulus for global plans to stop the escalation of global wars
5. The stress on pre-conflict peace-building
6. The search for a new principle of equilibrium
7. The shift from cohabitation to cooperation
8. The search for common goals for humanity
9. The expansion of intercultural understanding
10. The increasing scope for a religious contribution to the future world order

11. The weakening boundaries of the sovereign state
12. The growth of people's power

1. Increased Scope for International Action

The end of the Cold War has meant that a number of states that were teetering on the brink of survival now lack a patron to support them. Some of them have virtually collapsed, with no superpower rushing to their aid.

This provides the global community with a great new opportunity for concentrated international effort. Where formerly the dominant superpower might have resisted external intrusions, today the stage is set for a truly international effort to assist. The previous Secretary-General of the United Nations drew attention to this feature,[14] pointing out that rescuing failed states has become a United Nations responsibility. When the United Nations is involved in the task of rehabilitation, it has a unique opportunity to strengthen institutions, encourage political participation, protect human rights, and promote economic and social development.

As the positive duties of the world community multiply severalfold, so also do its opportunities, in a way not known in the era of superpower rivalry.

2. The Emergence of New States on a Note of High Idealism

The disintegration of the Soviet Union has seen the emergence of a number of new states, on a scale that can only be compared to the emergence of new states at the end of colonialism. Many of the opportunities that then existed for helping those states to structure themselves in accordance with principles of the rule of law were lost, owing to superpower rivalries and other factors. Today we have another such opportunity, with a helping hand that could be stretched out by the global community as a whole.

Despite their many problems, they start on a note of high idealism. Many of the states released from the former Soviet Empire have introduced into their constitutions a range of human rights clauses along the lines of the Universal Declaration of Human Rights, and many of them have pledged themselves to an acceptance of international law as part of their national law. This has also meant a renewed examination of their cultural roots, and a deeper search of their traditions and ideologies. There is great opportunity here for assisting these enthusiastic new players on the global stage—

who will soon be asserting themselves, once they overcome the initial problems of new nationhood.

3. Failed Ideologies

The Cold War divided the world on the basis of opposing ideologies. Socialist and communist states justified their overall control of society and the economy on ideological grounds. The state would care for the individual and see to his or her material needs. The individual, with full confidence in the paternalism of the state, could surrender to it many spheres of his or her freedom of action. The ideology of the state was all-embracing, and religious influences were discouraged.

With the end of the Cold War, socialism and communism could no longer hold their own as unquestioned state philosophies—creating an ideological vacuum. The philosophy of individualism and of the free marketplace was scarcely adequate to fill this conceptual void. A revived interest in religion and a search for traditional values partially filled the place formerly occupied by Marxism.

The dormant forces of religion, released from their sixty-year confinement under Marxist rule, are resurgent and spreading their nonmaterialist thought waves throughout these communities.

4. A Stimulus for Global Plans

With the two superpowers in effect policing the world, local wars could scarcely reach any proportions before the guardian power bestirred itself and took appropriate action to snuff out the flames. The withdrawal of superpower vigilance resulted in local wars escalating out of control to the point where war in half a dozen places in the world has become commonplace. Television screens relay them across the world, and one is no longer surprised at a war careering out of control. It is a normal phenomenon of the post-Cold War scene.

War has thus in a sense been devalued. It was once high currency, handled only by the superpowers. It is now small change in everyone's hands. Everyone seems to have the right to wage war, because the chances of getting away with it are great.

Waging war is no longer the monopoly of the few but has become a mass phenomenon, a means to live by and to self-affirmation. Everybody has the right to wage war with everybody else.[15]

This situation is so patently intolerable, and such a drain on the rest of the world, that the rest of the world is stimulated as never before to move into some sort of purposeful plan to diminish these conflicts—a situation that was beyond the reach of other nation-states during the era of two-power dominance.

5. The Stress on Pre-Conflict Peace-Building

In the speech of the United Nations Secretary-General already referred to, the point was made that a new concept that is emerging is the concept of peace-building. In place of the post-conflict peace-building of the past, the world in the future will need to explore pre-conflict peace-building as well.

When a nation shows signs of falling apart, a mending operation must be mounted to identify and consolidate structures creating greater trust and well-being among the peoples concerned. It may be possible in this fashion to forestall the splintering of the state through commercial, cultural, and educational projects aimed at consolidating its unity.

Just as preventive diplomacy can forestall wars between states, anticipatory peace-building can forestall wars within states. The world community has a role to play in such activity, for turbulence anywhere destabilizes peace everywhere.

6. The Search for a New Principle of Equilibrium

The old world order was based upon the age-old principle of balance of power. Kautilya in India, Cardinal Wolsey in England, Machiavelli in Italy, all extolled the virtues of this principle, which for two thousand years has been looked upon as the key to stability.

The Cold War was a manifestation of the ultimate in checks and balances, for two superpowers, each with the power to destroy the world a thousand times over, confronted each other and provided an uneasy balance of terror that prevented major war. That balance has gone. One superpower, with all the goodwill in the world, can scarcely hold the scales even in international conflicts of interest.

A new source of equilibrium must be found, and it perhaps lies in the acceptance of overarching principles rooted in the need for global survival. Such principles would bind all nations alike. Finding bases of agreement for such principles is a new conceptual challenge. The deep springs of the world's cultural traditions will need to be tapped, for superficial and temporary solutions will scarcely meet this new challenge.

7. The Shift From Cohabitation to Cooperation

This topic is closely related to the last.

The world can no longer live by mere coexistence. Under massive pressures such as global ecological threats and the proliferation of nuclear weapons, narrow notions of sovereignty have yielded before the broader global need for concerted action. Technological advances in communications, transport, and medical services render individual national action manifestly inadequate, however powerful the nation involved. Nations can therefore no longer stand passive, discharging their international obligations by noninterference with their neighbors—they need to join hands in active resolution of the common problems facing them all.

Under the Cold War dispensation, the cooperation of the two superpowers meant in practice that the large majority of nations followed suit. In the post-Cold War era, cooperative action needs to stem in greater measure from the independent volition of all states. All are called upon to be more active participants in the common task of pooling their positive energies for the construction of a better world for all.

Since nearly all major world cultures are bound up with religion, this is a time for exploring elements of commonality in religion which could thus provide a cement for linking global attitudes. Their common teachings on peace, human dignity, compassion, and service to others form a substantial core around which the spirit of global cooperation can be built.

8. The Search for Common Goals

During the period of the Cold War, there was a sharp cleavage and antagonism between the economic, political, and military goals of the two superpowers. This rendered it difficult to agree on common global goals for the world community. With the easing of that polarized situation, the formulation of common goals for mankind may perhaps be more easily achieved.

Such goals would transcend national boundaries and interests. National interests necessarily beget national rivalries. There are winners and losers in the race toward such interests. There are allies and opponents, friends and enemies. The pursuit of national interests has traditionally divided the world. It has also aggravated world problems, for it invariably leads to short-term solutions that temporarily satisfy national aspirations but create larger problems with international dimensions. Every country must, of course, have short-term national goals, but there is now a large slate of long-term global goals that every country can pursue with no detriment to its national interests.

The route to global survival, which the future dictates, is that all nations join together in setting for themselves collectively a series of global goals. This task is made easier also by the proliferation of areas where global cooperation is imperative and by the knowledge explosion and the information highways that will overcome barriers to the exclusiveness of knowledge.

In the formulation of these goals, traditional values and inspirations can play a significant role. Indeed, the task could well be described as the task of formulating a set of higher values to meet the needs of the new millennium—a task that must necessarily take account of the traditional values ingrained in the world's humane traditions.

9. The Expansion of Intercultural Understanding

One of the most positive outcomes of the end of the Cold War was the demolition of the Berlin Wall and the lifting of the Iron Curtain—symbolic of an opening up of all sections of the world to one another. Cultural exchanges are taking place on a scale never known before. China and its ancient civilization are taking America by storm. American music finds its way into the Red Square. The treasures of Russian culture are more freely seen in the West.

As with culture, so also with religion. The religions are opening out to one another. Interreligious conferences proliferate. Societies, such as the Assisi Society, recall the great interreligious dialogues of the past, as when during the Crusades Saint Francis of Assisi exchanged religious dialogue with Sultan Melek el Kamal, or when the Emperor Akbar, at the height of the Moghul Empire, had discussions with Christian theologians. The wisdom of Buddhism, Hinduism, Confucianism, Jainism, Zoroastrianism—

hitherto little known in the West—is sweeping through into one vast inter-cultural dialogue that is building up in all parts of the world.

With intercultural understanding comes political understanding, for it is only through an appreciation of other cultures that other political points of view can be understood.

10. The Increasing Scope for a Religious Contribution

The post-Cold War global configuration, as outlined above, opens up many opportunities for all religions to find common ground on the spiritual values inherent in them all, and not to be diverted by the rival claims of insti-tutionalized religious groups. They can thus make a greater inspirational input into matters of world governance. They also have opportunities as never before to lay to rest the notion that religion is necessarily a divisive factor, rousing emotions and fomenting wars. Undoubtedly religion has played this role frequently in history, and does so even today.

But that is precisely the opposite of the role it can and should be playing in these closing years of the century. This is the time for an appreciation of the great universal principles that lie behind all religions, rather than for a concentration on the dogmatic and ritualistic superstructures that divide the human family.

11. The Weakening Boundaries of the Sovereign State

There was a time when each nation-state attempted to be an island unto itself, and largely succeeded in doing so. What occurred within a country's borders was exclusively a matter for its rulers, who claimed the right and the ability to regulate it independently of external forces.

That has changed dramatically in the second half of this century. On the conceptual plane, human rights have pierced the wall of sovereignty, open-ing the human rights situation in any country to the legitimate scrutiny of the world community. On the physical plane, modern technology has made every country dependent upon others in the environmental and eco-logical fields. On the economic plane, the world economy is becoming integrated as never before. On the communications plane, all walls of se-crecy that formerly surrounded nations have come crashing down like the Berlin Wall. On the organizational plane, nonstate actors, such as various international organizations and groups, and even individuals, have become global actors and have penetrated into states, where they act routinely and legitimately.

In other words, we are moving toward one world, free of the traditional isolationism of the nation-state. Global ideas and movements will dominate the world, however much the individual nation-state may tend to resist this.

12. The Growth of People's Power

During the period of East-West rivalries, popular movements were extinguished in many of the client states falling on either side of the Great Divide. Some were suppressed with a heavy hand, as happened in Hungary in 1956, Czechoslovakia in 1988, and Poland in 1981; and many a dictatorial regime, unpopular in the country, was propped up by the dominant external power.

The people's wishes, demonstrated peacefully across political and sectarian divisions, are now coming to be openly expressed, which was impossible before. The new phenomenon of people's power peacefully manifesting itself en masse is asserting its authority across the world. With people of all walks of life becoming increasingly conscious of their political, economic, and social rights, there is increased hope that in the world of the future the people's innate sense of justice will find more opportunities for expression, free of compelling external pressures that they are powerless to resist. The moral force of a nation, expressed through an outpouring of people's power, peacefully asserted, is a new force to be reckoned with.

All of the factors set out above combine in our time to offer religion a cardinal role in elevating the moral tone of the processes and personnel of government. There has probably never been in history an opportunity such as now exists for the major religions to pause in their tracks and take stock of the elements of commonality that bind them and their neighbors into a common community pursuing the common goals of universal peace. There was never a greater need for concentrating their undoubted inspirational force upon the task of avoiding catastrophe and conserving hope.

Far from being a force in human affairs that authoritative governments can suppress or liquidate, resurgent religion has proved its enduring vitality. Far from being "some kind of petrification of values past,"[16] religion has proved it is in tune with the most imaginative visions of the future. Far from being the slave of political and economic interests, it has shown that it can rise above the political and economic currents of any age, surviving with all its vigor when those currents have spent their force.

Charged with a new wave of idealism, the population of the world has the potential to meet the challenges that lie ahead, elevating the standards by which, individually and collectively, human affairs will be governed. However great the obstacles in the way of achieving a common global sovereignty, we can certainly move far on the path toward envisioning a common global civilization. That aim must reflect a balance between development, the environment, security, equity, and human rights. Finding a solution that will be fair to all nations will be imperative. The end of the Cold War provides a more conducive setting for that task than the world has enjoyed for centuries.

CHAPTER 17

THE CALL TO ACTION

The Lord's Prayer does not rest with its formulation of concepts, but contains a powerful call to action. This follows clearly from the assumption that the Prayer is to be uttered in a spirit of commitment and sincerity.

The commitments to which the Prayer ties down its reciter are that they do what they can to keep God's name hallowed ("hallowed be thy name"), to make possible the advent on earth of the rules that obtain in God's kingdom ("thy kingdom come"), and to do what lies in their power to ensure that God's will is done on earth ("thy will be done"). It is to these commitments that we now turn.

A. "HALLOWED"

For those who believe in an omnipotent God, the divinity is not merely holy but also the embodiment of majesty, truth, justice, power, love, and compassion.

The process of hallowing is quite clearly not a merely verbal exercise. Charles de Foucauld, in his spiritual outpourings, commented thus on "hallowed" as used in the Prayer:

> What is it, Lord, that I am expressing in these words? I am expressing the whole object of my desires, the whole aim and purpose of my life. I want to *hallow your name in my thoughts, words and actions.* And this means that I want to imitate your Son, Jesus, since he hallowed your name in his every thought, word and action.[1]

Action must therefore follow the word, unless the Prayer is to be reduced to an empty verbal shell.

Concentration on God's Attributes

Affirmation of the hallowedness of God is an abbreviated way of affirming the hallowedness of God's attributes. A concentration on the qualities of God provides an appropriate mental background for the commitments that follow. As Sri Ramakrishna, the Indian savant, has said:

> The magnetic needle always points towards the north, and hence it is that the sailing vessel does not lose its course. So long as the heart of man is directed towards God, he cannot be lost in the ocean of Worldliness.[2]

John Wesley gave expression to a similar thought when he said, "If the loving eye of the soul be steadily fixed on God [the] temptation soon vanishes away."[3]

By thus fixing attention on the attributes of the Almighty, the utterer is, to use the observation of Ramakrishna, taken away from the ocean of worldliness where values of a transitory nature tend to submerge the values of a transcendental nature that underlie the attributes of God. With a mind focused on them, a thoughtful recital of the Prayer will extract a wealth of meanings and overtones from the word "hallowed."

God's Hallowedness a Widely Shared Concept

Due respect for God's hallowedness has been a cause of contention between different religions through the centuries, and much blood has been spilt over this issue. In the contemplation of God's attributes, it is therefore important to note that most of the great religions, such as Hinduism, Judaism, Christianity, and Islam, tread common ground in the contemplation of God's majesty, the attributes of God, and the praise of God's name. In Islam, every chapter of the Koran opens with the words "In the name of God, the compassionate, the merciful," and numerous other Koranic verses and prayers expand upon the attributes of God.[4] In Judaism, the psalms of the Old Testament are replete with praises of the Lord, and the *Vedas* call upon the believer to "Chant the Name of the Lord and His Glory unceasingly."[5]

The *Bhagavad Gita* speaks of the splendor of God in terms that:

If the radiance of a thousand suns
   Were to burst at once into the sky
   That would be like the splendour of the Almighty One.[6]

It likewise links splendor with notions of purity and ubiquity, as where it says, "Supreme God, your light is brighter than the sun, your purity whiter than mountain snow, you are present wherever I go."

One must not forget, either, the extent to which traditional religions and belief systems hallow God in their prayers, as Creator and King. For instance, many traditional religions in Africa share this belief in a supernatural and omnipotent creator—as exemplified in the following prayer of the Kalahari Bushmen:

   Lord, Lord, you are the Lord
     You created all things
     You are the master of the forest
     You are the master of the animals
     You are our master and we are your servants
     You are the master of life and death
   You rule, we obey.[7]

Father Leonardo Boff, in his work on The Lord's Prayer,[8] gives us a telling historical example from a work dealing with the Spanish occupation of Mexico, showing the Aztecs' appreciation of the majesty of God. When the Franciscans arrived there in 1524 and preached the Christian concept of God to some high-ranking Aztec officials in the courtyard of St. Francis Friary, an Aztec scholar spoke thus to the missionaries, politely reminding them that their own beliefs ran parallel with Christian beliefs on the majesty of God:

   You have said that we do not know the Lord...
     the one from whom came the heavens and the earth...
     Our ancestors...
     they offered worship
     they honoured the Gods
     We know who it is
     to whom we owe our lives
     to whom we owe our birth

to whom we owe our conception
to whom we owe our upbringing
how we are to invoke the gods
how we are to pray.[9]

Much intolerance of other religions and belief systems lies in a lack of awareness of the universality of this concept.

As Boff observes, having cited this dialogue, what is important is that we need to consider what underlies the expression of hallowedness. It is insufficient to be content with a mere recital of that hallowedness, without probing the meanings that lie behind it.

Translating Hallowedness Into Action

The linkage between the invocation of God's hallowedness and the performance of Christian duty has received attention from several commentators of the highest eminence, including Saint Augustine and Martin Luther.

Augustine commented that the name of God, which is always holy in fact, should be held holy among humans by appropriate *conduct* on their part. Luther pursues the same idea in his *Kleine Katechismus,* explaining it as meaning praising and honoring God in our way *by our own words and deeds.*[10] It is true the petition does not speak of the conduct of humans but the attributes of God. Yet it would be a contradiction of the spirit of the exercise if the praise of God's name were reduced to its mere incantation, without an accompanying resolve to translate the respect thus shown into appropriate deeds.

The phrase "hallowed be thy name" is thus a commitment that locks the reciter into all the other principles of conduct integral to the Prayer. Accepting God's hallowedness not only by word but by deed is a precondition to whatever else one may ask of God in terms of the Prayer.

One wonders how often throughout the recorded history of the past two thousand years the phrase has been solemnly repeated—particularly in high places—without the accompanying conduct that hallows the name of God through compassion, charity, restraint from temptation, forgiveness, and assistance to those in need.

The Attributes of Hallowedness

What, then, are the attributes of hallowedness to which we commit allegiance and matching conduct? And in what way are these attributes relevant to matters of law and justice? This section will consider the attributes of God, not as though one is examining those of a remote god upon a distant throne, but with an eye to the practical relevance of those attributes to the present condition of humanity.

In interpreting the Prayer, we must be aware of the context in which it was revealed. In the Sermon on the Mount, before teaching the Lord's Prayer, Jesus stressed the need for imitation of the qualities of God: "Be ye therefore perfect, even as your Father which is in heaven is perfect" (Matthew 5:48). This, no doubt, would be looked upon as an unattainable standard, but it endorses the theme that the attributes of God are the ideal, set by Jesus himself, toward which all should strive. They are not perfections monopolized by God, but perfections that all are invited to imitate.

God As Creator

Embodied in this concept are the eternal nature of God as existing before time began and as continuing after time as we know it comes to an end. God eternal and timeless is the source of creation, the source of life, the source of justice, and the continuing source of our sustenance.

The concept of God as the source of all creation, of all life, and of all sustenance is a point of legal linkage eliminating all differences and distinctions between races and nations, however ancient or modern. If God created them all, and continues to be the direct source of their life and sustenance, no one section of the human family is beholden to another for its sustenance. If those who have abundance assist those who are in want, they are doing so not from what they own in their absolute right but from what they themselves have received out of the generosity of God. As objects of generosity, they must also show generosity to others, and not take a false pride in their own abundance.

Just as we have read into the word "our" a lack of any political, racial, or other groupings that stand in the way of complete equality, so we can read into the fact that God is the common source of sustenance of all groups and nations the total absence of any form of preordained economic dependence.

This is not to say, however, that there do not exist all manner of *de facto* linkages and dependencies for supply, for the world is economically inter-dependent. Yet there is a total elimination of any concept of economic bond-age in the notion of God as the common provider of sustenance for all.

God As Power (Physical)

Boundless power is one of the attributes most commonly associated with divinity. God's power is not without relevance to human conduct, for by placing the individual against a cosmic perspective, it underlines the futil-ity of unprincipled self-advancement and false assertions of superiority.

Numerous passages of the Old Testament speak in ringing terms of the power of God. Indeed, the word for greatness and glory (*El*, the root word for Elohim) is used in the Bible around 2,500 times in association with God.[11] The scriptures of other religions are, likewise, eloquent on this topic. For example, Krishna says in *The Bhagavad Gita*:

> Be very sure of this
> Of the whole [wide] universe
> The origin and dissolution too am I
> Higher than I
> There's nothing whatsoever
> On Me the universe is strung
> Like clustered pearls upon a thread[12]

The first thinkers who foreshadowed monotheism, such as Akhenaton of Egypt (1353–1336 B.C.), were much inspired by the magnificence of the sun, which they saw as the source of all power. Modern science tells us that our sun is one amidst a sea of suns in the Milky Way, and that the Milky Way itself is one amidst a hundred billion comparable galaxies that form the visible universe. In terms of sheer power, we thus see an entity billions of times more powerful than any our forefathers visualized. Scientists us-ing an ultraviolet telescope orbiting through space reported in November 1996 that this visible universe may well be only one tenth of the reality.[13] Facts such as these must quell any feelings of self-importance that may tend to rise up in the individual psyche. A contemplation of God's power—one only of the qualities of the divinity—must breed humility in the thought-ful observer and veneration in the believer.

The epic progress of science in this century thus equips our generation above all others that have gone before us with hard scientific facts that prove how much more powerful the Creator is than could have been comprehended even by the best minds before our time. The more the knowledge revealed to us, the more the wonder grows. When the poets spoke of sermons in stones and the running brooks, they little knew how the learning of later centuries would confirm that there were more marvels locked into the composition and history of the smallest pebble than can be contemplated in a lifetime of sophisticated chemical, physical, geological, historical, or philosophical research.

The vastness of God's power has yet another social message for us, for it forces a consideration of our total dependence on the planet that is the common home of the community of mankind. Our sense of togetherness grows against the backdrop of the immensity of the universe. Living together on a little spaceship in the outer spirals of an insignificant galaxy, we are compelled to realize that sheer survival demands the very degree of brotherhood and sisterhood required by the Prayer. Modern research also emphasizes more than ever before the total dependence of all living things upon the complex interaction of myriad forces acting in unison to make life possible and sustainable.

All that we now know could not be communicated to an unsophisticated audience two thousand years ago, but is comprised in a contemplation of the power of the divinity—the all-powerful God or Creator, upon whose coordination of the required elements that make life possible all humans depend.[14] The increased realization that all life proceeds from this source, and that the continuance of all sustenance is dependent on the fine balance underlying the whole order of creation, must instill greater respect for the sanctity of life, greater attention to the means for its sustenance and the equitable distribution of those means, and a greater regard for the preservation of the ecology of the planet and its fauna and flora.

God As Power (Political)

Another aspect of God's power is power over all human institutions, and over nations and principalities. John of Salisbury wrote in 1159:

[F]or all power is from the Lord God and has been with Him always, and is everlasting. The power which the prince has is therefore from God, for the power of God is never lost, nor severed from him.[15]

In Christian Europe, the consecration of the ruler by the Church legitimized his or her power and authority, and the very titles of rulers (which often contained the phrase "by the grace of God") acknowledged this higher source of political and legal authority.

The principle that God is the ultimate source of all political and judicial authority receives powerful confirmation from Jesus' admonition to Pilate, "You have authority over me only because it was given to you by God" (John 19:11).

The social contract theories of rulership held that a ruler's power came to him through a notional contract he or his predecessor had made with his subjects. These theories were very much in vogue in seventeenth-century Europe. Yet, despite this acknowledgment of power coming from the people, nearly every European ruler was anxious to proclaim in his edicts and even on his coins that he held his power by the grace of God.

It is of interest that other theistic religions likewise acknowledge this principle. Thus in the Islamic books we read quite specifically that inasmuch as all political power comes from God, the political power of every ruler is held by him in trust and never in his own right.

God As Power (Punitive)

It is not necessary for the purpose of this discussion to consider the awesome punishments recorded in the Old Testament for disobedience to God's will. Quite apart from the question of punishments or sanctions, it is enough to note that the majesty and infinite power of God add majesty and authority to his command.

We should, of course, note here that the reason for obedience to God's law goes far beyond the mundane considerations of punishment and reward. Rather, it is the morality that lies behind the law that is the reason for obedience. Some schools of jurisprudence (for example, the Scandinavian school of realists) have in their exposition of the reasons for obedience to laws shown the psychological importance of the instinct to obey law that is internalized in the individual—quite apart, that is, from a consideration of the punishments that would follow disobedience.

The infinite precision with which the affairs of the universe are ordered, down to the minutest details of quasars and atomic combinations, and the coordination of myriad factors that make life possible even for a millisecond, prompt an important reflection on justice. No human judge can take into account the infinite range of factors leading to an act, which need to be assessed in the formation of a just judgment. The power of the divinity is our assurance that Divine justice takes into account every minuscule factor relevant to the assessment of blame. This has stimulated through the ages a realization of the fallibility of the human judge, and the need for an unrelenting search for improvement in the methods of justice we ourselves pursue. Divine justice is the ideal toward which human justice aspires.

The majesty and infinite power of God, and the wondrous works seen by the believer to have been performed by God, also reinforce belief in the *wisdom* of God, for it is difficult to conceive of such power being possessed and exercised without an accompanying wisdom that matches that power. It may be possible to think of a little object being created in vain, but the conviction is compelling that a gigantic structure like the universe as we know it, if indeed it was the subject of conscious creation, was not created lightly or by way of an aimless diversion, but that it had a serious purpose. To the mind of the theistic believer, power then links itself to ineffable wisdom in suggesting some grand design beyond the reach of human perception. Such sentiments produce within the individual a strong internalized reaction of instinctive acceptance that a Divine purpose, animated by a Divine wisdom, underlies it all. Righteousness as the principle prescribed by God for human conduct then commands allegiance out of the conviction that it is intrinsically right that a rule which such an author has endorsed should be obeyed.

The concept of boundless power prompts another law-related thought, for a characteristic of boundless power in human hands is that, unless checks and balances are externally imposed, that power tends to be abused. It is only perfect *virtue* that can handle unbridled power without abuse. As Lord Macaulay has observed, "The highest proof of virtue is to possess boundless power without abusing it."[16]

Looked at in this light, one can link God's power with the concept of virtue, for boundless though it be, it is exercised on certain principles rather than in purely arbitrary fashion. To conclude otherwise would be a derogation from the perfection of God. The absolute power of God stands in stark contrast to absolute power enjoyed by humans, of which the historian Lord

Acton made the memorable observation that "all power tends to corrupt and absolute power corrupts absolutely."

God As Truth

Mahatma Gandhi has written:

> There are innumerable definitions of God because his manifestations are innumerable. They overwhelm me with wonder and awe and for a moment stun me. But I worship God as Truth only. I have not found Him but I am seeking after Him. I am prepared to sacrifice the things dearest to me in pursuit of this quest.[17]

Thomas à Kempis thought in similar vein when he wrote, "O God, who art the truth, make me one with thee in everlasting love."

Truth, then, must be one of the essential attributes of the hallowedness of God, without which the concept of holiness is not complete.

A quality not given to humans is to perceive the truth on all things with absolute certainty. In the case of God, the believer goes one step further and sees God as more than a mere knower of truth but an embodiment of truth, for in God there can be no falsehood.

Plato stressed this twenty-four centuries ago when he said in his *Laws* that "To be absolutely sure of the truth of matters concerning which there are many opinions is an attribute of God not given to man."

Truth is reality, and falsehood a false perception or narration of that reality. Falsehood does not exist unless an aberrant perception distorts the true view of that reality. Humanity, limited as it is in its perceptive abilities, rarely sees reality except with some element of distortion. Truth, of course, is primordial and part of the order of the universe from its inception. In the words of John Hales, "Truth is more ancient than error, for error is nothing else but deviation and swerving from truth."[18] Thus truth is timeless.

A further element of distortion is introduced when that already aberrant perception is put into words, for words rarely coincide entirely with the perceptions they are meant to convey. For God these intervening distortions are not present. Horne Tooke, an early philologist, emphasized the frailty of words when he said: "Except only in words, there is nothing but truth in the world."[19] God sees reality as it truly is. God *is* reality. God is and embodies truth. If God embodies truth, disloyalty to truth is disloyalty to God. There must be a willingness to abide by the truth however inconvenient it may seem, for to do less is to offer disrespect to the Divine. As Calvin wrote, "If we reflect that the Spirit of God is the only fountain of truth, we would be careful, as we would avoid offering insult to Him, not to reject or condemn truth wherever it appears."[20] Where there is love of God, there is also a love of truth. As Confucius put it, "Those who know the truth are not equal to those who love it."[21] The lover of truth may have less knowledge than the knower of truth, but is more to be respected. He or she comes closer to God and to sincerity in uttering the phrase "hallowed by thy name," for he or she is saying, among other things, "hallowed be God as an embodiment of truth."

Since God is omniscient, all reality—as it truly exists—is known to God. All facts are seen by God as they truly are. In the words of the Hindu scriptures, "In God knowledge is infinite; in others it is only a germ."[22]

God As Justice

One of the highest yearnings of humanity throughout history has been for justice. While one can understand that the desire for justice is very strong among those who are victims of injustice, the nobler concept is the yearning for justice in the abstract—justice not only for oneself but for all, justice as a value in itself.

The assumption that justice is an attribute of God is widespread and turns up sometimes even in modern legal literature. In the leading case of *Cooper v. Wandsworth Board of Works,*[23] the court was considering the question whether the Wandsworth Board of Works could pull down a house without giving the owner an opportunity to be heard. Byles J. referred to the 1723 case of *The King v. The Chancellor of Cambridge*[24] in which Justice Fortescue observed that, "even God himself did not pass sentence upon Adam before he was called upon to make his defence, if he had any."

Such instances illustrate both the assumption that justice is an attribute of God, and the influence this assumption has exercised on the evolution of legal principles, especially in their developing phase. This example is drawn from the field of administrative law, but nearly every evolving department of the law—in its early stages, at any rate—manifested such an influence.

Both the New and the Old Testaments show justice as a special concern of God. The passages indicating this are simply too numerous to catalogue. Amos 5:21–24 is a powerful illustration:

> I hate your religious festivals; I cannot stand them!
> When you bring me burnt-offerings and grain-offerings
> I will not accept them...
> Instead, let justice flow like a stream,
> and righteousness like a river that never goes dry.[25]

Here is a reference to justice deep enough to override forms and technicalities, abundant enough to serve inexhaustibly, continuous enough to serve at whatever time, powerful enough to serve against the greatest repositories of temporal power. Justice must seek out those who have no one to speak for them and makes no distinction between races, for Deuteronomy says of God: "He makes sure that orphans and widows are treated fairly; he loves the foreigners who live with our people, and gives them food and clothes" (10:18).

Not surprisingly, the word righteousness and its variants—right, righteous, and justice—appear hundreds of times in the Bible. God's righteousness is everlasting (Psalm 119; 142–144), and the very foundations of his throne are righteousness and justice (Psalm 89:14; 92:2). In Daniel (9:7, KJV), we read, "O Lord, righteousness belongs to thee," and in Psalm 11:7 that "the righteous Jehovah loveth righteousness."

The New Testament is replete with sayings of Jesus rejecting the trappings of legality and pursuing the spirit of justice rather than the letter of the law. Likewise, Jesus is identified with righteousness in many New Testament passages. Of God, the New Testament says, "a sceptre of righteousness is the sceptre of thy kingdom" (Hebrews 1:8, KJV), and the following verse describes him as ruling over his kingdom with justice for ever and ever, loving what is right and hating what is wrong. And Peter describes him as "the Holy One and the Just" (Acts 3:14, KJV).

The centrality of justice to the concept of divinity appears in all religions. To cite an illustrative example from the Hindu scriptures:

> Men who put no faith
>   In this law of righteousness [*dharma*]
>   Fail to reach Me and must return
>   To the road of recurring death.[26]

Justice may in fact be described as a sister of truth, for unless the truth be fully known, justice cannot be administered. It is only the application of just principles to true facts that results in justice.

Human processes for achieving justice are full of fallibility at every point in the process of judgment. Error can enter the human judgmental process in all of its four stages. In the first place, the human judge can never be in absolute possession of that vast canvas of facts which go to make up the surrounding circumstances of a piece of conduct. Second, granted such a perfect and absolute knowledge of the facts, the human judge can err in the factual conclusions he arrives at upon that basis of primary fact. Third, the human judge can err in applying the principles of law to the factual conclusions reached. Fourth, even if the human judge passed through these three stages without error, there may yet be a range of choices available, all of which are acceptable principles of law. There is often a clash of competing principles, each of which has some appearance of validity. For example, the deterrence of further crime, the education of the criminal, the interests of the victim, and the interests of society—all of which are valid values—may compete with each other in the identical case; and it is difficult for the human judge to hold the balance true. He or she must choose, from among these alternatives, that which most accords with that individual's sense of justice. There is here a fourth stage of possible error.[27]

All these grounds of fallibility are avoided in a justice system that is perfect. None such exists on earth and the attribute of perfect justice has thus always been considered a quality of the Divine. Jurists throughout the ages have contrasted human justice with the Divine, and treated as self-evident the truth that no human judge has ever been infallible.

If the name of God be hallowed, one of the attributes in that halo of hallowedness must be the attribute of perfect justice, which rests in the divinity alone. Those who pledge themselves to hallow the name of God pledge themselves to do justice, to the best of their ability, to all fellow human beings in their relationships with them.

Another thought connected with justice is that justice is an attribute of God, and, if God is eternal, those principles are eternal. Particular rules of law may change from time to time, for changing circumstances produce changing laws, but standing above and below them as their aspiration and their foundation are principles of justice that are eternal. The constancy of justice is linked with the timelessness of God.

God As Love

The concept of God as the embodiment of love has already been sufficiently dealt with in these pages. Jesus places love in the forefront of his commandments—"Love each other as I have loved you." We read in 1 John 4:8, "Whoever does not love does not know God, for God is love." Again, "God is love and whoever abides in love abides in God, and God abides in him" (1 John 4:16).

Perhaps the English word "love" is inadequate to convey exactly the depth of meaning contained in the scriptural references to "love." We use the word to cover the several meanings for which Greek has at least four distinct words: *epithemia* (desire or yearning); *eros* (sexual love); *philia* (affectionate love, as between brothers, sisters, and friends); and *agape* (total dedication and devotion to the welfare of another, regardless of sacrifice and personal cost).[28] It is this last meaning—total dedication, irrespective of the consequences to oneself—that is invariably the scriptural meaning; and that is the love involved in the concept of hallowedness.

As with all the attributes of God, we can read various legal connotations into this one.

If God is love, and the guiding rule for Christian conduct is to love our neighbor as ourselves, the duty to assist those in want becomes imperative. In the words of Saint Thérèse of Lisieux: "The love of God must not be built up in our imagination but must be tried by works." One is not Christian in one's conduct if one fails to do so, for Christ has specifically stated that whatever is done to the least of his people is done to himself. Where the hungry are fed or the naked are clothed or the shelterless are housed, this is something done for God himself. Such help is a law of Christian life. On a global scale when we see the deprivations to which many a well-meaning person is unwittingly a party and when he or she does nothing about it, the first law of Christianity is violated and the hallowedness that is recited in the Lord's Prayer rings hollow.

There are other law-related implications as well. For example, abstention from force, from war, from violence of all kinds, is a characteristic of love. In the words of Mahatma Gandhi:

Nonviolence is therefore in its active form goodwill towards all life. It is pure love. I read it in the Hindu scriptures, in the Bible, in the Koran.[29]

Socrates described love as the messenger between the gods and man. Saint Paul tells us that it is from the commandment of love that all the other commandments follow. Love suffuses all the other virtues.

If love is the soul of Christian existence, it must be at the heart of every other Christian virtue. Thus, for example, *justice* without love is legalism; *faith* without love is ideology; *hope* without love is self-centeredness; *forgiveness* without love is self-abasement; *fortitude* without love is recklessness; *generosity* without love is extravagance; *care* without love is mere duty; *fidelity* without love is servitude. Every virtue is an expression of love. No virtue is a virtue unless it is permeated, or informed, by love (1 Corinthians 13).[30]

God As the Sender of Peace

We read in Leviticus, "If you walk in my statutes...and do them...I will give peace in the land, and you shall lie down, and none shall make you afraid" (26:3,6, KJV). Of the future Jerusalem and its glory, Isaiah says, "For thus saith the Lord: Behold, I will extend peace to her like a river" (66:12, KJV). So, also, says David, "The Lord gives strength to his people and blesses them with peace" (Psalm 29:11).

The New Testament likewise frequently identifies God with peace. The "God of peace" is referred to in the Epistle to the Romans (15:33), the Corinthians (2 Corinthians 13:11) and the Hebrews (13:20). The Old Testament speaks of the Messiah as the Prince of Peace (Isaiah 9:6), and Jesus speaks of "my" peace—"My peace I give unto you" (John 16:33). Jesus is identified with peace from his birth when a multitude of the heavenly host sang "peace on earth" (Luke 2:14).

Peace is also identified with righteousness for, "The work of righteousness shall be peace" (Isaiah 32:17).

God As Perfection

Perfection in all things is a characteristic of the Divine. We have already dealt with perfection in justice as an aspect particularly apposite to the theme of this work. Perfection in other qualities, such as beauty and goodness, are equally important; but those themes fall outside the specific purview of this work. As this work has attempted to show, the Prayer reveals upon analysis a series of principles and standards that are component elements of justice. As God is perfect in the whole, He is perfect also in each of these component elements. By definition we cannot achieve perfection in any of these, but the perfection of God offers us a constant standard toward which to direct our efforts.

God As Supporter of His People

There is no need to elaborate here: For the believer, God is a rock of refuge and a source of strength. One puts one's trust in God in the sure expectation that the principles God stands for will be upheld and not change from day to day. God's word is an ever-present source of wisdom and counsel. If one searches deeply enough, that word will be seen to contain the basic principles on which wisdom and counsel rest.

The words of Saint Francis of Assisi, in a prayer inspired by the Lord's Prayer, serve as a fitting summary:

May our knowledge of you become ever clearer, that we may know the breadth of your blessings, the length of your prowess, the height of your majesty, and the depth of your judgments.[31]

The commitment to hallow God's name, an operative part of the Prayer, is thus a total commitment to Christian conduct. One might as well not recite the Prayer if one is not prepared to make this commitment.

B. "BE THY NAME"

The discussion of "hallowed" would be incomplete without a brief consideration of the accompanying words "be thy name," a phrase that creates difficulties of understanding for those not familiar with the scriptural use of the word "name."

We are reminded of the importance attaching to the name of God when we see the Ten Commandments spelling out that "Thou shalt not take the name of the Lord thy God in vain"—for there was profanity in the misuse, the assumption, or the desecration of the sacred name of God. Likewise, we see other clues to the true meaning of the word in such passages as

"They that know thy *name* will put their trust in thee" (Psalm 9:10, KJV), or "Some trust in chariots, and some in horses, but we will remember the *name* of the Lord, Our God" (Psalm 20:7, KJV). Clearly the word "name" has attributes beyond the concept of naming its subject, for merely knowing the name of God, without more, cannot instill the trust mentioned in the second quotation, nor can the mere sound or enunciation of the Lord's name induce the confidence reflected in the third.

All this is part of a habit of expression known in many cultures by which the name of an entity is used not merely to name it but to describe its essential qualities. The name becomes almost a substitute for the characteristics of the object named, and, where a person is named, a way of referring not only to the name but all the attributes of a person. "By the grace of your name, may humanity find itself lifted higher and higher," say the sacred writings of the Sikhs in a thought that captures the power of the name of God.[32]

In their seminal work *The Meaning of Meaning*, Ogden and Richards point to the fact that in many ancient texts words are treated as having a personality like a living being. They point out that in the ancient Pyramid texts, a god called Khern (meaning Word) had a personality like a human being;[33] and refer to Revelation 11:13 ("There were killed in the earthquake names of men seven thousand") of which a modern rendering would be "seven thousand people were killed." The former gives a clear indication that names were identified with the persons they represented.

The Meaning of Meaning cites several examples from the Egyptian, Hindu, Jewish, Greek, Roman, and Abyssinian cultures to illustrate the same point.[34]

A seventeenth-century commentator on the New Testament[35] answered the question we are addressing in the words "the name of God is God himself" (*nomen Dei est Deus ipse*). Numerous passages in the Old and the New Testaments confirm this view. As the biblical scholar Ernst Lohmeyer observes, "God's name describes him in the totality, the uniqueness of his being and action."[36] The identity of the name with its owner's full personality comes out also in such passages as "Behold, the name of the Lord comes from afar, burning with his anger...his lips are full of indignation" (Isaiah 30:27). The learned editor of the *Vocabulary of the Bible* expresses a similar conclusion in these words: "In the Old Testament, far from being a mere label, just an external description, a name expresses the profound reality of the being who carries it."[37]

It is thus clear that the word "name" in this expression must not be taken purely at face value but as meaning something more. Perhaps it can fairly be paraphrased, "Hallowed be Thou and all Thy attributes."

Aldous Huxley's approach to this clause[38] is to consider the word "name" as being used in two senses and to consider the hallowing of it as linked in a twofold way to the other objects and purposes of the Prayer.

The two meanings of the word "name" are explained as follows:

1. As with other peoples of antiquity, the Jews regarded the name of a thing as identical with its inner principle or essence. Thus the phrase simply means "God."
2. For us the name of something is essentially different from that which is named, words being merely devices to enable us to think about things. When we hallow the name of God we are therefore hallowing our verbalized concepts of God—not in an incantatory or magical sense but as a means of directing the mind to those attributes and keeping them in contemplation.

So also the twofold linkage between this clause and the succeeding clauses of the Prayer is as follows:

1. The hallowing of God and his name is an indispensable condition for achieving the other aims mentioned in the Prayer: the realization of God's kingdom; the doing of his will; the receiving of grace; forgiveness and liberation.
2. Conversely, the better we succeed through liberation, forgiveness, and grace in doing God's will and realizing his kingdom, the more we shall be enabled to hallow God's name and God himself.

In short, the phrase "hallowed be thy name" must not deflect our attention from the Reality we are praising, to the mere word that expresses that reality. Shorn of its ancient associations, this form of expression tends in our day to make us concentrate on the word God, rather than on the immense and majestic verity behind that word, on which our attention should be fixed. If we fix our thoughts on God rather than his name we are more likely to pay due attention through our conduct to the qualities of hallowedness that we are pledging ourselves to respect.

C. "THY KINGDOM COME"

The attributes of God's kingdom—the kingdom we wish to have on earth as it is in heaven—are considered in the final chapter. But first we need to examine the commitment to do what lies in one's power to bring this kingdom down to earth: a call to action, as contained in the word "come." Indeed, the word "come" is a resounding call to action. One does not passively intone the hope that God's kingdom come on earth. One actively works toward it. One makes it come on earth.

The word "come" contains an injunction to each individual to do for his community, his country, and the international community what William Blake so eloquently captured in his words:

> I will not cease from Mental Fight,
>> Nor shall my Sword sleep in my hand,
>> Till we have built Jerusalem,
>> In England's green and pleasant Land.[39]

The primacy of the duty to work toward such ideals is stressed by Jesus himself, for he teaches "Seek first the kingdom of God and His righteousness, and all these things shall be added unto you besides" (Matthew 6:33, KJV). That may in a sense be said to be the primary teaching of the Lord's Prayer. One is asked to seek to achieve the kingdom of God by one's actions. It seems self-evident that one does not have to wait till one's sojourn on earth is over to put the Prayer into action.

The kingdom to which we must seek to come is the kingdom of righteousness. That is the New Jerusalem that such conduct brings down to earth. The thoughts underlying "thy kingdom come" interlock with those of "thy will be done," and both interlock again with the vision enshrined in the words "on earth as it is in heaven."

Unfortunately, too seldom are these words seen in this light. The ideal they express is clearly accepted—but it remains at the level of a spiritual ideal and is not seen as the practical call to action that is part of its essential message.

"The harvest is great but the laborers are few" refers not merely to the call to holy orders, but also to the task of planting a regime of righteousness on earth. Jesus' mission on earth was not merely to found a priesthood, but to banish iniquity and establish justice "on earth as it is in heaven." That was an important part of the harvest that the Lord of the harvest wanted to gather in. If "the goal of the universe is…'a Kingdom of God' in which values are realized,"[40] that goal requires an army of workers committed to bringing earthly justice into line with the law of love that Jesus proclaimed.[41] The Prayer is a rallying call to that army of workers. This law of love provides the basis of justice, not only between individuals but also between nations.[42]

The Words Constitute a Pledge

Each time the Prayer is recited, the utterer is pledging his or her effort toward achieving its goal of God's kingdom on earth. "Thy kingdom come" is not only the expression of a hope. It is not only a call to action. It is also a commitment and a pledge. Indeed, this could not be clearer. Other parts of the Prayer express one's beliefs or one's appeals or one's aspirations, but these three words in particular are a specific pledge. Apart from belief, entreaty, and aspiration, all of which are important, the heart of a prayer is the promise of the devotee to do something or make a commitment to a course of action. "Thy kingdom come" is clearly such a pledge. Indeed, the commitment could scarcely be more explicit.

The commitment in the Prayer is a commitment also to do what lies within one's power to construct a community that knows no distinction between its scale of values and that of God. When this happens, there is complete harmony, integration, and unity between the two kingdoms that have strayed far from each other: the kingdom of the created and that of the Creator. The world of the created is then subsumed, so to speak, into the world of the Creator, with a common scale of values and a common dedication to justice and righteousness. That world is then in tune with, and part of, the Infinite. For its citizen, "the kingdom of God" has "come."

The faithful who pray that "thy kingdom come" are thus giving utterance to a thought as lofty as any conceived by the mind of man.

Fusion of the Two Kingdoms

An important theme lying concealed in these words is the theme of an eventual fusion of the two worlds—the kingdom of heaven will come upon earth, thus resulting in a fusion of the two kingdoms, or, alternatively, that the wayfarer on earth will find his way to a unity or merger with the kingdom of heaven and all it stands for.

Either way, there is the notion of a merger with the Infinite, the time-lessness and the idealism of the kingdom of heaven. It's similar to the Hindu comparison of the soul of the wayfarer on earth to a drop of water rising from the ocean into a cloud, descending as rain upon the earth, flowing into a river and thence back to its primeval source. In the expressive simile of Charles de Foucauld, if we "desire earth to be a mirror of heaven," we must guard against acts that tend to "break that mirror."[43]

A beautiful practical thought, closely related to the theme of this book, which appears in Buddhism and Hinduism, is the concept that one day the entire world order will be ruled not by a temporal or physical sovereign, but by the "kingless authority of the law."[44] This is another method of capturing the idea of bringing God's kingdom on earth.

The connotation of identification implicit in the word "come" is a key concept of the Prayer.

Ongoing Process

No one would suggest that the kingdom of God can be brought down to earth by a mere wish or resolve. It would require a considerable effort to reshape the material attitudes that dominate the governance of matters on earth. The world of human affairs where realpolitik and force are the order of the day, and the kingdom of God where moral righteousness prevails, are far apart. It is only through an ongoing process that the bridge can be achieved.

We do not need to dwell in this work on the claim of theologians that the phrase is used in the eschatological sense of the ultimate achievement of perfection, when God's kingdom will, in the fullness of time, descend on earth. The eschatological sense of the words cannot be a barrier to starting to plant God's kingdom on earth so far as lies in the power of each individual to contribute to this process. The kingdom of God has for this reason been described as a process. It is a mission for which preparation is required.

This brings to mind the parable explaining the kingdom of heaven through the illustration of the ten maidens who took their lamps and went to meet the bridegroom. Five were wise and five were foolish. The foolish took no oil with them while the wise took flasks of oil for their lamps. The bridegroom was delayed, and when his arrival was announced at midnight, the foolish asked the wise for some oil as their lamps were going out, but the wise observed that there would not be enough both for themselves and the others. The foolish maidens went out to purchase oil and missed the bridegroom and could not go with him to the marriage feast (Matthew 25:1–13). Thoughtful preparation well ahead of the event is therefore essential.

Whatever view one takes of the word "come," entry to the kingdom of heaven can thus be achieved only by thoughtful preparation—which means compliance with the codes of conduct prescribed, including doing away with hypocrisy and pretense and legalism and going to the heart of good conduct as prescribed. One must "not heap up empty phrases as the Gentiles do" (Matthew 6:7). We are told that we must not lay up "treasures on earth, where moth and rust consume and where thieves break in and steal." Instead, store up "riches for yourselves in heaven where moths and rust cannot destroy and robbers cannot break in and steal" (Matthew 6:19–20).

The world has a way of getting around even such clear indications against the pursuit of wealth for its own sake, which is one of the principal causes of the world's predicaments. Interpretations, sometimes very subtle, sometimes plainly ludicrous, place a gloss upon such passages and seek to explain them away. For an extreme attempt to do so, the reader is referred to the following example, which would be amusing were it not a serious reflection of attitudes not infrequently adopted in real life. This is an example of a pastor's preaching which, through the efforts of Mr. Upton Sinclair, has now become classic:

> Jesus did not say "Lay not up for yourselves treasures upon earth." He said "Lay not up for yourselves treasures upon earth *where moth and rust doth corrupt and where thieves break through and steal.*" And no sensible American does. Moth and rust do not get at Mr. Rockefeller's oil wells, and thieves do not often break through and steal a railway. What Jesus condemned was hoarding wealth.[45]

By its very absurdity, this example highlights the principle that the coming of the kingdom is totally impeded by sanctimonious attitudes—emphasizing the letter of the text, while completely contradicting its spirit. Elevating the letter of the law in such a manner as to defeat its spirit was the target of some of Jesus' strongest condemnations.

The Kingdom of Heaven Is Within Oneself

Implicit in such reflections is the thought that the kingdom of heaven can be enjoyed while we are on earth. The usual presupposition, that we enter that kingdom only upon our physical death, is a convenient device for shrugging off the load of present responsibility undertaken by one who utters the Prayer.

Being part of the kingdom of heaven must not be an ideal reserved for the dead. To resign oneself to this attitude is to abdicate all hope that it would be possible to establish a regime of justice on earth. Granted the necessary state of mind, the Christian takes the view that paradise can be created here on earth. All the instruments of technology and wealth necessary for creating this possibility are here at hand, at the disposal of the present generation more than any in the long succession of generations past. All that is lacking is the will to implement the proper set of values. The kingdom of heaven is thus not a distant dream, but a reality lying within human reach more closely now than ever before.

To take the view that the solace of heavenly joy is not available while we are still on earth would be a mournful doctrine indeed. Saint Augustine writes:

I was wandering like a lost sheep, searching outside myself for that which was within. I ran through all the streets and squares of this great city, the world, searching for Thee, O God, and I found Thee not because I sought Thee wrongly. Thou wast within me and I sought Thee without.[46]

In like vein, Meister Eckhart (1260–1327) wrote, "God is near us, but we are far from him. God is within, we are without, God is at home, we are in the far country."[47] Similar thoughts can be found expressed in other religions. Thus the *Adi Granth*, the holy book of the Sikhs, says, "The True One is not far from us, but resides within us;"[48] and Sri Ramakrishna (1836–1886) wrote, "I have come to the stage of realisation in which I see that God is walking in every human form and manifesting himself alike in the sage and in the sinner."[49] Likewise, Mahatma Gandhi (1869–1948): "I know God is neither in heaven nor down below, but in everyone."[50]

Just as "stone walls do not a prison make, nor iron bars a cage," so also the bodily frame does not imprison humans in an earthly kingdom to which the Divine has no access. "If a man loves me," said Jesus at the Last Supper, "he will keep my words: and my Father will love him, and we will come under him and *make our abode with him*" (John 14:23, KJV). Even more explicitly, when he was asked by the Pharisees when the kingdom of God should come, he said, "the Kingdom of God is within you" (Luke 17:21). Pursuing this same concept, the apostle Paul, in his First Epistle to the Corinthians, asks: "Know you not that you are the temple of God and that the spirit of God dwells in you?" (6:19).

The enjoyment of God's kingdom is thus proclaimed by Christianity to be within reach while the individual concerned is still on earth. It is there for those to construct who enjoy a frame of mind that links their values to those of God.

Concluding this review of the implications of the word "come," we need to note, finally, the message of hope it contains. The Prayer tells us in express terms that the kingdom of heaven can be achieved on earth. We do not have to resign ourselves to the prevalence of iniquity in this world, shrugging our shoulders helplessly at our inability to make the slightest dent on the wickedness we see around us.

D. "THY WILL BE DONE"

Dual Connotations

The expression has both an active and a passive meaning. Traditional recitals of the Lord's Prayer tend to concentrate on the passive. The ancient wisdom that "man proposes, God disposes" affirms one's resignation to the will of God. Humans can only strive. The eventual result of their endeavors is not for them to determine. "[T]he race is not to the swift, nor the battle to the strong...; but time and chance happeneth to them all" (Ecclesiastes 9:11, KJV). The ultimate result is part of a grand design, which it is not always given to mortals to see. This acceptance of a grander design and the resignation to that will are part of the Christian faith.

After acknowledging that God's will is supreme, the supplicant tends to lapse into a state of inaction, forgetful of the fact that the phrase also contains a powerful call to individual action to do what one can to bring the kingdom of God to earth. This is the positive side of the affirmation, no less important than the resignation to God's will. In short, alongside of resignation to God's will, one is also pledging positive action to do God's will — to the limit of one's ability and free will. While theistic faith lays all things at the feet of the Divine, human effort is called for in the pursuance of one's goals. It is this active meaning that concerns us here.

The Range of Human Free Will

It is of the essence of Christian teaching that humanity is endowed with a measure of free will. In this context it is well to remember also that human free will enjoys a virtually limitless range of choice from the sublime to the barbaric. Forty centuries of recorded history demonstrate that humans can soar aloft with the angels or wallow in the brutality of beasts. While the higher reaches of human conduct cause a glow of pride at being human, the long catalogue of human crime that stains the pages of history places a grave question mark over human claims to superiority in behavior. Its massive scale, calculated cruelty, refined tortures, and sheer sadism often reduce human conduct even below the bestial. All history demonstrates this, and the century now drawing to its close perhaps more than most others.

Endowed with this enormous range for the operation of free will, each human being makes an individual choice as to the level at which to pitch his or her conduct. In the vast spectrum of human conduct the highest levels are those concerned with the implementation of heavenly principles upon earth. If heaven is to be brought down to earth, no lesser standard of conduct would suffice. Every human being, however humble, can contribute his or her share toward bringing about this result.

Free will is not an attribute with which human beings were endowed in vain. Each individual's will is momentous and valuable in the scheme of things—not inconsequential and ineffective. No individual is entitled to take up the position that his or her impact will be so slight or uncertain as to be irrelevant. It is out of the cumulation of individual wills that even the major political will of a nation is forged. Speaking in global terms, world opinion is likewise the cumulation of an infinity of individual wills. If all individual wills of those who seek a better world remain passive, so also will the state of the world; and righteousness within it will atrophy.

The May 28, 1994, edition of *The New York Times* carried a full-page notice by Amnesty International regarding the slaughter in Burundi entitled, "Listen. Can You Hear the Silence?" The page displayed a large picture of dozens of dead bodies, many of them children, spread-eagled on a road. The road runs through "a field as green as any English meadow....Far above you summer clouds in a perfect sky." The message states, "Do you know what our deadliest enemy is? It's not the guns of vicious tyrants. It's the silence of good people....Do not be part of the killing silence." A purely passive reading of the words "thy will be done" can lead to such a killing silence, not only in Burundi but elsewhere. The killing fields can spread.

Dedicating One's Actions to the Will of God

However well intentioned our actions may be, they need to be dedicated to the performance of God's will, not ours. To quote an illustration from an epochal event in modern history, when King George VI committed his country's forces to battle in the invasion of Europe in June of 1945, he said, "I solemnly call my people to prayer and dedication." In the hushed expectancy of one of the solemn moments in history when one of the greatest military expeditions of all time was about to be launched, he continued, "We shall ask not that God do our will, but that we may be enabled to do the will of God."[51]

Assisting the Weak and Needy

It is not the will of the Father that the "little ones" should perish (Matthew 18:14). The "little ones" of this quotation, while clearly covering children, is not limited to children only. There are many who are as helpless as children and consequently need external support if they are to survive. Indeed, if one is to take Jesus' teachings in their whole context, one recognizes that it is important to help those who are unable to help themselves.

The parable of the Lost Sheep is so important that major Christian orders, such as the Order of the Good Shepherd, are based upon it. It powerfully conveys the idea of the helpless one, the little one, who needs support if he or she is to be kept from harm. Who are the lost sheep? Who are the little ones?

First to come to mind are the children who have run away from home and live on the streets. The story of America's exploited street kids has been movingly written by Father Bruce Ritter, founder of Covenant House, who has saved tens of thousands of them from exploitation.[52] His book is appropriately dedicated "to the thousands of good and brave and beautiful bought and sold kids who never made it back because no one has reached out to them in time." As with the American street kids, there are millions across the globe in prostitution, slavery, forced military service, children perishing from famine, outcasts, children who have seen their parents killed in cold blood before their eyes, young people whose world has collapsed.

Beyond the ranks of children, the weak and needy include the aged, the paralyzed, those stricken with incurable diseases, and the oppressed who live under the yoke of tyrannies of various sorts—economic, political, and military. As scripture expounds it, "I myself will be the shepherd of my sheep...I will look for those that are lost, bring back those that wander off, bandage those that are hurt, and heal those that are sick..." (Ezekiel 34:15–16).

If it is God's will that none of the little ones shall perish, "thy will be done" is pregnant with meaning and, if that will be done, the words "on earth as it is in heaven" acquire a profound meaning. "Not everyone who calls me 'Lord, Lord' will enter the Kingdom of Heaven, but only those who do what my Father in heaven wants them to do" (Matthew 7:21).

In his powerful book, *Where God Weeps*, Father Werenfried Van Straaten summarizes the essence of the duty owed to the oppressed in these terms:

> The Savior, once born in the City of David, is disgusted with our piety, with our streamlined liturgy, and with all the important or unbalanced reforms which we think indispensable for the prosperity of the Kingdom of God, if we refuse to the victims of lawless aggression, to the peaceful who suffer violence, to those who are helplessly trodden down in the struggle for political power, to the parishioners of Tri Tam, to Mary Thoi's newborn baby, and to all the outcasts of the world the love for which the Child in the crib has been waiting for two thousand years.[53]

The Essence of Christian Action

"I have food to eat that you know nothing about....My food...is to obey the will of the one who sent me and to finish the work he gave me to do" (John 4:32,34).

Doing the will of God was Jesus' mission on earth. If one is seeking for guidance in the interpretation of these words of the Prayer, that guidance is there in abundant measure from such pronouncements by the Master himself. In the beatitudes, this message, likening the duty of service to food, is reemphasized, for we are told, "Blessed are they that hunger and thirst after righteousness." One does not satisfy the hunger for righteousness except by action toward righteousness. The Prayer is only the profession of a faith that needs to be translated into action. By such action one identifies oneself with the divinity, for such action makes the actor "brother and sister and mother" of Christ himself (Matthew 12:50). No closer identification, no closer merging of personalities is possible.

It is not words that get one into the kingdom of heaven, but deeds.

Averting the Path of Selfishness

These words of the Prayer take the focus of practical Christianity away from oneself. It is not only one's personal conduct, such as avoidance of immorality and sin, that is the center of the Prayer. With the words "thy kingdom come" the Prayer goes outward from oneself to the wide world beyond. Of those who recite the Prayer with themselves only in view, it has been observed, "The selfish element infects and enfeebles all their Christianity."[54] The duty to assist others is not merely a duty to assist out of one's surplus. That entails no sacrifice. The gospel standard is to give, even at sacrifice to oneself. "Sell all your belongings and give the money to the poor" is the ideal specified (Luke 12:33).

"Love one another as I have loved you," the command left by Jesus to his followers, ties in with this concept and leaves no room for selfishness. That love consists not of protestations of love but action in furtherance of the spirit of oneness with all others. This is the practical operation of the law of love that lies at the core of Christianity. The will of God is the infinite will of love which, in the words of the writer already quoted, "will fill the little vessel of our will out of its own living stream and make the will of God indeed our will."[55]

"...I have come down from heaven to do not my own will but the will of him who sent me" (John 6:38) drives this point home.

Keeping the Law of God Is Only Part of Doing the Will of God

Viewed narrowly, the law of any institution or state can be seen as a series of commands and prohibitions. So long as one keeps on the right side of such law, one does not get into trouble.

But law viewed in its broader sense consists of principles that go beyond mere compliance with the letter. Behind the letter of the law is the spirit of the law, which reaches out to a broader canvas of duty and obligation than can be reached by mere adherence to the letter.

Too often, doing the will of God is seen as mere adherence to a set of commands and prohibitions. In one sense, one may conceivably comply with the law of God by such behavior, but that falls far short of doing the will of God. The will of God extends much further. Beyond mere prohibitions, it is a clarion call to active service. Beyond specific formulations, it offers the broader guiding principles within which they are set.

For failure to see this distinction, "Many Christians never learn to understand the difference between the law of God and the will of God,"[56] and "It is indeed a change in the life of the believer when he fully grasps and experiences the difference."[57]

God As Partner in Good Works

The New Testament is replete with the idea that there is work of God to be done on earth—the work of feeding the hungry, clothing the naked, healing the sick, reforming the sinner, helping the weak, teaching the young, comforting the afflicted. All of these are part of the work God expects to be done on earth and to which he calls humans into partnership with Him. What is done for all of these people is done for God. It is a continuing partnership between God and man, and it is the will of God that this should be so.

> I was hungry and you fed me, I was thirsty and you gave me a drink; I was a stranger and you received me in your homes, naked and you clothed me; I was sick and you took care of me, in prison and you visited me. The righteous will then answer him, "When, Lord, did we ever see you hungry and feed you, or thirsty and give you a drink? When did we ever see you a stranger and welcome you in our homes, or naked and clothe you? When did we ever see you sick or in prison, and visit you?" The King will reply, "I tell you, whenever you did this for one of the least important of these brothers of mine, you did it for me!" (Matthew 25:35–40).

The Lord's Prayer contains an invitation to share in this partnership of good works, for God identifies completely with those in need. We are accepting God's will and desire to help others when we pray "thy will be done on earth." The lesson could not be emphasized more strongly than in the words that follow shortly after the scriptural passage just cited.

> The King will reply, "I tell you, whenever you refused to help one of these least important ones, you refused to help me." These, then, will be sent off to eternal punishment, but the righteous will go to eternal life (Matthew 25:45–46).

The Scope for Individual Action

The gospels exude a supreme belief in the strength of the individual will. Where there is determination to achieve some benefit for the wider world, as opposed to oneself, or indeed for humanity in general, the scriptures teach that one is working for God, for one is about God's work of feeding the hungry and helping those in want. When that determination is present, the worker can take heart from the stirring gospel message that the individual acting alone and with determination can make a mountain move (Matthew 21:21). True determination in the pursuit of that ideal will not be deterred by the magnitude of the task or the obstacles that stand in the way.

We see all around us the power of the concerned individual to achieve lasting good on a global scale. Individual initiative can have a worldwide impact. Martin Luther King, Jr., Nelson Mandela, Albert Schweitzer, and Mother Teresa are but a few examples. Other dedicated individuals like Hugo Grotius, Henri Dunant, and Mahatma Gandhi have through their sheer individual determination achieved results far transcending the national scene of their respective countries. Grotius started the discipline of international law, and Dunant's work triggered off the Red Cross movement. Gandhi's work for the dignity of the people of India spread through the entire colonial world and resulted not only in the independence of India, but also in the liberation of dozens of countries under the yoke of colonialism. Martin Luther King, Jr.'s work for civil rights gave dignity to every disadvantaged person everywhere—not merely in the United States.

Of special interest here is the growing concern of international law with the idea of individual duty and individual responsibility. Individual conduct, hitherto a region into which international law did not intrude, is now becoming an important and integral section of it. The traditional view of international law was that it concerned the rights and duties of states rather than individuals. Today there is a growing view that international law itself must take note, not only of the rights of individuals (human rights), but also of the duties they owe to the international system. Indeed, the Preface to a recent report on the role of the individual in international law states that:

> The present stage of international law should be considered as a transitory period towards a new legal order in which the individual will be called upon to play a more important role as a subject of international rights and responsibilities.[58]

"Thy will be done on earth as it is in heaven" acquires a new significance in the light of this shift of emphasis to the individual. The individual can no longer wring his or her hands in helplessness, pleading that matters of global import are beyond the reach of his or her individual conduct.

It might be helpful here to touch briefly on some of the areas covered in this report as being within the reach of individual conduct. All of them, international matters of high importance, were formerly left out of the domain of individual responsibility as pertaining to high affairs of state, for which states alone bore responsibility. Today we see more clearly the individual's role in them, and through this perception, a greater role for conduct according to God's will. It is not merely in a personal, parochial, or domestic sense that action can be taken to help God's will to be done.

1. War crimes and crimes against humanity. The London Charter of 1945 creating the Nuremberg Tribunal established the responsibility of individuals for war crimes even though they be committed under superior orders. States can commit such crimes only through individuals. The horrors of the concentration camps, the ill treatment and torturing of prisoners of war, the killing of hostages, the plunder of property, the wanton destruction of towns and villages—all these acts require the active participation of individuals and, just as they are morally accountable for their acts, so also international law holds them legally responsible. Participation in such acts even under state orders is not doing God's will on earth.

2. Genocide. Article IV of the Genocide Convention makes persons

responsible for genocide personally accountable and punishable, whether they are constitutionally responsible rulers, public officials, or private individuals.

3. Acts against the peace and security of mankind. The International Law Commission, at the request of the General Assembly, has prepared a Draft Code of Offenses against the Peace and Security of Mankind. The draft code specifies individual responsibility and enunciates the principle that individuals can be punished. The individual, even when acting as the organ of a state, is a subject of international duties. Offenses include aggression, the illegal use of force, or the threat of force.

4. Apartheid. The International Convention on the Suppression and Punishment of the Crime of Apartheid treats apartheid as one of the most oppressive manifestations of slavery in our time and as a crime against humanity. It is a violation of international law and a serious threat to international peace and security. Those committing the crime are declared personally and individually responsible. The numbers of people across the world who reaped the benefits of apartheid without protest, though not perhaps being direct perpetrators of apartheid, were legion. So also were those who practiced a subtle form of apartheid by social discriminations of various sorts. Such apartheid-like discrimination still continues globally, though apartheid in South Africa has been banished from the statute books.

The Ethical Content of God's Will

God's will is not capricious, but is steadfast. Since God is righteous, his will is based upon the concept of justice. As Immanuel Kant philosophized, God is the guarantor of the moral order, the embodiment of the binding character of the moral law.[59]

In the Greek cosmos, man seems a plaything of the gods who, without rhyme or reason, but to suit their passing fancies, would subject humans to a variety of fates ranging from the depths of suffering to the peaks of happiness and prosperity. An eminent authority on classical learning, Professor Gilbert Murray, gives us the following insight into the Homeric gods of the Greek pantheon, which helps us to understand better the Christian concept of the will of God:

The gods of most nations claim to have created the world. The Olympians make no such claim. The most they ever did was to conquer it....

And when they have conquered their kingdoms, what do they do? Do they attend to the government? Do they promote agriculture? Do they practice trades and industries? Not a bit of it....They are conquering chieftains, royal buccaneers. They fight, and feast, and play, and make music; they drink deep, and roar with laughter....[60]

Such were the gods whose wills determined the fates of humans: They punished those who offended them and rewarded those they liked, but no thread of common principle or policy ran through their action. In the monotheistic religions, by way of contrast, all the higher qualities of righteousness and justice inhere in the divinity. The will of God, though inscrutable, has some deeper reason behind it not always visible to humans. The resignation to God's will is thus resignation to a higher grand design, rather than to the quirks of whim and caprice.

CHAPTER 18

THE WORLDWIDE RELIGIOUS REVIVAL AT THE TURN OF THE MILLENNIUM

In an earlier chapter we noticed a dozen factors on the international political scene that enable humanity to make a break with the past and chart out a new course. Here we shall look at several factors that incline humanity, as it charts out this new course, to lean away from materialism and turn to higher sources for its values.

It was once thought that unaided human reason could provide humanity with the keys to that kingdom of equality and justice that has through the ages been the philosopher's dream. That belief, stubbornly prevalent despite its proven shortcomings, lies now in tatters, destroyed beyond redemption by the primitive brutalities surfacing all around us. An age of unprecedented knowledge and unimaginable technology is dredging up from the depths of the human character a ruthlessness in the exercise of power, long supposed to have been left behind in the earliest stages of the ascent from barbarism. Far from being left behind at the foothills, that baggage has been carried up to the very peaks of "civilization" and is here with us to blight all hopes of a just social order based on reason alone.

As a result, many who derided religion are turning once more to the world's great faiths, hoping their ineffable wisdom may yet guide humanity to a more peaceful future. The signs are everywhere around us that a revived interest in religion is becoming a dominant factor in shaping tomorrow's world. As we approach the next century, a remarkable confluence of factors is creating a climate in which an unprecedented spiritual revival is in the making. Vast numbers of people, including some of the most concerned and progressive elements in every nation, are falling back upon religion when the alternatives that offered hope in the past seem, one by one, to fail.

A survey by *Life* magazine, reported in its issue of March 1994, showed that people today are praying in astonishing numbers, and that nine out of ten Americans pray frequently or earnestly. Fifty-one percent pray once or twice a day, and twenty-four percent three or more times a day. While most (forty-seven percent) pray for five minutes or less, twenty-eight percent pray for one hour or more. A vast proportion (92 percent) have in their prayers asked for forgiveness. To the question, "Have your prayers ever been answered?" 95 percent have responded in the affirmative.

In the context of such a resurgence of prayer, it becomes vitally important that renewed efforts be made to relate the lofty values of religion to the practical problems of law and order. How could this best be done? Has the separation of law and religion, central to modern—and, particularly, American—political thinking, blocked the penetration of religious values into the public arena? If so, can the partition be made porous, allowing the values to penetrate, without the dogma and the ritual? The Lord's Prayer has a great part to play in this osmosis of transcendental values into the world of practical affairs. It provides a route for the absorption of precept into practice, vision into reality, religious teaching into legal order.

Here are some of the several circumstances leading to the current flood tide of religious revival.

The Worldwide Breakdown of Law and Order

Both internationally and domestically, we are witnessing a deluge of violence. A world torn with disputes resolves those disputes in blood. Our newspapers and TV screens are filled with the most poignant demonstrations of humanity's capacity for inhumanity. Planes are hijacked; hostages are executed; villages are put to the torch; governments are held to ransom.

As a result, the principles of civilization, developed through forty centuries of suffering and effort, resemble garden flowers being strangled in a wilderness of weeds. In nearly every mind there lurks the fear that the new century could well be one of precipitous decline, rather than the upward-soaring century made possible by the knowledge and power at our command.

As the temperatures of dissatisfaction with the existing order rise to dangerous levels, we seek a means by which the wisdom of the past can speak to the present in terms that translate into social and political stability. Amid a chaos of jarring influences, amid systems of government that are long on promises and short on performance, we search desperately for a guide to the translation of morality's lofty principles into the practical language of law and order.

The Millennial Factor

Historically, the beginning of a new century has focused the collective mind on the role that religion can play in the brand-new century about to dawn. This was so at the beginning of this century and in preceding centuries. However, the start of a new millennium has much deeper religious connotations.

One of the meanings of the word "millennium," according to the *Oxford Dictionary*, is that it is the period of one thousand years when (according to one interpretation of Revelation 20:1–7) Christ will reign in person on earth. This meaning gives religious overtones to reflections on the beginning of a new millennium. The importance of this aspect is indicated by the number of words associated with the concept of a millennium of peace and justice—such as "millennial" (relating to Christ's anticipated reign of a thousand years), "millennialist" (meaning one who believes in this reign), "millennialism" (belief in the coming or the present existence of the millennium), "millennian" or "millenniary" (one who believes in the millennium). A wave of millennialism is sweeping the world.

In the history of Europe, millennialism has been an important factor not only at the beginning of the second millennium, but from time to time in history when various visionaries and religious leaders believed that the biblical millennium was about to dawn. At the beginning of another millennium, this historical and religious linkage to the promised age of justice surfaces once again in a more acute form.

Unable to project our vision into the infinity of the future, we tend to speculate on the future in convenient parcels of time. Most individuals philosophize at the commencement of a new year on what the year holds in store for them. At the commencement of a new decade, one tends to extend one's vision, taking in ten years at a time. At the commencement of a new century, there is naturally a magnification of the decade factor into what we may call "the century factor." At the commencement of a new millennium, there is a similar magnification of the century factor into what we may call "the millennial factor." We are witnessing this phenomenon now. There is a volcanic eruption of prophecies, both gloomy and optimistic, and of analyses, both prospective and retrospective. There is a plethora of prescriptions and resolutions. The collective mind is focused on the hopes of the future and the mistakes of the past in a manner not easily reproduced at any other period.

At the dawn of the second millennium, there was what has been described as "the vision of the year 1000."[1] Many thought in terms of the end of the world and the Last Judgment. Others used the occasion to focus on the ways in which religion could be better entrenched in the lives of people and of nations. Indeed, millennarianism has been an important concept throughout the history of Christianity, and many millenarian movements have existed even outside Europe—in Africa, the Caribbean, South American, and Asia.[2]

Nor is millennialism a concept confined to Christianity. There have also been millenarian movements quite unrelated to Christianity, such as the Taoist movements in the first century B.C. and the first and fourth centuries A.D.; also Buddhist-influenced popular millenarian white lotus movements from the twelfth through the nineteenth centuries A.D. So, also, in Japan there have been the *yo-naoshi m*ovements of the Tokugawa and Meiji periods. Elsewhere, millennial movements have existed among the Tupi-Guarani in the interior of Eastern Brazil, in Melanesia, and among the Plains tribes in North America in the late 1880s, culminating in the defeat of the Sioux Indians at the Battle of Wounded Knee in 1890.[3]

The mood for religious reflection at the commencement of a new millennium may therefore be described as globally widespread and deeply rooted in many traditions. One of the aims of this book has been to offer to this outpouring of millennial enthusiasm a perspective on the power and wisdom of the Lord's Prayer that may be harnessed toward world order in the new millennium.

Disillusionment With Established Religion

Paradoxically, one of the causes of religious revival is disillusionment with religion. We have noted already the feelings of youth who see organized religion as having failed to stem the tide toward godlessness, violence, and war that is endemic in the world today. They see churchgoing people everywhere complying with the forms of worship, but being party to the grossest iniquities—whether in the form of economic exploitation or arms dealing or environmental devastation—which are fast leading the world to irreversible tragedy. Many believe the new barbarisms seething all around them are possible only because, in their perception, the well-meaning, God-fearing and churchgoing public of the world lets its Christianity stop at the boundaries of their local church. As a result, they see religion as not reaching deep enough into their spiritual soul. They cast around, sometimes frantically, for an alternative that will combine spirituality with practical effectiveness.

Within mainstream religion, many adherents lean toward more intense and spiritually oriented versions, such as the charismatic movement in Catholicism, which now has many millions of adherents. Outside mainstream religion, people turn to avenues that will foster their personal spirituality. Among Christians, vast numbers are turning to such denominations as Jehovah's Witnesses, Seventh-Day Adventists, Mormons, and Assemblies of God, all of whose numbers have doubled, or even quadrupled, in the last two decades. Furthermore, a number of unorthodox sects gain ascendancy, both within Christian belief and external to it.

Some turn to other religions and to cults and sects that they see as guides to the deeper development of the personal and spiritual aspects of religion. Spirit mediums and "channels" gain a following. The search for the spiritual takes even the most unusual forms, even to the extent of preparedness to sacrifice oneself in the cause, as manifested in Jonestown in Guyana, the Waco compound in Texas, and by certain religious cults in Japan. Such is the dissatisfaction with the existing world order that some even see an escape to outer space as the only solution. In diverse places and in myriad ways the search is on for a key that will unlock the prison of humanity.

All of this drives vast numbers, not away from religion, but toward some form of it that they see as more acceptable and as squaring spiritual development with practical necessities.

The Collapse of Marxism

Marxism provided the world for a century with a set of values alternative to those of religion and a means of achieving them that was free of dependence on the religious moralities. It discouraged religious instruction and denied the legitimacy of demands for conformity between religious precept and public conduct.

By dividing the world into two evenly matched camps, it offered a haven and a refuge to those seeking the jettisoning of religious values. Another reason for its thriving was the fact that many a regime avowedly devoted to Christian principles behaved with scant regard for them, oppressing poor countries through a vicious colonialism and permitting their commercial conglomerates to exploit the underprivileged in both the rich and the poor worlds. Even regimes as iniquitous as that of apartheid in South Africa relied upon scriptural justifications, worked out by established churches such as the Dutch Reformed Church.[4]

Marxism therefore seemed to reign triumphant for three quarters of a century, attracting more and more of the oppressed within its fold. They came to see religion as a source of oppression rather than a means of relief.

We have already noted the political implications of the collapse of the Soviet Union. On another level, it means a fresh search for ideologies. Within the former Soviet camp, the latent religious spirit of the people is reviving. Religious practices and thought processes, heavy with the mold of decades of disuse, are being dusted out and refurbished.

A thousand years of Christianity had not been completely destroyed by that regime, but had only lain dormant, waiting for release from the forces belittling religion. A vast segment of the world, thus swept into the fold of resurgent Christianity, is reexamining the deep roots of its religious inheritance. Outside the former Soviet bloc, the collapse of Marxism has been viewed as a reminder that a century of public disavowal of religious values is historically only a passing episode against a backdrop of millennia of well-accepted religious wisdom. Throughout the former Soviet world, and indeed releasing its energies beyond that world, there surges a mighty tide of revitalized religion.

Humanity's Move Into Uncharted Waters

Environmental problems were scarcely envisaged until this century, because it was thought the seas, the atmosphere, and the land were vast enough to absorb any punishment that people could inflict on them. As America expanded westward, it was thought there were land, resources, and opportunities unlimited for all comers to take their fill. As science took its first halting steps, it was thought it could eventually find the answers to all our problems.

Hundreds of generations of humanity had relied on the wisdom of experience to deal with the problems encountered by the human race up to their time. The answers might not all have been correct, but past experience provided sufficient wisdom to guide each generation on its way. That is, until the present.

As humanity sails into uncharted waters we are very much like the legendary Odysseus, encountering at every turn phenomena that all the sailing experience of his forebears could not help him to handle. The one-eyed Cyclops whose tread would shake the earth, the magic of Circe who could convert the speech of men into the squeals of pigs, the tempting sirens who could lure men to their deaths by the most enchanting melodies, the whirlpools that could splinter to smithereens the stoutest work of man, the lethal contents of the secret bag of Aeolus, Ruler of the Winds, which curiosity opened, the wild paradise of Calypso, are all metaphorically awaiting our generation. It cannot yet conceive of the strange phenomena it will encounter as its fragile vessel sails through the uncharted waters it must traverse on its journey.

Odysseus had no recourse but to turn to the higher powers for guidance in the midst of these incomprehensible forces. Humanity, likewise, conscious of its helplessness, may have no other option. If it relies upon its own navigational skills, it will not weather the tempests and the whirlpools that await it. Nor will it be able to face those problems lying ahead, which are entirely without precedent in the long annals of our race.

A growing realization of human helplessness is driving many into what they see as a source of inner strength. It guided Odysseus to his destination. There may yet be in these higher values a cornucopia of untapped practical wisdom. Without it, we may be destroyed on the way, for there lies ahead of us a varied assortment of gambits of disaster.

Proliferation of Areas of Individual Moral Responsibility

We've already looked at the vastly increased number of situations in which, unpoliced by law, an individual is thrown back upon his or her own moral responsibility. Not everyone has a moral sense sturdy enough to make a moral code for himself or herself. Even if he or she should have a moral code, it will not be so finely nuanced as to afford a clear-cut answer in these difficult situations. Help is needed, which is sought from others in the field and from ethicists. As has already been noted, nearly every major hospital now has an ethics committee. Nearly every university has such a committee to oversee the area of human experimentation. In various walks of life, persons in positions of responsibility are casting around for moral guidance and inspiration as never before. This stimulates much thought about spiritual and religious values.

Scientific Insights Into the Wonderworld of Creation

There was a time when it seemed as if science would unravel the mysteries of the universe. Everything could be understood on the basis of the rational explanation that science would, in due course, unfold. The sense of mystery that surrounded our understanding of the universe would soon be dissipated as the cold inquiring light of science penetrated the veils that surrounded it. Consequently, the need that had existed from the most primitive stages of history for the interposition of a supernatural element between our understanding of the state of things and of the cause of things would disappear.

Contrary to expectations in the early days of science, we now face the paradox that the more science discovers, the more problems it reveals of a nature never contemplated before. With each new discovery, the question marks have multiplied. New enigmas have emerged in every shape and size. The sense of mystery that confounded our forefathers has intensified a hundredfold.

Whether in relation to the composition of the atom, or the workings of the human brain, or the size of the universe, or the nature of time, the wonders proliferate. We know, for example, that the trillions of cells that make the human body trigger chemical reactions every millisecond, totalling an inconceivable number of trillions of chemical reactions, which are needed every second to keep a human body alive. What force or genius coordinates these? "Which of you," we are asked in scripture, "by taking thought can add one cubit to his stature?" (Matthew 6:27, KJV). "Which of you," asks the modern inquiring mind, "can coordinate even a millionth part of these chemical reactions so as to keep the body alive and functioning for one second?"

The more than two hundred billion neurons in the human brain, each of which has up to one hundred thousand receptor sites for connections with other neurons, offer trillions of possible electrical circuits per second that keep the human brain functioning. No supercomputer can match the number of pathways available. Studies of human psychology and of the human brain and its workings "fill everyone who sees them with wonder and awe."[5]

The National Center for Human Genome Research is engaging in a search to map and identify every one of the 100,000 human genes and to determine the exact sequence of the three billion nucleotides that form the building blocks of human DNA. Such a colossal undertaking quite clearly will raise thousands of new problems not known before and, in particular, reemphasize the great question: How did all this fall into place?

Billions of universes, each containing billions of solar systems spread out across the known universe with an infinite number of similar universes, possibly stretching beyond, reveal a power far greater than our forefathers could have contemplated. Continuing research is only throwing up fresh wonders, as when, a few years ago, the galaxy called Abell 2029 was discovered, which alone contains a cluster of about a thousand galaxies, each with billions of stars. The Milky Way, which includes the sun and its solar system, contains only (!) about three billion stars, as opposed to Abell 2029's more than one hundred trillion stars.

The awe that our forefathers felt at seeing the sun, the moon, and the stars drove them to speculate on the nature of the divinity or supreme power who created them all. In our time, the microscope and the telescope have increased this sense of wonder in exponential terms. Science is driving this generation to philosophical speculation on the nature of the Divine.

Einstein demonstrated that time and space are interlocked in ways we never conceived. The physical and metaphysical implications of this discovery are constantly stimulating fresh speculation on the origin of the universe and the nature of the supreme power that regulates it. So, also, does his discovery of the convertibility of matter into energy ($e = mc^2$), which fuels speculation as to whether that supreme power, embodying an infinity of energy, could, in scientific terms, convert some of that energy into matter, the stuff of the universe.

The more we know, the more the wonder grows. We thus witness the paradox of a resurgence of religion stimulated by the triumphs of science. When the knowledge of future generations grows to proportions that will dwarf our knowledge, as our knowledge dwarfs that of our forebears, the drive toward religious speculation may well become ever more intense.

The Advance of Science to the Borders of Metaphysics

That confident era is past when science seemed able to roll back the frontiers of mystery and in the fullness of time reveal the fallacies that lay behind every superstition and spiritual belief. We have discussed that aspect in the preceding section. It is necessary here to note that these expectations went even further. As science took us away from religion and in the end exposed its hollowness, science would become the new religion—the religion of all rational thinkers. Indeed, belief only in logical reasoning and science would, in the next millennium, be the ultimate religion—a religion of experiential knowledge, as tested under the laser beams of relentless intellectual scrutiny. The scientist, a passionless thinking machine, would be the high priest of the new religion.

Science itself has snapped that daydream. The converse is in fact occurring. As seen in the last section, the scientific inquirer, as he or she proceeds further on the quest for empirical knowledge, finds not only that vast new areas open up for inquiry, but also realizes that the most sophisticated findings of modern science take the inquirer back to the realms of metaphysics. Flashes of intuition or inspiration often light the path to new discoveries. Quantum physics shows an unknown interaction between the mind of the experimenter and the substance of the material under investigation. Studies of the brain reveal that the intuitive function plays as important a role in the acquisition of knowledge as the rational—indeed, that a whole cortex of the brain subserves this purpose. Studies of the theory of probability lead to what is known as the "chaos factor," which defies all scientific prediction.

The world of quantum physics, by defying empirical investigation, throws us back upon metaphysical speculation. This has led to numerous studies of the interrelationship between modern physics and some of the transcendental principles foreshadowed by past metaphysical thought. *The Tao of Physics* by Fritjof Capra[6] is a well-known example of the attempt to trace a correspondence between modern physics and ancient metaphysics. It will suffice here to refer to Paul Davies' Templeton Prize-winning recent work—*The Mind of God*—on science and the search for ultimate meaning. The author concludes that:

> It seems at least worth trying to construct a metaphysical theory that reduces some of the arbitrariness of the world. But in the end a ratio-

nal explanation for the world in the sense of a closed and complete system of logical truths is almost certainly impossible.

Observing that the mystical path is possibly a way to an understanding of the universe, he observes:

> We, who are children of the universe—animated stardust—can nevertheless reflect on the nature of that same universe, even to the extent of glimpsing the rules on which it runs. How we have become linked into this cosmic dimension is a mystery. Yet the linkage cannot be denied.[7]

Scientific inquiry has taken us full circle back to the metaphysical kingdom out of which it sought to lead us.

The Ascendancy of Individualism

Edmund Burke said of the French Revolution that, by wiping the slate clean of all the collective groupings of society that had protected the individual in the past, it had left the individual defenseless and alone to face the might of an all-encompassing state.

In the past two centuries, in the wake of that revolution and others, many of the old collective groupings that sheltered the individual and fostered collective decision-making have broken down. No longer does the group make decisions for the individual in many areas that were once the prerogative of the group. The individual makes these decisions in reliance on the individual's own moral resources.

The demise of the totalitarian state structure in Eastern Europe has released into the realm of individual autonomy hundreds of millions of individuals for whom, in the previous dispensation, decisions on many matters touching their lives were made by the authority of the state. The world of state control has been transformed into one in which each individual must fend for himself or herself.

The closing days of the twentieth century thus witness a worldwide strengthening of individualism: in the Western world, an accentuation of individualistic values; and in the former Communist bloc, a release of the individual to seek his or her own destiny.

In all these societies, the individual is experiencing a newfound strength.

Whether as entrepreneur or campaigner for environmental conservation, women's rights, consumer protection, or the myriad other causes that have surfaced, the individual has come into his or her own, and become an independent, autonomous decision-maker on a variety of issues of great moment to the general public. Vast numbers of private individuals have become independent and responsible performers on the stage of public affairs. With decision-making also comes accountability, and this is again an exercise in justifying actions and decisions on the basis of values.

It is true that some segments of this new autonomous group are so commercially oriented that, to adapt Oscar Wilde's witticism, they "know the price of everything and the value of nothing." Yet it is also true that another considerable segment is deeply concerned to base its judgments upon values. For their values, they turn to religious systems, both familiar and unfamiliar.

Many segments are identifiable within this latter group. For example, a sizeable segment, known as the New Age movement, is estimated in the United States alone at between ten and twenty million. They are thought to represent "the most affluent, well-educated, successful segment of the baby boom."[8] The first principle of the New Age movement is individual responsibility. It is a Westernized version of the Eastern dogma of *karma*: that every action generates consequences the actor will eventually have to face. As the Bible puts it, "As you sow, so shall you reap." Individual responsibility stresses the present: "Each individual is responsible for everything he or she does."[9] In short, we have here the notion "forgive us our trespasses as we forgive them that trespass against us" deeply believed in and sincerely acted upon.

This new generation of influential decision-makers is turning increasingly to religion. They are globally linked by journals, books, and magazines—of which *New Realities, Yoga Journal, East West Journal,* and *New Age Journal* are examples. They "are trying to create a more harmonious world by seeking spiritual fulfillment, by demanding the best of themselves and others...."[10]

Across the world, like-minded influential young people who are molding tomorrow's world are looking to religion for inspiration. Computer technology helps them to network with one another. Together they form a powerful influence forging a better future through a new mix of idealism and practical skills.

Humanity's Capacity to Destroy

Never before, as a new century commenced itself, has humanity possessed the power to destroy itself. Its future balances on a razor's edge. The self-same power that can create a bountiful world for all of humanity can also destroy all of humanity, taking with it to a common destruction all the achievements of all the benefactors of humanity through all the centuries. Which way the choice will fall will depend on humanity's ability to restrain itself in the exercise of its newfound power. No laws or governmental struc-tures have thus far been devised, sufficient to hold back that little nudge that can tilt humanity over the brink. The fate of the race seems very much to rest in the lap of the gods, and some other guidance seems necessary—no matter what the religious belief of the person contemplating this awful prospect.

There is, therefore, a turn toward religion, not only for the moral prin-ciples that will hold back hearts and minds from the fateful decision, but also for help in the form of supernatural or Divine intervention to save humanity. Our dependence on the unbounded powers that created us seems greater now than when our earliest ancestors worshiped the unseen hand that rent the earth or threw the thunderbolt. We are back in an age when our dependence on the supernatural seems more naked than ever before.

Since the end of the Cold War, with its threat of a nuclear holocaust, other scenarios have surfaced, many of them more difficult to control than the nuclear button that could have set off global Armageddon. Nuclear exper-tise is spreading throughout the world, part of it escaping in unauthorized fashion from the unemployed scientific expertise of the former Soviet Union. Nerve gas and weapons of bacteriological warfare are produced, sometimes independently and sometimes with know-how stolen from the great pow-ers. Incidents like the release of nerve gas in the Tokyo subway show how brittle are our protective structures. Everywhere there is an indication that some higher guidance is required.

In a world in which it is so easy to set a match to an explosion that will end life upon the planet, the thinker turns increasingly to other more transcen-dent values than the materialism that has governed the world all these mil-lennia. Nothing prompts the mind to such reflections more sharply than the nearness of catastrophe; and the possibilities of catastrophe seem day by day to multiply and to come ever closer to home. The ground is ready, more than ever before, for the spiritual seeds that are sprouting all around us.

"Televangelization"

Preachers and popes, evangelists and hot gospelers, throughout the ages, could address audiences only within earshot. Thousands might have filled the public square to listen to the greatest preachers of their times, but that was the limit of their immediate reach.

Today's preacher can, in one hour, directly reach an audience of twenty million or more—a vaster audience than Martin Luther or Pope Gregory the Great could address throughout their lifetime. The messages go out morning, noon, and night and penetrate into the inmost recesses of the home. The preachers are many and the audiences are unlimited.

It may be that one in a hundred continues to listen when the program comes on and that many turn away from them. It may be that some of the captive audience feel open hostility to the message. Yet far more are exposed to the religious message—and far more frequently at that—than ever before in religious history.

The test of the extent of their listening public in a hard commercial activity is the success of these programs, for they would not be put on the air except to beam this message to a listening audience. The programs multiply. Televangelization is a force to be reckoned with, and it not only wins converts but constantly flashes a religious message into the consciousness of millions who would never step into a place of formal worship.

There may be a tendency to decry the televangelist and his message. In fact, some of them have had their insincerity exposed. Yet many do win converts and impress by the sincerity of their message and their call to high principle and noble purpose. As with Oliver Goldsmith's vicar, it cannot be gainsaid that many among "Those who came to scoff remained to pray"— the difference being that the village preacher's congregation is magnified a millionfold.

The Growing Satisfaction of Basic Needs

Most people are preoccupied with finding shelter, food, and clothing. They then need to find basic education for their children and basic medical support. The daily grind consumes their energy and time. What sociologists describe as "the hierarchy of needs" gives such urgent priority to these basic requirements as to leave no leeway for the pursuit of anything higher.

However, in the developed world and even in the poorer countries, a society has emerged that is free of the drudgery of satisfying these basic needs. An affluent class on a scale never before known in history has surfaced. For example, in India alone, it is estimated that this affluent class may comprise between two hundred and three hundred million people. This means that a large and significant element of the global population now has the freedom to turn from the pursuit of basic wants to the pursuit of the higher values.

When the mind is to a large extent freed from the daily grind that blocks out opportunities for contemplation and self-improvement, it turns to the higher values: art, culture, and philosophy. Throughout history the release of energies from the pursuit of daily wants has stimulated the pursuit of the higher values.

Self-scrutiny, self-improvement, and the search for more lasting sources of satisfaction can lead to, among other things, a turn toward religion. A class with time and money to spare is, in unprecedented numbers, imbibing afresh the strengthening influences of religion and spirituality.

Evidence of this trend is all around us. One example is the booming spiritual market—whether it be books, cassettes, or courses in spiritualism and self-improvement. In nearly every capital city in the world, the self-improvement courses that are advertised are legion; and in most of these the element of spirituality looms large. The mind of this affluent, powerful, decision-making group is tuned into religion in a manner not known before.

Environmental Devastation

We have referred to the ways in which the scale of modern corporate enterprise, the headlong rush of modern technology, and the pursuit of the wasteful lifestyle are converting much of the planet into an ecological desert. Holes in the ozone layer, the melting of the polar icecaps, the extinction of living species by the hour, deforestation and desertification, chemical and nuclear pollution of the seas and the atmosphere, combine to produce a possible apocalyptic vision of the collapse of all life-support systems. The clock of human destiny accelerates toward catastrophe, so long as these trends remain unchecked.

There is urgent need to turn back upon the tracks that are leading us to the brink. How do we change course?

Pursuit of the materialist paths only takes us further along the road to destruction. We need to take the road "less traveled."[11] A change of direction requires a change of perspective. A change of perspective requires a change of values. A change of values requires a search for the ultimate verities that lie beyond our material existence. The rush to destruction of our material inheritance can lead us back to the preservation of our spiritual inheritance.

Moreover, there lie within that spiritual inheritance a number of practical principles with great potential to address this particular problem. For example, most religions stress the concept of the good steward. We are the trustees of the earthly inheritance we receive and must hand it over to those for whom we hold it in trust—namely, the next generation—in as good a condition as we received it. The Islamic, Melanesian, Polynesian, African, and Amerindian religious traditions are particularly strong on this concept.

There is also the strong thrust of religious thought toward the simple lifestyle. Jesus taught his followers the values of simplicity and opposed the craving for material possessions. Buddhism teaches its followers to sit lightly upon the earth. The citizen of today's affluent societies has sometimes been assessed as putting two hundred times the pressure on the environment that is put upon it by the citizen of a country of the poor world.

The pursuit of what Lewis Mumford described as the "Pentagon of Power,"[12] namely, progress, profit, productivity, property, and publicity, is fast leading toward the spoliation of the inheritance of future generations. We have already discussed how these have become titanic forces that leave the human factor out of the balance sheet. Mumford, one of the foremost interpreters of civilization in this century, sees these forces as a mega-machine that is creating an ecological, cultural, and personal desert and a pollution of all that is human. We need a reexamination of the five forces identified by Mumford, which have become contemporary thought's most sacred convictions and have in fact become the idols of our time. The facts and arguments he assembled in 1970 have grown exponentially in their ominous portent in the quarter century that has elapsed since then. The necessary change of course and change of values is driving humanity to the pursuit of higher principles than those of this pentagon.

Cross-Fertilization of Cultures

The shrinkage of the globe through air travel and instant communication has meant that cultures insulated from one another through all recorded history are now in immediate contact. There is no room in the global village for the self-centered belief systems of the past. For the Western world, in particular, this means an exposure to spiritualism and other religions in a manner that makes it understand with a deeper significance the spiritual nature of its own inheritance. The breakdown of insularity brings greater richness of understanding.

Also, the immense depth of Eastern spiritualism has operated as an eye-opener. Here were vast dimensions of inner development, philosophical perspectives of the universe, techniques of meditation, and reflections on the nature of the supernatural that struck an answering chord in the idealism of the young.

Those hungry for spiritualism have begun to derive benefits from this new fare—from books, seminars, and classes. Popular journals and the media have picked up the message and beamed it to a wider public. The spark of spirituality, hitherto latent in the general public, has begun to be rekindled.

Notions of charity, humility, and oneness with humanity—deeply embedded in the Christian message, but smothered by the self-centeredness of centuries—have been strengthened by the realization that these values are universal.

> "Alas! for the rarity,
>   Of Christian charity"

wrote Thomas Hood (1799–1845) in his famous poem "The Bridge of Sighs." The suicide of a helpless young girl in a crowded city stimulated him to a poignant attack on the complacencies of the time. His anguished lament continued:

> "O! it was pitiful!
>   Near a whole city full,
>   Home she had none"

That was a protest against the uncaring attitude of a Christian community to its waifs and strays. There are many Thomas Hoods in contemporary society, protesting at the absence of Christian principles in their inward-looking cultures. The tendency to take one's religion for granted, or to relax, has been disturbed by the proximity of other religions. As already suggested, wisdom previously overlooked is now being perceived in the cultures of Africa, Melanesia, Polynesia, and Amerindia. All but those who were not prepared to see are being enlightened and are seeking more information. They read across the cultures as never before and the process of cross-fertilization, now only just begun, is likely to proliferate as millions of people of all countries link up with one another through computer networks. It is indeed an exciting time to be alive as the universal forces of hope, charity, compassion, and global fellowship coalesce and gather strength. They form a mighty tide of planetary goodwill. That force may well be unstoppable.

Transnational Forces of Evil

From the positive side of the global village, we turn now to the negative, which, ironically, is also promoting a resurgence of religious consciousness.

The global village is increasingly the arena of new international forces whose rampant immorality provokes a reversion to higher universal values to control them. Among these forces, which spread their malefic influence as if national boundaries do not exist, are the drug trade and terrorism. They have assumed a position so powerful that even governments cannot control them.

The drug trade, in particular, has driven whole communities back to their moral roots. Presidents and prime ministers across the world, in their attempt to counter the addiction to drugs, are striving to reach deeper into the moral heritage of their communities, and reminding the young in particular that there are other routes to mental calm and contentment than the escape route of drugs.

But these are not the only such forces. The armaments trade is another. It crosses national boundaries and often stimulates unrest and civil war with a view to increasing its sales. It is another example of immorality that is rampant and uncontrolled, which again provokes speculation on the higher morality that alone has power to hold it in check.

It is a sad reflection on the supposed refinement of the closing years of this century that the two greatest industries upon this planet, in terms of their turnover, are those that deal in armaments and narcotics. The one sells death and the other sells mental and physical degradation. Indeed, the latter seems set to overtake the former, with a turnover approaching a trillion dollars annually. No wonder governments all over the world are marshaling their resources as the surest means to meet its threat. Strongest among these resources are the spiritual heritage of their respective cultures.

Likewise, international gambling is spreading its tentacles as casinos sprout in the most unlikely places. This arouses a deep religious sentiment of resentment.

A Growing Awareness of Religion's Practical Importance

Whether one accepts religious principles or not, one must accept the practical fact that the moral code of over four billion of the world's population is shaped by religion. The principles embodied therein are principles that they will not dare deny publicly, and will, in fact, accept in the privacy of their conscience.

The traditional dismissal of religion as irrelevant to the world of practical politics has been the subject of serious reconsideration in recent times. As President Jimmy Carter has stated, in his Foreword to a book already cited,[13] his personal experience has convinced him that religion can be significant for peacemaking. At Camp David, for example, the religious beliefs of the three principals involved—Jimmy Carter, Menachem Begin, and Anwar el-Sadat—exercised such an influence on the course of the negotiations that a failure to understand that fact could, according to President Carter, have had an incalculable impact upon the talks. The rigorous separation of church and state in the United States and other countries has desensitized many citizens to the deep interaction of religious and political considerations in many parts of the world.

The various case histories presented in that study—from the Philippines, South Africa, Nicaragua, Nigeria, East Germany, Zimbabwe—all show the positive role religion can play in the process of peacemaking and the negative impacts that follow from the failure to accord religion a role.

If it is true that religion and cultural background play a practical role in the hard world of *diplomacy*,[14] it can likewise play a practical role in the world of law, for law, like diplomacy, aims at the peaceful settlement of disputes. The uplifting value of religious principle amid the down-to-earth concerns of practical statemanship cannot be without its impact in the world of law. If religion has been proved to be the missing dimension in politics, it can likewise be the missing dimension in law, for humanity's pursuit of its ultimate goal of peace cannot move only to the drumbeat of force and realpolitik. The caring society of the future cannot be founded on legal systems divorced from the fundamental values, the higher values, that have throbbed through the uplifting moments of human history.

There will always be those who see religion as an exercise in futility, deriding it in the most scornful terms as, for example, that it is "a daughter of hope and fear, explaining to ignorance the nature of the unknowable." Similarly, philosophy will be derided in such terms as that it is a "route of many roads leading from nowhere to nothing."[15]

Yet behind these veils of cynicism, skeptics realize that religion and philosophy cannot so easily be tossed out the window. Howsoever the tides of fortune have risen or fallen, these factors have played a role in human history; and the force of their impact upon human affairs is by no means spent. Even those who scoff realize its power. They know that they cannot define it or get to grips with it, but they know it is there. They know that a yearning for religious, philosophical, and transcendent values has been implanted in the human mind from the very hour when first it was capable of independent thought.

In short, deep within them, many of the doubters doubt their doubts. They do not openly give expression to them, but in the face of all the forces outlined above, their doubts increase. Many are the thinkers in history for whom transcendental values, once despised as being as slender as cobwebs, have turned into cables of steel.

CHAPTER 19

"ON EARTH AS IT IS IN HEAVEN"

E verything that has been said in this book is to prepare us for the ultimate practical goal we set for ourselves when we recite the Lord's Prayer: to establish God's will on earth, which we interpret as a quest for as near a reproduction as possible on earth of the qualities of the kingdom of heaven.

By doing God's will, we practice on earth to the best of our ability the values that prevail in the kingdom of heaven. The ideal is thus to create a regime upon earth, wherein hatred, envy, and selfishness are not the springs of human conduct. This is what we seek in the public arena. This macro-entity of public life is made up of millions of micro-entities. These are the wills of the hundreds of millions of citizens who make up the body politic of each state and of the world community. It is at that level that the Prayer can and will make an impact as we move into the next century.

The Kingdom of God and the Kingdom of Man

The notion of God's kingdom, ruled by the law of God, and man's kingdom, ruled by man-made law, lies at the heart of vast theological and legal discussions that have taken place down the centuries. The theme in one form or another has been central to legal thought. The philosophers of the Church equated the laws of God with natural law, thus joining up with an even more ancient stream of juristic writing, going back to Greek philosophy and even beyond—for the dichotomy between natural law and positive law has the most ancient of philosophical origins.

When, therefore, the supplicant prays that "God's kingdom come" he or she is praying for a bridge between these two orders, a bridge by which God's law, the law of the kingdom of heaven, becomes human law as well, governing the lives of men and women on this earth even before they reach the heavenly kingdom.

Thought about the city of God specially intensifies at times of great crisis as, for example, during the fall of Rome in the fifth century or during the Nazi subversion of all Christian values in the twentieth. The present time is also a time of crisis when all established values and the very continuance of civilization are brought into question by titanic forces that may well destroy them.

Saint Augustine propounded the doctrine in 413 A.D., three years after the sack of Rome by Alaric the Goth. He had seen a great legal system overthrown and taken over by a barbaric and lawless regime, and this may have sharpened his sensitivity to the starker contrast between the law of heaven—which stood far higher than even the well-organized Roman law— and the lawlessness he saw all around him.

Long before Augustine, Cicero had spoken of "a society coterminous with the universe which transcends all limited associations of state, race or class, and of which all men are qualified to be members simply in virtue of their common humanity."[1] Augustine was thus tapping a perennial stream of legal philosophy and at the same time giving it a new and more dramatic formulation in the light of Christian teaching.

> And thus it has come to pass that though there are very many and great nations all over the earth, whose rights and customs, speech, arms and dress, are distinguished by marked differences, yet there are no more than two kinds of human society, which we may justly call two cities according to our scriptures. The one consists of those who live after the flesh, the other of those who wish to live after the spirit....True justice has no existence save in that republic whose founder and ruler is Christ...

When all Europe was astir with the Reformation, Martin Luther made the doctrine of the two kingdoms the center of his theory of law, Church, and the state. The two kingdoms are locked in bitter conflict until the end of the world. Yet the dualism of the two kingdoms is not absolute and complete, for there is a unifying point: God's plan for law and love for all mankind.[2] Here is a bridge available to the faithful when they pray "Thy kingdom come."

Provoked by the godlessness of the Third Reich, Protestant theologians such as Erik Wolf, Johannes Henkel, and Hans Dombois worked out major new theories, analyzing the duality of the law of God's kingdom and that of the kingdom of man from a variety of standpoints. They drew upon history, sociology, philosophy, and jurisprudence to construct a variety of new approaches, Henkel emphasizing God's unifying plan based on love, Wolf emphasizing Christian brotherhood, and Dombois emphasizing the role of the Church as the institution par excellence concerned with man's relationship to God.

We are now historically at such a time of reflection on fundamentals.

Prayer and the Kingdom

The vision of the kingdom, "the city on the hill," "the New Jerusalem," is so beautiful and idealistic that there can be a strong tendency to relegate it to the apocalyptic future, to the will of God, to circumstances beyond humanity's control. This causes a lack of effort, a passiveness in the face of iniquity, a spirit of resignation to the evils of this world, until such time as God in his infinite wisdom decrees that the time has come. This attitude needs to be countered. Indeed, it denigrates the value of prayer in general and the Lord's Prayer in particular, for the Prayer expressly sets as its goal the attainment of a state "on earth as it is in heaven."

Passivity and inertia dominate the attitudes of many people, even when confronted with spectacles such as malnourished children perishing of starvation in faraway countries; aged refugee women painfully picking up grains of rice one by one from the dust of a passing food truck; patients gasping in the agonies of terminal lung cancer induced by smoking; bright young students demonstrating for an ideal who are at the receiving end of police batons and bullets; mass graves of victims of genocidal slaughter; people battered and scarred beyond recognition by military, police, or prison torture. Should there be a charge of apathy, any number of self-exonerating reasons is instantly drawn upon:

> "What impact can I make?"
> "What resources do I have to fight such a problem?"
> "It is an international problem"
> "The government should look after the problem"
> "I have my own problems"
> "It's not my business"

"I'm already overcommitted"

"I am not a charitable institution"

"We have done all we can for them"

"There are some people who just cannot be helped"

"If they can't look after themselves, they deserve their fate"

"I give enough charity"

"Some people can't look after themselves"

"It is entirely their fault"

"They had their chance and busted it"

"They wanted freedom and got it. Let them sink or swim"

Are such excuses in keeping with the Prayer? Can people offering them meaningfully recite the Prayer? Indeed, can they recite the Prayer at all, except as a mechanical repetition of a beautiful string of words?

It is necessary to fight against such feelings of futility, and avoid denigrating the power to transform the world that is given to people through prayer.[3] To pray the Lord's Prayer and not believe that the kingdom is attainable is a contradiction in terms. It is a negation of the faith and commitment that are the very essence of the Prayer.[4]

Such attitudes represent the antithesis of God's kingdom on earth. In their totality these attitudes form the substance of governmental attitudes, just as a body is made up of millions of cells. The health of the body depends upon the health of the cells, for sick cells do not make a healthy body. Each cell has a vital contribution to make to the whole. If, as we are taught, love is the essence of Christianity, this phrase means the institution of an earthly regime based upon love.

We shall not achieve God's will on earth as it is in heaven if we turn our gaze away from the major iniquities that give the kingdom of earth its seemingly permanent contours of evil. The iniquities dealt with in Part Two of this book hem in the promised land like a ring of mountains, preventing people of goodwill from entering it.

We conclude with a brief examination of the *characteristics* of the kingdom of heaven that we promise in the Prayer to replicate on earth.

"Thy kingdom," the kingdom of heaven or the kingdom of God, is a regime wherein justice, peace, and harmony prevail. As Paul reminds us in his Epistle to the Romans (14:17) the kingdom of God is not of worldly

things, but of "the righteousness, peace, and joy which the Holy Spirit gives."
That is the kingdom the supplicant asks to see on earth in contrast to the
vastly different kingdom of man wherein mundane values prevail. "Glorious things are spoken of thee, O City of God," says the psalmist (87:3,
KJV), thus capturing the spirit of God's kingdom which we would wish to
see on earth.

Commenting on Matthew 3:2, John Wesley observed:

> The Kingdom of Heaven and the Kingdom of God are but two phrases
> for the same thing. They mean not merely a future happy state in
> heaven, but a state to be enjoyed on earth.... In some places of scrip-
> ture the phrase more particularly denotes the state of it on earth; in
> others, it signifies only the state of Glory; but it generally includes
> both.[5]

As the *New Jerome Biblical Commentary* puts it, "The Prayer expects
an earthly, this-worldly realization of God's will."[6] However, this realization could not possibly be achieved except by human effort. In Martin
Luther's words, in the Fifth Wittenberg Sermon, of 1522: "[T]he kingdom
of God—and we are that kingdom—consists not in speech or in words, but
in deeds, in works and exercises."

> Every baptized Christian is taught to pray "Thy kingdom come" and
> that is interpreted to mean, Let thy will be done by men on earth as it
> is done by angels and saints in heaven. The Kingdom then is just the
> heavenly life brought down to earth, and its aim and standard is noth-
> ing short of the perfection of God Himself, "Be ye therefore perfect—
> especially be ye perfect in love—even as your Father which is in heaven
> is perfect" (Matthew 5:48).[7]

Love, therefore, seems to be a central characteristic of the kingdom of
heaven. How love was understood by Jesus appears in succinct summary in
the Sermon on the Mount. Hence, "the sermon is very important for a right
understanding of the kingdom."[8]

Of special interest to a justice-oriented study are the fourth, fifth, and
seventh beatitudes, dealing respectively with "those that hunger after righteousness," "the merciful," and "the peacemakers." All of these categories
are declared to be blessed and, if the beatitudes represent the spiritual atti-

tudes of the kingdom of heaven, righteousness, mercy, and peace rank high among them.

The beatitudes do not speak in terms of a heaven that is to come in the future to persons of designated categories. It is conceived of as being present here and now, "for theirs *is* the kingdom of heaven."

Also noteworthy, as indicating the lack of importance attaching to rank, is the third beatitude—"blessed are the meek." There is thus no place in the kingdom of heaven for pride of power, intellect, birth, race, culture, or wealth. "He has put down the mighty from their seat and exalted the humble and meek."

If special identification with the divinity were required in the midst of this high elevation of all the categories of beatitude, some special significance may be attached to the seventh beatitude—"blessed are the peacemakers." In their case the identity with the Divine is carried even further, for "they shall be called the children of God."

Jesus' entire life and teaching constituted a repudiation of the mundane values of this world, a repudiation dramatized in his rejection of the suggestion that all the kingdoms of the world could be his if he bent the knee to those values (Luke 4:5–9). He chose, rather, the lasting beatitudes of his own kingdom, the kingdom of heaven, which he sought to replicate on earth.

Jesus' Descriptions of the Kingdom of Heaven

How did Jesus himself view the kingdom of heaven that we are to emulate?

The phrase "kingdom of heaven" does not occur as such in the Old Testament. It is, however, "a central motif of Jesus' teaching."[9] Jesus constantly referred to this concept in his teachings. The phrases "kingdom of heaven" or "kingdom of God" appear fourteen times in Mark, thirty-two times in Luke, and thirty-seven times in Matthew.[10]

Time and again Jesus reverts to this theme. In Matthew 13:24, for instance, there is the parable of the kingdom of heaven being likened to a man who sowed good seed in his field. When his enemies sowed weeds among the wheat, and his servants, on discovering this, suggested that all be gathered up, the master said, "Let the wheat and the weeds grow together until harvest. Then I will tell the harvest workers to pull up the weeds first and burn them, and then gather up the wheat and put it in my barn." An inexorable process of justice would sort out the weeds from the wheat, giving each its proper place.

A similar idea permeates the parable of the net thrown into the sea, to which the kingdom of heaven is likened in Matthew 13:47–48. It gathers fish of every kind, and when it is drawn ashore, the fish are sorted out, the good being stored in vessels while the bad are thrown away, in the same way as evildoers will be separated from the righteous.

Since there is no passport to the kingdom of heaven for any but the righteous, it is axiomatic that righteousness reigns therein.

We've seen in an earlier chapter that the parable of the Ten Maidens also carries implications for entering the kingdom. In other descriptions of the kingdom of heaven Jesus stresses its infinite value. It is a prize beyond compare, for which all other prizes and values must be forsaken. The kingdom of heaven is like "a treasure hidden in a field." Its discoverer sells all he has and buys that field (Matthew 13:44) or, again, "a pearl of great price," for the purchase of which a merchant in search of fine pearls will sell all that he has (Matthew 13:45).

Yet again, it has leavening or transforming qualities, uplifting the vast mass with which it comes in contact, for a little leaven transforms and uplifts the entire loaf (Matthew 13:33). So, also, the kingdom of heaven is like a mustard seed. "It is the smallest of all seeds, but when it grows up, it is the biggest of all plants. It becomes a tree so great that the birds of the air come and make nests in its branches" (Matthew 13:31–32).

These last two parables emphasize the fact that the kingdom of heaven is scarcely visible or, to the superficial observer, of very small proportion, like the leaven and the mustard seed. In however small a degree these are present, they can influence the whole of society and grow to great proportions, just as the leaven can elevate the whole loaf, or the mustard seed become an enormous tree providing a place of rest and shelter. The extent of their potential is not discernible to the human eye.

Those with the power of discernment can thus see how far a little speck of goodness can influence and benefit the whole world. Anyone can see how many seeds there are in an apple, but it is wholly beyond our power to see how many apples there are in a seed. That is a potential, vast and unknowable, which lies beyond the power of any human being to assess. Such is the kingdom of heaven. It can only start with small beginnings in individual acts of kindness and love. From such beginnings it grows to great proportions, but the leaven or the seed, however small, are necessary to

make the beginning. That leaven or seed comes from individual wills activated to the right course of conduct by the principles set out in the Prayer.
What each individual can contribute may be infinitely small, but it is infinitely important that that contribution be made.

Also, we are told, membership of the kingdom of heaven is an extremely
privileged state, for he who is least in the kingdom of heaven is greater than
even John the Baptist, who is described in the same verse, "among those
born of women there has risen no one greater than John the Baptist."

In other words, the greatest on earth are lesser than the least in heaven.
To the question, "Who is the greatest in the kingdom of heaven?" Jesus
answered:

> The greatest in the Kingdom of heaven is the one who humbles him-
> self and becomes like this child (Matthew 18:4).

Race and tribe, rank and privilege, birth or learning count for nothing
against those fundamental qualities that are prized in heaven and amid which
the Father reigns.

When viewed in succinct form, we see in the parables a clear and useful
summary of the characteristics of the kingdom of heaven.

Analogies Used by Jesus	*Implications of Analogy*
1. a pearl of great price	The kingdom of heaven does not come easily. It has to be earned.
2. a treasure hidden in a field	One has to search for it
3. leaven, which causes a loaf to rise	It transforms
4. a grain of mustard seed	It grows gradually within oneself; if one has it in the littlest measure, it can grow to vast proportions
5. a tree full-grown from the mustard seed in which the birds of the air seek shelter	From small beginnings, it can grow to become a place of shelter and rest
6. a net thrown into the sea, from the catch of which fish are chosen or discarded	A place of judgment, where justice is not only determined, but also implemented

7. a man sowing good seed in his field. The weeds are gathered and burned and the good seed is stored in the barn.	There is no place in it for any but the good
8. you must be like children to enter the kingdom of heaven	Humility is the essence of the qualifications for membership. Aristocracies of every kind are done away with
9. the ten bridesmaids	A state to be carefully prepared for
10. a king settling accounts with his servants	A place of absolute justice where the measure you have given will be the measure you will get

The Revolutionary Nature of the Kingdom of Heaven

Of the kingdom of heaven, as taught by Jesus, H. G. Wells has written[11] that it is remarkable that, despite the enormous prominence given to it by Jesus, it has been of considerable insignificance in the procedure and teaching of most of the Christian churches. Even in the Lord's Prayer, it occupies pride of place, for it is thrice repeated in the midst of the economy of words characteristic of the Prayer.

This doctrine of the Kingdom of Heaven, which was the main teaching of Jesus, and which plays so small a part in the Christian creeds, is certainly one of the most revolutionary doctrines that ever stirred and changed human thought. It is small wonder if the world of that time failed to grasp its full significance, and recoiled in dismay from even a half-apprehension of its tremendous challenges to the established habits and institutions of mankind…For the doctrine of the Kingdom of Heaven, as Jesus seems to have preached it, was no less than a bold and uncompromising demand for a complete change and a cleansing of the life of our struggling race, an utter cleansing without and within.[12]

"[T]here were no chosen people and no favorites in the Kingdom of Heaven" and "there are no privileges, no rebates and no excuses in the Kingdom of Heaven." Jesus

> was like some terrible moral huntsman digging mankind out of the snug burrows in which they had lived hitherto. In the white blaze of this kingdom of his there was to be no property, no privilege, no pride and precedence; no motive indeed and no reward but love. Is it any wonder that men were dazzled and blinded and cried out against him?[13]

The notion of the kingdom of heaven was not a simple notion of the separation of the forces of good from those of evil and a preservation of the former. Rather, it was an ongoing struggle, where virtue prevailed over evil. In the words of the philosopher Alfred North Whitehead, it was "The overcoming of evil by good."[14]

On Earth...Peace

The Prayer requests that God's will be done, not merely in respect of the individual, and not merely in respect of the individual's immediate family or society, but "on earth." The Prayer is thus for the whole world; and if God's will be a regime of justice, it is a prayer for justice for the whole world. As Saint John Chrysostom put it:

> [H]e did not say "thy will be done in me or in us," but "on earth," the whole earth so that...earth no longer differs from heaven.[15]

That, briefly stated, is the highest ideal toward which the Prayer teaches its reciters to aspire, and that encapsulates the theme of this work.

Christianity is saturated with the notion of peace, and it is in this light that the entire message of the Lord's Prayer must be read. It will be remembered that peace on earth was the song of the angels at the birth of Christ. "My peace I leave you" was the message left to the disciples shortly before the death of Christ. "The Prince of Peace" was a favored description of the mission of Christ. The thought underlying "on earth as it is in heaven" is thus a thought deeply rooted in the notion of peace—peace in the family, peace among the flock of the good shepherd, peace in the nation, peace among the nations.

The Kingdom of God is by definition a kingdom of peace. If the kingdom of God is to be instituted on earth, a primary requisite must be peace. If peace is a requisite, the requisites of peace must, in turn, receive attention, and a primary requisite of peace is forgiveness and resistance to temptation. The United Nations Charter puts peace in the forefront of the requisites necessary "to save succeeding generations from the scourge of war."

The Universal Declaration of Human Rights, and numerous other human rights documents, have given fine and elegant expression to the fundamentals of peace and human rights as agreed upon by the community of nations. Yet there is a danger that even these formulations are often looked upon with more emphasis upon their letter than their spirit.

We are now within sight of our goal. We have come a long way from the mere recitation of the Prayer as a spiritual exercise, to its translation into practical precepts.

Peace, forgiveness, abstention from trespasses and temptations, recognition of human dignity, love, brotherhood and sisterhood, righteousness, universalism—all of these are built into the Prayer as they are built into the kingdom of heaven. The Prayer, by enshrining these values, constructs a bridge that will span the gulf between the two kingdoms. It shows us the way, if we will only take it. We are given the free will to choose the way we shall proceed.

As the moving hand of history is poised to write a new chapter in the story of humanity, we are being given a renewed—and perhaps a final—opportunity to transform into reality the fondest vision of the ages: the vision of a kingdom of justice "on earth as it is in heaven." If we can etch the majestic principles of the Lord's Prayer into the future history of humanity, we shall truly create for our posterity a world that "is charged with the grandeur of God."[16]

APPENDIX

THE PRAYER'S TREASURY OF HUMAN RIGHTS

We have seen in the preceding pages how the Prayer, interpreted in the light of the life and teachings of its author (see chapter 4), captures every aspect of human life. Looked at in this light, it indeed contains, embedded within it, a boundless treasury of human rights.

Throughout this book we have noted the power of the Prayer and the world's neglect of its principles of practical conduct. We have seen the reach of its teaching of forgiveness and the damage caused to the human prospect by hatred, the opposite of forgiveness, which dominates the world order. We have noted the many trespasses and temptations that beset our path as we commence our preparations for the next century, our century of last opportunity.

The road map with which the Prayer furnishes us runs through human rights territory, for it is through a recognition of the dignity and worth of each human being that we can build the New Jerusalem. That recognition, and the respect on which it is based, can come only from the internalization of these values in each individual. Power to restructure the world comes not from the barrel of a gun, as Mao taught, but from the depths of the heart. The Lord's Prayer is an established route to the hearts of millions. If its principles of action take root there through adequate reflection, we have at our disposal the necessary power to restructure the world.

The main thoroughfare indicated on this road map is togetherness: We are not isolated individuals praying for our own personal needs, but a group praying for *our* daily bread, entreating *our* common father, seeking forgiveness of *our* trespasses. One cannot sincerely utter the Prayer while building walls around oneself; we are required, rather, to demolish such egotistic walls as currently exist, and make common cause with humanity.

The world of the future, requiring as it does this feeling of fellowship, imposes a requirement of participation, assistance, service, abandonment of lame excuses, and interest in the problems of our neighbor, however geographically remote.

This book has aimed at translating the lofty spiritual principles of the Prayer into rules of practical conduct for our age. A powerful means of doing so is to enmesh those principles into the global human rights system. That system is today uplifting and inspiring national legal systems throughout the world, by providing them with a universally accepted set of norms to which they should adhere.

The linkage between the Prayer and the human rights system is thus critical if the Prayer is to penetrate into the legal system itself—as is essential if there is to be a just national order within countries, and a just international order between them.

What follows are some of the pathways charted out in the Prayer, expressed in the idiom of modern human rights. By formulating them in this fashion, we reap the double advantage that the practical strengths of the Prayer are more clearly perceived and, at the same time, the human rights movement throughout the world is considerably strengthened.

Concepts Relating to Basic Human Rights

- A duty-related, rather than rights-related, view of human rights
- The concept that rights inhere in people by virtue of their very humanity
- The concept that duties inhere in people by virtue of their very humanity
- Equality of all human beings as members of a common family, irrespective of differences in status, learning, ability, race, nation, clan, caste, creed, gender, or age
- Nondiscrimination among all human beings (a corollary of the above)
- The concept that an intrinsic dignity inheres in all human beings by virtue of their very humanity
- Since human rights are a birthright of every human being, no authority, however powerful, can take them away (the concept of inalienability, or of "certain inalienable rights," in terms of the American Declaration of Independence, 1776)
- The notion that these rights cannot in principle be suspended, even temporarily (nonderogation of basic rights)

- Every person is possessed of a personality before the law which the legal system must fully recognize
- Every person has a direct right of access to authority
- There is a duty of affirmative action to assist those in distress
- There is a duty to observe nonviolence in the settlement of all disputes
- Every person is possessed of economic rights ("daily bread")
- Every person is entitled to social rights
- Every person is entitled to cultural rights
- There is a basic entitlement of everyone to the necessities for survival—food, shelter, etc. ("daily bread")
- Every employee is entitled to a fair wage
- Apartheid in every shape or form is prohibited
- Slavery in every shape or form is prohibited
- Torture in every shape or form is prohibited
- Forced labor in any shape or form is prohibited
- Each person's privacy (an adjunct of dignity) is to be respected
- All persons are entitled to protection from all forms of exploitation
- Children are entitled to special protection
- Disadvantaged persons and groups are entitled to special protection
- Condoning iniquity to another involves condoning the principle lying behind that iniquity, and is thus a condonation of an iniquity to oneself
- A need exists to address not only the deprivations of human rights, but also the economic and social causes lying behind those deprivations
- There is a duty to assist in the upliftment of those in need and hence to assist in their development toward economic independence
- There is an obligation of humanitarian conduct in all situations of life and toward all people, including particularly such groups as prisoners, refugees, the disabled, the aged and infirm, foreigners, and, not the least, one's enemies

Concepts Relating to the Judicial Process

- Justice is impartial and applies to all equally
- Every person enjoys equality before the law

- The principles of justice do not vary from age to age, but are eternal
- Every individual is entitled to the recognition of his or her free will and is consequently individually accountable for his or her actions
- Formalism and literalism are not in accordance with true justice
- All decisions must be made with justice and fairness and not blindly in reliance on the strict letter of the law
- Every person against whom an accusation is made is entitled to a fair trial
- Judgments must always conform to justice and must not be arbitrary or induced by fear or favor
- Punishment must fit the offense, and degrading, cruel, or unusual punishments are prohibited
- The redress and punishment afforded by law are often inadequate to right the wrong that has been done and, hence, society and the offender have a duty to go beyond this in order to rehabilitate the victim.
- The test of the legality of an action is not the test of its justice
- There is a wide gulf between the concept of "legal" action and "just" action
- There is a higher law or a higher set of standards standing over the particular laws of each state
- There is a need for reconciliation between the parties to a dispute which formal justice tends to ignore
- Many human rights violations and disputes result from the rancor and hatred which remain as a legacy of disputes that are only formally solved without reconciliation and forgiveness
- Right conduct should not be the result of fear of punishment, but of a conviction of its moral correctness
- Formal justice can police only a small segment of the area of wrongful conduct
- Formal justice requires a combination of action and intention to constitute a wrongful act, but moral rightness or wrongness does not necessarily require an external act
- Formal legal systems can be used as an instrument of oppression and a means of entrenchment of privilege. It is the duty of all those playing a part in their administration to ensure that they are not used for such purposes

- Those in prison must be well looked after with due regard to their dignity as human beings

Concepts Relating to Social Rights and Responsibilities

- The concept of brotherhood and sisterhood implicit in the Prayer leads to mutual duties and responsibilities
- The concept of brotherhood and sisterhood implicit in the Prayer implies the concept of collective or social responsibility on the part of the group to which one belongs, for the wrongful acts of individual members of that group
- The concept of social solidarity resulting from the two prior concepts
- The prohibition of the hoarding of social resources
- The concept of a right to social progress and to the economic development necessary for this purpose
- The concept of the socially oriented use of property
- The concept of environmental duties
- The concept of the duty to assist those in distress (the "Good Samaritan" attitude)
- The duty of active assistance to the disadvantaged
- The duty of intergenerational fairness in the use of earth resources
- The duty of intergenerational fairness in conserving the environment
- The concept of trusteeship of earth resources
- Regard for all who would be affected by one's acts or omissions, however remote they may be, and not merely those with whom one is in direct relationship
- Resistance to insensitivity to the great global problems of our time
- Active cooperation with one's neighbors in the solution of common problems
- The concept that those who are in power over society—executive, legislative, or judicial—hold that power in trust, to be used according to the principles of justice
- The concept of respect for other religions
- The concept of respect for other cultures

Concepts Relating to Individual Conduct

- To use as the standard of one's actions and attitudes toward one's neighbors the rule that we should love our neighbors as ourselves
- At the very least to act toward our neighbors as we would have them act toward us
- One cannot ask forgiveness from others of wrongs done to them unless one practices forgiveness oneself
- The duty to attempt so far as is possible to understand the problems of others
- The duty to attempt so far as is possible to understand the background of other groups and races
- The duty to ensure that one's actions do not have the effect, even remotely, of taking the "daily bread" out of the mouths of others
- The duty to acquaint oneself with information relating to the sufferings of others, rather than turning a blind eye to them
- The principle that condonation of wrongdoing is close to aiding and abetting such wrongdoing and thus involves a measure of personal responsibility
- The duty to translate the "Good Samaritan" concept of assistance to those in distress into a principle of daily living
- The importance of the active performance of good, rather than the merely negative abstention from evil
- The need to have due regard to considerations of justice in all the actions of daily living
- The recognition of the notion of a moral duty which reaches beyond the requirements of the letter of the law
- The observance of good faith in all one's dealings and relationships with others
- The importance of fair dealing in all one's dealings and relationships with others
- The immorality of using the legal concept of freedom of contract to extract unfair advantages from the weaker contracting party
- The immorality of using the legal concept of property ownership in justification of the antisocial use of property
- The immorality of using freedom of speech to promote such activities as unfair advertising or the dissemination of half-truths in the media or otherwise

- The immorality of using screens of corporate registration to shield one from the moral responsibility for corporate decisions to which one is party
- The duty to ensure that one's daily bread is not earned in unrighteous fashion, contradictory to the principles of the Prayer
- The duty of affirmative action to redress handicaps and inequalities
- The avoidance of taking cover under group responsibility for one's own violations of moral duty
- To avoid discriminations of race, color, religion, class, sex, etc. in all one's dealings
- So to use one's property as not to cause harm to others
- Each individual himself or herself chooses the standards by which his or her individual conduct is judged
- The avoidance of literal and legalistic interpretations of one's rights and duties
- The duty of each individual to work toward the peaceful resolution of all disputes, domestic as well as international
- The duty of every one to do what is in their power to bring about a regime of righteousness on earth

Concepts of International Law

- The concept of universalism
- The concept of peace
- The duty of environmental protection
- Recognition of the right to development as a human right
- A higher or universal law standing above the laws of states
- The recognition of a universally binding code of human rights
- The principle of intergenerational fairness
- The observance of fair international trading practices
- Humanitarian conduct in peace and war
- The criminality of genocide
- The rejection of colonialism in all its forms and practices
- The principle of mutual respect of states and peoples for each other
- The duty of active cooperation of each state with all other states in the solution of global problems, rather than contentment with mere passive coexistence with them

- The equitable sharing of earth resources
- The principle of trusteeship of earth resources
- The peaceful resolution of disputes
- The observance of good faith in all international dealings
- As a consequence of good faith, the observance of a state's promises to other states, and hence the sanctity of treaties

Many more items could certainly be added to this list. But these in themselves constitute an invaluable road map. It is endorsed with all the *Authority* of one of the greatest moral systems the world has seen. It proceeds from a *Personality* symbolizing human dignity in the face of repression, human values in the face of tyranny, love and compassion in the face of hatred. With unwavering moral certitude His finger pointed the way and, in the present plight of humanity, it seems clear—even at this eleventh hour—that the route He pointed out can ensure our survival.

From its realm of eternal light, the Prayer streams rays of practical guidance upon us, yet century after century we have shut them out and moved from blunder to blunder in the resulting darkness. When we are under the pressure of forces threatening our very survival, it is time to open the shutters and let the light stream in.

NOTES

Chapter 1

1. For example, *Religion, the Missing Dimension of Statecraft*, Douglas Johnston and Cynthia Sampson (eds.), Oxford University Press, 1994.
2. President Carter, in his Foreword to *Religion, the Missing Dimension of Statecraft*.
3. See, for example, Samuel T. Huntington's *The Clash of Civilizations and the New World Order*, Simon & Schuster, N.Y., 1996.
4. See R. Müllerson, *Human Rights Diplomacy*, Routledge, 1997. See, especially, Ch. 3.
5. H. G. Wells, *The Fate of Homo Sapiens*, Martin Secker & Warburg Ltd., 1939, p. 312.

Chapter 2

1. *Catechism of the Catholic Church*, St. Paul's, 1994, p. 665, para. 2776.
2. *Exegesis in Rhyme of the Lord's Prayer*, by Hugo Grotius, to be sung to the tune of the twelfth Psalm, Bruyn Harmansz Schinckel, Delft, 1619.
3. On this aspect, see the thoughtful study *God and Utopia: The Church in a Technological Civilization*, by Gabriel Vahanian, Seabury Press, New York, 1978.
4. 2nd ed., 1989.
5. Michel de Montaigne, *Essays*, LVI, 1580.
6. The Catholic Encyclopedia, Vol. IX, p. 356.
7. Ibid.
8. See Per-Olaf Sjögren, *The Jesus Prayer*, St. Paul Publications, Bangalore, 1978.
9. C. G. Jung, *Modern Man in Search of a Soul*, Ark Paperbacks, 1933, p. 278.
10. *Why We Can't Wait*, Signet Classics, 1963, p. 92.
11. See, on this aspect, the *UN Declaration on the Promotion among Youth of the Ideals of Peace, Mutual Respect and Understanding among Peoples*, GA Resolution 2037 (XX), 1965, which points out that it is the young people who suffer most in the conflagrations of our time.
12. John and Charles Wesley, *Poetical Works*, 13 vols., ed. G. Osborne, London, 1868–1872, Vol. 1, pp. 230–231.

Chapter 3

1. *New Jerome Biblical Commentary, supra.*, p. 702.
2. Ernst Lohmeyer, *The Lord's Prayer*, Collins, 1965 (tr. John Bowden), p. 285.
3. Romans 2:19–20, cited by Lohmeyer.
4. 1st series, 1931.
5. Lohmeyer, *supra.*, p. 285.
6. Robert Schuller Ministries, 1990, p. 5.
7. Pierre Lefevre, *One Hundred Stories to Change Your Life*, St. Paul Publications, 1989, p. 81.
8. *The Interpreter's Dictionary of the Bible*, p. 155.
9. See, generally, Concilium, *The Dignity of the Despised of the Earth*, Seabury Press, N.Y., 1979, Jacques Pohier and Dietmar Mieth (eds.), pp. 12–20, on the importance for fundamental moral theology of Jesus' relationship with the poor and the outcasts.
10. Gilbert Murray, *Five Stages of Greek Religion*, Watts & Co, The Thinker's Library, 1935, p. 218. See also p. 181.
11. William Barclay, *The Plain Man Looks at the Lord's Prayer*, Collins, London, 1964, p. 45.

12. *Devotions.*
13. Dummelow (ed.), *The One Volume Bible Commentary*, Macmillan, New York, 1973, p. 646.
14. Ibid.
15. *The Lord's Prayer: the Prayer of Integral Liberation*, trans. from Portuguese by Theodore Morrow, Orbis Books, New York, 1983, p. 28.
16. *Mahatma Gandhi, Selections From*, N.K. Bose (ed.), 1948.
17. Emerson, *Essays*, 1841.
18. Konrad Braun, *Justice and the Law of Love*, Swarthmore Lectures, George Allen and Unwin, 1950, p. 29.
19. Ibid., p. 30.
20. *De Veritate*, 1259.

Chapter 4

1. *New Jerome Biblical Commentary*, p. 1149.
2. Ibid., p. 1147.
3. Ibid., p. 1151.
4. Ibid.
5. Ernest Lohmeyer, *The Lord's Prayer*, op. cit., p. 1.
6. Ibid.
7. See, for example, Leonardo Boff, *The Lord's Prayer: The Prayer of Integral Liberation, supra.*
8. Julius Stone, *Human Law and Human Justice*, Stanford University Press, 1965, p. 25.
9. *Concilium*, October 1969, p. 12.
10. Keith Mason, *Constancy and Change*, Federation Press, Sydney, 1990, p. 29.
11. *The Cambridge History of the Bible: The West from the Reformation to the Present Day*, S.L. Greenslade (ed.), 1963, p. 51.
12. See *Harper's Bible Dictionary* under "Justification."
13. In the Preface to his translation of the Indian classic *Sakuntala*; see also *Sakuntala*, tr. by Michael Coulson, Folio Society, 1992, introduction by William Radice.
14. M. M. Pickthall, *The Glorious Koran*, London, George Allen & Unwin, 1930.
15. *The Bhagavad Gita*, tr. from the Sanskrit, with an introduction by Juan Mascaró, Penguin Books, 1962, p. 35.

Chapter 5

1. *Catechism, op. cit.*, para. 2844.
2. Ibid., para. 2841; *Matthew, 6:14–15.*
3. *Sermons on the Lord's Prayer*, (*La preghiera del Signore: omelie sul Padre nostro*), introduction, trans. and notes by Giuliana Caldarelli, Edizioni Paoline, Roma, 1983, p. 5.
4. *Life Thoughts*, 1858.

Chapter 6

1. Note: Luke [11:4] speaks of "sins" and Matthew [6:12] speaks of "debts." This discussion uses the phraseology of the Book of Common Prayer.
2. Richard P. McBrien, *Catholicism*, revd. ed., 1994, Collins Dove, p. 888.
3. *The Challenge of Peace*, para. 244.
4. For the different theoretical views on the media problem, see the author's *Justice without Frontiers: Furthering Human Rights*, Kluwer Law International, 1997, chs. 13 and 14.
5. Yale University Press, 1964.
6. [1932] A.C. 562.
7. Kahlil Gibran, *The Prophet*, Heinemann, 1928, pp. 49–50.
8. See Gregory Baum, *Theology and Society*, Paulist Press, New York, 1987.
9. Cf., also, the pastoral letter of twenty–five American bishops of the region of Appalachia entitled "This Land is Home to Me," analyzing what social sin means in that comparatively poor region of the US.
10. See Baum, op. cit., p. 287.
11. A. N. Allott, "African Law," in J. D. M Derrett (ed.), *An Introduction to Legal Systems*, Sweet & Maxwell, 1968, p. 140.
12. See Walpola Rahula, *What the Buddha Taught*, Gordon Fraser, 1959, p. 48.
13. Sri Aurobindo, *The Foundations of Indian Culture and the Renaissance in India*, Sri Aurobindo Ashram, Pondicherry, 1971, p. 91.

Chapter 7

1. See Boff, op. cit., p. 97.
2. *A Plain Man Looks at the Lord's Prayer*, pp. 115–117.
3. *Catechism of the Catholic Church, op. cit.*, p. 514, para. 2845.
4. *The Sermon on the Mount*, 2:9.
5. Migne, *Patrologia Graeca* 10, 1601.
6. Plato, *Phaedrus*. See, Harvey, *Oxford Companion to Classical Literature*, 1940, p. 319.
7. *Rgveda*, I.89, emphasis added. See, on this sentence, Georg Feuerstein, *Introduction to the Bhagavad Gita*, Rider & Co., London, 1974, p. 22.
8. See Barclay, op. cit., p. 119.
9. Origen, *On Prayer*, 29.5.

Chapter 8

1. Pt. II, 4.
2. Al Ash'ari, died 935 A.D.
3. St. Basil (c. 329–379), *Hexamoron*.
4. *Selected Writings of William Law*, Stephen Hobhouse (ed.), reprinted 1972.
5. *Dhammapada*, 5th century B.C.
6. *Catechital Lectures*, 350.
7. François de La Rochefoucauld, *Maxims*, 1665.
8. *Catechism of the Catholic Church*, op. cit., p. 516, para. 2850.
9. Ibid., para. 2854.

Chapter 9

1. Lohmeyer, op. cit., p. 203.
2. Thomas Pakenham, *The Scramble for Africa*, Weidenfeld and Nicholson, 1991, p. 611.
3. Pakenham, ibid., p. 602.
4. Lucien Bodard, *Green Hell: Massacre of the Brazilian Indians*, Dutton & Co., New York, 1971, p. 161, trans. from the French.
5. Ibid., p. 5.
6. Anchor Books, 1966.
7. *War and Peace*, Signet Classics, 1980, pp. 1414–1415.
8. B. V. A. Roling, *International Law in our Expanded World*, Amsterdam, 1960, p. 27, cited also in R.P. Anand, "Attitude of the Asian African States towards certain problems of International Law" (1966), 15 *International and Comparative Law Quarterly*, p. 55, at p. 60.
9. United Nations Charter, Preamble.
10. Rachel Ehrenfeld, *Narco Terrorism*, Basic Books, 1990, p. xx.
11. A. Whittaker, "Enslaved Children," *Anti-Slavery Reporter*,1990, Series 7, Vol 13, No. 6, pp. 77–85, at 82.
12. Ibid., p. 83.
13. P. Bond, "The Sale of Tatip," *Anti-Slavery Reporter*, 1989, Series 7, Vol. 13, No. 5, pp. 26–36, at 27.
14. "Sex Tourism," *Anti-Slavery Newsletter*, No. 18, Feb. 1992, p. 3.

Chapter 10.

1. For an examination in greater depth of the responsibilities of nuclear scientists, see this author's *Nuclear Weapons and Scientific Responsibility*, Longwood Academic, 1984. See also his draft of a "Proposed UN Declaration of Scientific Responsibility in Relation to Nuclear Weaponry," in the *Encyclopaedia of Social Inventions*, London, 1989, pp. 194–5.
2. *Faith and Violence*, University of Notre Dame Press, 1968, pp. 6–7.
3. See the author's *The Slumbering Sentinels: Law and Human Rights in the Wake of Technology*, Penguin, 1983, p. 151.
4. See an article by the present author titled "Traffic in Armaments: A Blind Spot in Human Rights and International Law" (1987), 2 *Development Dialogue, Journal of the Dag Hammarskjöld Institute*, Sweden, p. 68.
5. See Ralph Lapp, *The Weapons Culture*, Pelican, 1968.
6. *Redemptor Hominis*, Ch. 16.
7. Russell Scott, *The Body as Property*, Allen Lane, 1981.
8. See June Goodfield, *Playing God: Genetic Engineering and the Manipulation of Life*, Hutchinson, 1977.

9. For a layman's account of this see *Time Magazine*, 19 January 1994, pp. 20–38.
10. *Herald Tribune*, 11 June 1997.
11. The mining of Nauru presents a classic case of denudation of topsoil. See this author's *Nauru: Environmental Damage under International Trusteeship*, Oxford University Press, 1992.
12. By the International Union for the Conservation of Nature and the World Conservation Union.
13. *Guardian Weekly*, October 20, 1996, p. 17.
14. The Revelation of St. John, Chs. 7, 8, and 9. For strikingly similar descriptions, see E. R. Ehrlich *et al*, *The Cold and the Dark: The World After Nuclear War*, Norton & Co., 1984.
15. See Charles Birch, *Confronting the Future*, Penguin Books, 1975, p. 130.
16. In an article written for *Inter Press Service*, and cited in Bangkok's *The Nation*, March 27, 1994, p. A11.
17. See, generally, Susan George, *How the Other Half Dies: The Real Reasons for World Hunger*, Penguin, 1976, pp. 158–191. On the relationship between Christian teaching and the world food shortage, see Jack A. Nelson, *Hunger for Justice: The Politics of Food and Faith*, Orbis Books, 1982.
18. Gerald McKnight, *Computer Crime*, Michael Joseph, 1973, p. 13, emphasis added.
19. Arthur R. Miller, *The Assault on Privacy: Computers, Data Banks and Dossiers*, University of Michigan Press, 1971, p. 25.
20. Arthur R. Miller, ibid.
21. Cited in Lapp, *The Weapons Culture*, op. cit., p. 16.

Chapter 11

1. See, for example, "Global Apartheid," Gernot Köhler, in Falk, Kim and Mendlovitz (eds.), *Toward a Just World Order*, Westview Press, Boulder, Colorado, Vol. 1, 1982, p. 315.
2. G. R. Taylor, *The Doomsday Book*, Thames & Hudson, 1970, p. 297.
3. International Publishers, N.Y., reprint, 1970. It refers, *inter alia*, to punishments such as amputations, crucifixions, and the like.
4. *Mabo and others* vs. *State of Queensland*, [1992] 107 ALR 1.
5. Vatican II, para. 63.
6. *Mater et Magistra*, paras. 169–170.
7. See, also, this author's *Equality and Freedom: Some Third World Perspectives*, Hansa Publishers, 1976, p. 92.
8. Alfred A. Knopf, *The Quest for Law*, 1941, pp. 368–369.
9. On the injustice of international trade, see *Concilium, Option for the Poor: Challenge for the Rich Countries*, Leonardo Boff and Virgil Elizondo (eds.), T&T Clark Ltd., Edinburgh, 1986, pp. 3–16; and Susan George, *How the Other Half Dies*, op. cit.
10. Norma McRae, "The Future of International Business," *The Economist*, London, 29 January 1972, p. xxi.
11. Even by 1975 the revenue of General Motors was higher than the GDP of 130 nations (*L'Etat du Monde*, 1997 edition. p. 47).
12. *The Consumer and Corporate Accountability*, Harcourt Brace Jovanovich, N.Y., 1973.
13. Simon Schama, *The Embarrassment of Riches: An Interpretation of Dutch Culture in the Golden Age*, University of California Press, 1988, p. 337.
14. See, for an early discussion, G. Goyder, *The Responsible Company*, Basil Blackwell, Oxford, 1961, p. 62 *et seq*.
15. *Reader's Digest*, April 1993, p. 67, "Teaching the World to Smoke," at p. 68.
16. Ibid., p. 70.
17. Guardian Weekly, December 1, 1996, p. 15, reporting article in the *Washington Post*.
18. Stewart Firth, "German Firms in the Western Pacific Islands 1857–1914" (1973), 8 *Journal of Pacific History*, p. 10 at p. 13.
19. See *The International Herald Tribune*, 4 December 1996.
20. Giorgio Giacomelli, *The International Herald Tribune*, 4 December 1996.
21. See Susan George, *How the Other Half Dies: The Real Reasons for World Hunger*, op. cit., pp. 192 *et seq*.—"Food Aid?…Or Weapons?"
22. Susan George, ibid. See also Teresa Hayter, *Aid as Imperialism*, Pelican, 1971.
23. *Guardian Weekly*, October 13, 1996, p. 31.
24. *Populorum Progressio*, 34.
25. *Sollicitudo rei socialis*, 1987, paras. 27–32.
26. Ibid., paras. 33–35.
27. Ibid., para. 10.

Chapter 12

1. Adolf Hitler, *Mein Kampf, Complete and Unabridged*, R. Hitchcock, New York, 1939, p. 606.
2. Dutch Reformed Church Publishers, Cape Town-Pretoria, 1974, ISBN 0 86991 158 9. See, further, this author's *Apartheid: The Closing Phases?*, Lantana, Melbourne, 1980, pp. 88–93.
3. *The Greening of America*, Random House, 1970, Ch. 4.
4. Ibid., p. 26.
5. Ibid., p. 36.
6. L. Mumford, *The Pentagon of Power*, Secker and Warburg, 1964.
7. On the Buddhist theory of development, see further *Human Development in its Social Context*, C. A. Mallmann & O. Nudler (eds.), Hodder & Stoughton, 1988, pp. 233–247. See, also, J. Galtung, *Buddhism: A Quest for Unity and Peace*, Honolulu, Dae Won Sa Buddhist Temple of Hawaii, 1988.
8. Galtung, ibid.
9. George Scott, *The Rise and Fall of the League of Nations*, Hutchinson, 1973, p. 401.
10. Allan Bloom, *The Closing of the American Mind: How Higher Education Has Failed Democracy and Impoverished the Souls of Today's Students*, Simon and Schuster, New York, 1988.
11. Macaulay's Minute on Education, 1835.
12. A criticism so seriously taken at the time that the English lawyer and scholar, John Woodroffe, wrote a book in reply—*Is India Civilised?* and the Indian savant Sri Aurobindo countered it with an essay condemning "the strong reigning idols of rationalism, commercialism and economism, the successful iron Gods of the West" (Sri Aurobindo, "The Foundations of Indian Culture," *Centenary Edition of Aurobindo's Works*, Vol. 14, pp. 1–12).
13. The French philosopher, Léon Duguit (1859–1928), brought this out well in the context of the industrialized society of southern France, where each worker performed a very specialized assignment and was dependent for all the rest of his needs on the other members of society.
14. Quoted by Lord Lugard in *The Dual Mandate in Tropical Africa*, 2nd ed., 1963, p. 60.
15. Lord Lugard, ibid., pp. 60–61.
16. Quoted in L. Dewar and C. E. Hudson, *Christian morals: a study in first principles*, Hodder & Stoughton, 2nd ed., 1948, p. 209.
17. R. H. Tawney, *Religion and the Rise of Capitalism*, Merton Books, 1956, pp. 156–157.
18. Encyclical *Justice in the World*, art. 49.
19. *The Way: A Quarterly Review of Christian Spirituality*, London, 1961—June 1963.
20. Rock Edict V, Vincent A. Smith (trans. and ed.), *The Edicts of Asoka*, Essex House Press, 1909. See also H.J. Carroll et al. (eds.), *The Development of Civilisation*, Scott Foremann, 1961, Vol. 1, pp. 468–469.
21. Zend-Avesta, tr. M. Muller, cited in *The Fount Book of Prayer*, Robert van de Weyer (ed.), Harper Collins, 1993, p. 399.
22. John M. Zane, *The Story of Law*, Doubleday, 1927, p. 202.
23. Abul-Fazl, *Sayings of the Prophet Muhammad*, Award Publishing House, New Delhi, 1980, Saying 580.
24. *History of Western Philosophy*, 2nd ed., 1961, p. 420.
25. Confucius, 6th–5th century B.C.
26. [1919] AC 211, at 233–4.
27. Martin Buber, *I and Thou*, A Scribner Classic, Collier Books, Macmillan Publishing Co., N.Y., 2nd ed., 1986, p. 75.

Chapter 13

1. 23 August 1990, E/CN.4/Sub.2/1990/44.
2. In *Humanitarian Law of Armed Conflict: Challenges Ahead*, edited by Astrid J. M. Delissen and Gerard J. Tanja, Martinus Nijhoff Publishers, 1991, p. 613.
3. See Oliver Ransford, *The Slave Trade*, Redwood Press, 1971, pp. 190–196. On the linkage of slavery with power, and the social life of the affluent, see Edward W. Said, *Culture and Imperialism*, Vintage Books, 1994, pp. 94–97.
4. E/CN/.4/1994/84 of 14/1/94.
5. Op. cit., para. 22.
6. *New York Times*, May 3, 1978, cited in this author's *Human Rights in Japan*, Lantana, 1974, pp. 31–32.
7. See, generally, Guy S. Goodwin-Gill, *The Refugee in International Law*, OUP, 1990.

Chapter 14

1. *Newsweek*, August 12, 1996, special interview before an address to the First World Congress on Business and Ethics, Tokyo, July 1996.

2. See Milton Friedman, "The Social Responsibility of Business is to Increase its Profits," *New York Times*, September 13, 1970, cited in Robert C. Solomon, *Ethics and Excellence: Co-operation and Integrity in Business*, Oxford University Press, 1993.
3. Robert C. Solomon, ibid., ch. 1.
4. See, in particular, Solomon, ibid., ch. 22, "Justice: The Ultimate Virtue of Corporate Life," citing John Rawls: "Justice is the first virtue of social institutions as truth is of systems of thought" (John Rawls, *A Theory of Justice*). See, also, G. Goyder, *The Responsible Company*, Oxford University Press, 1961.
5. *Ethics and Excellence*, op. cit., p. 241.
6. See, for example, Anthony Sampson, *The Sovereign State: The Secret History of ITT*, Coronet Books, 1976, likening a modern business empire to a sovereign state. Also, Berle and Means, *The Modern Corporation and Private Property*, 1932. See also Bertrand Russell, *Power*, Unwin Books, 1960, p. 87.
7. See I.G. Waddell, "International Narcotics Control," (1970) 40 *American Journal of International Law*, p. 311.
8. R.W. Reid, *The Tongues of Conscience*, Constable, London, 1969, p. 103.
9. Ibid., p. 214.
10. On the inability of the law to restrain science and technology, see generally the author's *The Slumbering Sentinels: Law and Human Rights in the Wake of Technology*, Penguin, 1983; and the more recent publication, *Justice without Frontiers: Protecting Human Rights in the Age of Technology*, Kluwer Law International, 1998.
11. Jacques Ellul, *The Technological Society*, John Wilkinson (tr.), Vintage Books, New York, 1964.
12. For further details, see the author's *Justice without Frontiers: Protecting Human Rights in the Age of Technology, supra*, ch. 1.
13. On this aspect, see C.G. Weeramantry (ed.), *Human Rights and Scientific and Technological Development*, UNU Press, 1990, especially Chapter 3.
14. R. W. Reid, *The Tongues of Conscience*, op. cit., p. 105.
15. See, generally, Julius Stone, "Knowledge, Survival and the Duties of Science," 23 *American University Law Review* (1973), p. 231. See also the present author's *Nuclear Weapons and Scientific Responsibility*, 1987; and *The Slumbering Sentinels, supra*.
16. See, generally on this aspect, James Antonellis, *A Journalist Looks at the Lord's Prayer: The Our Father in the Mass Media*, St. Paul Publications, 1990.
17. Reprinted as *Communication for All: New World Information and Communication Order*, Philip Lee (ed.), Maryknoll, New York, 1988.
18. Carlyle, *On Heroes, Hero-Worship, and the Heroic in History*, p. 34.
19. See, on these aspects, Johan Galtung, "Social Communication and Global Problems," in *Communication for All: New World Information and Communication Order, supra*, pp. 7–9.
20. W. Schramm (ed.), *Mass Communications*, University of Illinois Press, 2nd ed., 1972, p. 78; Michael Symons, *New Journalist*, No. 16, Sept. 1974.
21. W. Schramm, *Mass Media and National Development*, Stanford University Press, 1964, pp. 58–69.
22. Herbert Marcuse, *A Critique of Pure Tolerance*, Beacon Press, 1965; W. Schramm, *Four Theories of the Press*, University of Illinois Press, 1972, p. 105.
23. Popularly known as the Hutchins Report, from its Chairman's name.
24. On this aspect, see further the author's *The Law in Crisis: Bridges of Understanding*, Capemoss, London, 1975.
25. See, for example, Bruce Wasserstein and Mark J. Green (eds.), *With Justice for Some: An Indictment of the Law by Young Advocates*, Beacon Press, 1972.
26. See this author's *Nauru: Environmental Damage under International Trusteeship*, Oxford University Press, 1992, p. 37, quoting *Australian Archives*, File GD19 2.18 and 2.24, in relation to the annexation of Nauru by Proclamation in the name of the German Emperor.
27. *Tito* vs. *Waddell*, (1977) 3 *All ER* 129, at 150.
28. (1992) 107 *ALR* 1.
29. Ibid., p. 21.
30. Ibid., p. 26.
31. Ibid., p. 18.
32. Mr. Justice Brennan in "The Christian Lawyer" (1992), 66 *Australian Law Journal*, p. 261.
33. *Harpers Bible Dictionary*, op. cit., p. 519.
34. See such works as Anthony Sampson's *The Arms Bazaar*, Hodder and Stoughton, 1977.
35. *Guardian Weekly*, October 20, 1996, p. 1.

Chapter 15

1. *Redemptor Hominis*, ch. 17.
2. Thomas J. Emerson, *The System of Freedom of Expression*, Vintage Books, New York, 1970, p. 5.

3. See this author's *Law: The Threatened Peripheries*, Lake House, 1984, p. 152.
4. See this author's *The Law in Crisis*, op. cit., p. 223.
5. Werner Herzog's film *The Enigma of Kaspar Hauser*.

Chapter 16

1. Machiavelli, *The Prince*, Quentin Skinner and Russell Price (eds.), Cambridge University Press, 1988, p. 62.
2. Ibid., pp. 51–52.
3. Carl von Clausewitz, *On War*, tr. J.J. Graham, New & Revised Ed. by F.N. Maude in 3 vols., Kegan Paul, Trench Trübner & Co. Ltd., London, 1908, Vol. I, p. 23.
4. Ibid., p. 2.
5. Ibid.
6. Michael I. Handel (ed.), *Clausewitz and Modern Strategy*, Cass, 1986, p. 213.
7. Ibid.
8. *Documents concerning the action taken by the Council of the League of Nations under Article 14 of the Covenant and the adoption by the Assembly of the Statute of the Permanent Court*, 1920, p. 233.
9. See Charles Allen, *The Savage Wars of Peace: Soldiers' Voices 1945–1989*, Michael Joseph, London, 1989.
10. Alvin and Heidi Toffler, *War and Anti-War: Survival at the Dawn of the 21st Century*, Little Brown & Co., 1993, p. 14.
11. See, for example, "Law and Religion: Is Reconciliation still Possible?" by R. Randall Rainey, S.J., (1993) 27 *Loyola Law Review*, p. 147.
12. *The Great Democracies* (Part 4 of the *History of the English Speaking Peoples*), Cassell, 1967, p. 223.
13. Martin Luther King, Jr., *Strength to Love*, Collins, 1963, p. 34.
14. Boutros Boutros-Ghali, "Maintaining Peace and Security: The United Nations as Forum and Focal Point" (1993), 16 *Loyola International and Comparative Law Journal*, No. 1, p. 4.
15. Alberto Quatrucci, "Religions, From Conflict to Coexistence," *Cooperazione*, Monthly Publication of the Italian Ministry of Foreign Affairs, English Ed., No. 136, May 1994, p. 24.
16. Quattrucci, op. cit., p. 26.

Chapter 17

1. *The Fount Book of Prayer*, op. cit., p. 145.
2. *Sri Ramakrishna, 1836–1886, His Life and Sayings*, ed. F.M. Muller, 1899.
3. *The Works of John Wesley*, 14 vols., 2nd edn., ed. Wesleyan Conference Office, London, 1958-9, vol. V, p. 232.
4. For example, the verse of The Throne Q.2.255: "God, there is no God but Him, the Living, the Eternal One. Neither slumber nor sleep overtakes Him. Who can intercede with Him except by His permission? He knows what is before and behind men. They can grasp only that part of His knowledge which He wills. His throne is as vast as the heavens and the earth, and the preservation of both does not weary Him. He is the Exalted, the Immense One."
5. Isherwood (ed.), *Vedanta for the Modern World*, p. 32.
6. *The Bhagavad Gita*, 11.2. These words were made familiar to Western readers by Oppenheim, the nuclear scientist, when he referred to them in the context of the devastation caused by the nuclear bomb and followed it with the later words from the same source:
   "I am become Death
   The shatterer of worlds."
7. *The Fount Book of Prayer*, op. cit., p. 221.
8. At pp. 41–42 of the English translation by Theodore Morrow, op. cit.
9. The intolerance towards the Aztecs which resulted appears from the rest of the Aztec address:
   "Hear this O Lords, do nothing to our people
   that will bring them harm
   that will destroy them…
   Consider quietly and considerately, O Lord
   what is really necessary."
   [From "Diálogos con les sabios indígenas" in M.L. Portilla, *El Reverso de la Conquista* (Mexico City, 1970) pp. 23–8, cited by Boff, ibid.]
10. See, generally, Lohmeyer, op. cit., pp. 78–79.
11. On this aspect generally, see Reginald Klimionok, *How to Pray*, Triune Publishing, 1991, ch. 3: "Hallowed be thy name."

12. VII, 6 & 7, *Hindu Scriptures*, R.C. Zaehner (tr. & ed.), Everyman's Library, Dent and Sons, 1972, pp. 279–281.
13. *Guardian Weekly*, December 1, 1996, p. 11.
14. On the marvels locked within the human body, as revealed by the latest computerized research, see *Life*, February 1997, "A Fantastic Voyage through the Human Body."
15. *Policrations*, John of Salisbury, 1159.
16. *Edinburgh Review*, July 1843.
17. *An Autobiography or the Story of My Experiments with Truth*, London, 1949, citing *The Imitation of Christ*, Ch. III 'Of Truth.'
18. John Hales, [1584-1606], *Private Judgement in Religion*.
19. *The Diversions of Purley*, 1786-1805, Pt. II, ch. V, 'Of Abstraction.'
20. John Calvin, *Institutes*, II 536.
21. Confucius, c. 500 B.C.
22. Patanjali, 2nd century B.C., *Yoga Aphorisms*, I.
23. (1863) 14 CBNS 180.
24. 2 Lord Raymond 1334.
25. Cf. the Hindu scriptures which capture with beauty and clarity the notion that we must commit ourselves to this concept of righteousness when they say, "May the stream of my life flow into the river of righteousness" (*Rigveda* 11.28.1–9).
26. R. C. Zaehner (tr. and ed.) *Hindu Scriptures*, op. cit., p. 285.
27. See, generally, this author's "The Importance of Philosophical Perspectives to the Judicial Process," 6 *Connecticut Journal of International Law* (1991), p. 599.
28. See Richard P. McBrien, *Catholicism*, New Ed., Collins Dove, 1994, pp. 937–938.
29. Gandhi, *Young India, 1921–1922*, S. Ganesan, 1922, p. 285.
30. Richard P. McBrien, *Catholicism*, op. cit., p. 939.
31. *The Fount Book of Prayer*, op. cit., p. 149. See, further, *Francis of Assisi, the Complete Works*, tr. R. J. Armstrong & I. C. Brady.
32. Words of Guru Nanak, founder of the Sikh religion—see M.A. Macauliffe, *The Sikh Religion: its Gurus, Sacred Writings and Authors*, New Delhi, 1963, Oxford University Press, 1909; *The Fount Book of Prayer*, op. cit, p. 268.
33. C. K. Ogden and I. A. Richards, *The Meaning of Meaning*, 1923, Ark Paperback edition, 1985, p. 27.
34. See ibid., pp. 26–29.
35. Calov, *Biblia Novi Testamenti Illustrata*, 1676, 1, 231, cited by Lohmeyer, op. cit., p. 74.
36. Ibid., p. 75.
37. J. J. von Allmen, *Vocabulary of the Bible*, Lutterworth Press, 1958, p. 278.
38. "Reflections on the Lord's Prayer" in *Vedanta for the Modern World*, Christopher Isherwood (ed.), Unwin Books, 1963, pp. 203–4.
39. Preface to "Milton."
40. A. E. Baker, *The Divine Christ*, 1937, p. 62.
41. See, generally, Konrad Braun, "Justice and the Law of Love," *Swarthmore Lectures*, 1950, George Allen & Unwin.
42. Ibid., pp. 50–51.
43. Cited in *The Fount Book of Prayer*, op. cit., pp. 145–146.
44. For Buddhism, see K. N. Jayetilleke, "The Principles of International Law in Buddhist Doctrine," 120 *Recueil des Cours* (1967–I), p. 539; *Anguttara Nikaya*, 1 Pali Text Society, p. 109; for Hinduism, see B.A. Saletore, *Ancient Indian Political Thought and Institutions*, New York, 1963, p. 139.
45. Cited by C. K. Ogden and I. A. Richards in their *Meaning of Meaning*, op. cit., at pp. 16–17. They go on to comment that, "When moth and rust have been eliminated by science the Christian investor will presumably have no problem!"
46. *Soliloquies*, 387.
47. *Sermons*.
48. *Adi Granth*, 421/4. See Piara Singh Sambhi, *Sikhism*, Stanley Thornes & Hulton, 1989, p. 72.
49. See further *Ramakrishna, Prophet of the New India*, Harper, New York, 1948.
50. See further *The Essential Gandhi*, L. Fischer (ed.), George Allen & Unwin, 1963.
51. *The Times*, 6 June 1944.
52. Father Bruce Ritter, *Sometimes God has a Kid's Face*, Covenant House, 1988.
53. *Aid to the Church in Need*, 1970, p. 62.
54. Andrew Murray, *God's Will: Our Dwelling Place*, (formerly *Thy Will be Done*), Whitaker House, 1982, p. 32.
55. Ibid., p. 33.
56. Ibid., p. 24.
57. *Ibid.*, p. 25.

58. Study Series 4 on the Status of the Individual and Contemporary International Law by Erica-Irene A. Daes, Special Rapporteur, UN, NY, 1992.
59. Immanuel Kant, *Religion within the Limits of Reason Alone*, reissued New York, 1960, Part IV, pp. 182 ff. Harper and Row, 1960, New York.
60. *Five Stages of Greek Religion*, Watts & Co., 1935, pp. 46–47.

Chapter 18
1. Oscar Halecki, *The Millennium of Europe*, Notre Dame University Press, 1963, p. 128.
2. *The Perennial Dictionary of World Religion*, Harper Collins, 1981, p. 480.
3. For these references, see *The Perennial Dictionary of World Religion*, op. cit.
4. See this author's *Apartheid: The Closing Phases?*, Lantana, 1980, pp. 292–293, for a scriptural justification of apartheid, citing extracts from the 1974 Synod Report of the Dutch Reformed Church in South Africa.
5. These are the concluding words of Robert Ornstein and Richard F. Thomspson's *The Amazing Brain*, Chatto & Windus, 1984.
6. Fritjof Capra, *The Tao of Physics: An Exploration of the Parallels between Modern Physics and Eastern Mysticism*, 2nd ed., Bantam Books, 1984.
7. Paul Davies, *The Mind of God*, Simon & Schuster, 1992, p. 231.
8. Naisbitt and Aburdene, *Megatrends 2000: the New Directions for the 1990's*, Morrow, N.Y., 1990, p. 316.
9. Ibid., p. 322.
10. *New Age Journal*, February 1988, p. 50.
11. Robert Frost, "I took the one less traveled by, And that has made all the difference." Also the title of the best-selling book by Dr. M. Scott Peck, Simon & Schuster, 1978.
12. See Lewis Mumford, *The Pentagon of Power*, Secker and Warburg, 1970.
13. *Religion, the Missing Dimension of Statecraft*, Douglas Johnston and Cynthia Sampson (eds.), Oxford University Press, 1994, pp. 4–5. See Chapter 1 above.
14. See R. Müllerson, *Human Rights Diplomacy*, Routledge, 1997.
15. Both these definitions are taken from Ambrose Bierce, *The Devil's Dictionary*, World Publishing Co., 1911, pp. 283 and 251.

Chapter 19
1. *Masters of Political Thought*, Vol. 1, Michael B. Foster (ed.), Harrap, 1942, p. 201.
2. See W. Steinmuller, "Divine Law and its Dynamism in Protestant Theology of Law," *Concilium*, Vol. 8, No. 5, October 1969, p. 15.
3. See Charles Elliott's *Praying the Kingdom*, Darton, Longman and Todd, 1985, p. 20.
4. Ibid.
5. John Wesley, *Explanatory Notes upon the New Testament*, London, Epworth Press, 1948, p. 22.
6. Op. cit., p. 644.
7. Dummelow, (ed.), *The One Volume Bible Commentary*, Macmillan, New York, 1973, p. 637.
8. Ibid.
9. *Perennial Dictionary of World Religions*, Harper, San Francisco, 1981, p. 408.
10. A. M. Hunter, *The Work and Words of Jesus*, SCM, 1973, p. 90, cited in Frank Field, *The Politics of Paradise*, Collins, 1987, p. 27.
11. *The Outline of History*, 1920, p. 526.
12. Ibid., pp. 526–527.
13. Ibid., p. 531.
14. *Religion in the Making*, 1927.
15. As cited in *Catechism of the Catholic Church*, p. 678, para. 2825—*Homiline in Matthaeum* 19.5; PG 57, 280.
16. From Gerald Manley Hopkins, *God's Grandeur*.

INDEX

ABOUT THE AUTHOR

Christopher Gregory Weeramantry, born in Sri Lanka in 1926, earned a Doctor of Laws degree from the University of London and has been a lawyer for fifty years. He has experience in all branches of the legal profession, having been a trial lawyer, a Justice of the Supreme Court of his country, a law professor, and a legal author. He is now a Judge of the International Court of Justice and the Vice-President of that Court.

Weeramantry has written nearly twenty books, as well as around a hundred articles that have been published in legal journals on five continents. In addition to having lectured extensively throughout the United States, he has also taught at universities around the world and has spoken on law-related topics to a variety of audiences: from school children, to the general public, to members of academic, scientific, and other professional organizations.

Judge Weeramantry's writings have covered such areas as human rights and the philosophy of law, including law-related studies of Buddhism and Hinduism. Among his books are *Islamic Jurisprudence: An International Perspective* (published simultaneously in London and New York); *The Slumbering Sentinels: Law and Human Rights in the Wake of Technology; The Law in Crisis: Bridges of Understanding; Apartheid: The Closing Phases;* and *Equality and Freedom: Some Third World Perspectives.*

He is married, has five children and several grandchildren, and spends most of the year in the Netherlands at The Hague, which is the seat of the World Court.